THE
SHRIEK
OF SILENCE

THE SHRIEK OF SILENCE

A Phenomenology of the Holocaust Novel

DAVID PATTERSON

THE UNIVERSITY PRESS OF KENTUCKY

Copyright © 1992 by The University Press of Kentucky
Scholarly publisher for the Commonwealth,
serving Bellarmine College, Berea College, Centre
College of Kentucky, Eastern Kentucky University,
The Filson Club, Georgetown College, Kentucky
Historical Society, Kentucky State University,
Morehead State University, Murray State University,
Northern Kentucky University, Transylvania University,
University of Kentucky, University of Louisville,
and Western Kentucky University.

Editorial and Sales Offices: Lexington, Kentucky 40508-4008

Library of Congress Cataloging-in-Publication Data

Patterson, David, 1948-
 The shriek of silence : a phenomenology of the Holocaust novel / David Patterson.
   p. cm.
 Includes bibliographical references and index.
 ISBN 978-0-8131-6013-9
 1. Holocaust, Jewish (1939-1945), in literature. 2. Jewish fiction—History and criticism. I. Title.
PN56.H55P38 1992
809'.93358—dc20   91-17269

This book is printed on acid-free paper meeting
the requirements of the American National Standard
for Permanence of Paper for Printed Library Materials.

Contents

Prologue / 1

1 Theoretical Background / 3

2 The Word in Exile / 29

3 The Death of the Father / 54

4 The Death of the Child / 77

5 The Splitting of the Self / 98

6 The Resurrection of the Self / 123

7 The Implication of the Reader / 145

Epilogue / 168

Works Cited / 170

Index / 177

For Miriam and Rachel
and, with deepest love
and gratitude, for my
wife, Gerri

Prologue

"And it came to pass in those days that terror denied all languages and frontiers" (Wiesel, *Six Days* 5). For those were days invaded by night, the days of the reign of the Kingdom of Night. They are days that haunt and harrow all subsequent days, words, and deeds, cutting through the frontiers of language and meaning that might once have divided light from darkness. Terror has undone time and with it that being that once inhabited the heart of human being, the being of the word. "There is no peace for the darkened valleys," Amos Oz has said, "something is rising up in the night, something is mounting, gathering, something is silently happening" (144). Something—*davar-mah* in the Hebrew text (153)—"some word" that is not a word, a sound that is not a sound, bursts forth between word and word in a shriek of silence. From this emerges the Holocaust novel.

"It is true," Elie Wiesel once told me, commenting on the event of the novel's creation. "I descend . . . somewhere." He, like the others addressed in these pages, beckons us to follow—to a place that is no place, where the word is swallowed up into words. It is a place where there is "no connection," to borrow a phrase from Martin Buber, "rather shriek, shriek, and in between them the abyss" (*Daniel* 86). By what method shall we proceed to such a place? How shall we undertake such an investigation? Buber offers a suggestion: "Imagine that at some dreadful midnight you lie there, tormented by a waking dream: the bulwarks have crumbled and the abysses scream, and you realize in the midst of this agony that life is still there and I must merely get through to it—but how? how? Thus feels man in the hours when he collects himself: overcome by horror, pondering, without direction" (*I and Thou* 120). Life is still there; the heart continues to beat when it should have come to a stop. Holding these novels in our hands attests to that. Yet in the text that we hold in our hands lurks the horror that threatens us, the exile that implicates us. The method, therefore, settles nothing. Indeed, it is unsettling in the extreme, and that is the point: to speak and break in the effort to respond to the testimony entrusted to us. For unless we are broken by our response to the voice and the event of the Holocaust novel, we can never open up to its outcry. Only by becoming such a wound do we gain even the tiniest access to these wounded ones.

It is from the midst of a wound that Ka-tzetnik 135633, for instance, writes, "I shoot up from the launch-pile of skeletons into the tempest of my own cry of Passion" (*Shivitti* 104). The outcry that arises from the skeletal remains of life and language constitutes the Holocaust novel and the voices that inhabit it. Aharon Appelfeld, for example, creates a character in *Tzili: The Story of a Life* who harbors the very outcry of which the novel is made. In an endeavor indicative of the author's own endeavor, the character struggles to articulate to his friends the prospect of redemption. But no one listens to him. And so, "the whole night he sat and wailed. Through his wailing the history of his life emerged" (146). In a similar way Mordi bespeaks his author's effort to speak in *The Chocolate Deal* by Haim Gouri when he describes the days and nights that he spent hiding in a cellar: "I thought that periodically I'd shriek one day-long shriek which would earn me the title of Champion Shrieker" (56). The character, however, remains silent; yet it is just through his silence that the author's shriek makes itself heard.

What, we ask, is the substance of that shriek? One more example, from Ka-tzetnik's *Star of Ashes*, will tell us. "Children," he writes, "push against their mother's belly, as if seeking to get inside once more. Their scream, embryonic, unuttered, howls out of their mother's eyes" (53). Thus the author pushes against the belly of life's origin, his shriek of silence howling through the invisible eyes of his character. We read the words, but we do not see those eyes; we encounter the silence, but we do not hear the shriek. The task of this book is to make those eyes visible, to make that shriek heard. What, then, is curled up in this shriek that frames and infiltrates the novel? What do we now set out to hear, if we can find the courage? A passage from Elie Wiesel's *Somewhere a Master* may offer a response: "An appeal, an outcry to God on behalf of His desperate people and also on His behalf, an offering to night, to heaven, an offering made by wise old men and quiet children to mark the end of language—a burning secret buried in silence" (201). So we take up the pursuit of the secret and its fire and go in quest of the silence and its shriek.

1
Theoretical Background

"Let him who wants fervor not seek it on the mountain peaks," the Maggid of Mezeritch once said. "Rather let him stoop and search among the ashes" (see Wiesel, *Souls* 71). Since 1945, however, the world has lived on a mountain of ashes—the ashes of children, ashes of God's chosen, ashes of God Himself. The winds of Auschwitz have quite literally, quite graphically, scattered the people of the Covenant, and with them the Covenant itself, over the face of the earth. The people inhabit the soil that yields our bread; they haunt the air we breathe. I have heard at least one survivor declare that, when the breeze blows from a certain direction, she can still smell the odor that oozed from the chimneys of the death camps. As Arnost Lustig expressed it in his novel *A Prayer for Katerina Horovitzova*,

These ashes would be indestructible and immutable, they would not burn up into nothingness because they themselves were remnants of fire. . . . No one living would ever be able to escape them; these ashes would be contained in the milk that will be drunk by babies yet unborn and in the breasts their mothers offer them. . . . These ashes will be contained in the breath and expression of every one of us and the next time anybody asks what the air he breathes is made of, he will have to think about these ashes; they will be contained in books which haven't yet been written and will be found in the remotest regions of the earth where no human foot has ever trod; no one will be able to get rid of them, for they will be the fond, nagging ashes of the dead who died in innocence. [50-51]

What the translator rendered as the "expression" of every one of us is in the original Czech *pohled*, which means "look, glance, sight, view"; the very image of the human being is cast in these ashes. The phrase "have to think about" bears in the Czech text a stronger moral and existential injunction in the word *povinen*, suggesting duty, obligation, compulsion (41). Failing to answer to these ashes would mean falling short of human being.

Hearing such testimony, one cannot help but recall the outcry raised by Nelly Sachs: "O the chimneys . . . And Israel's body as smoke through the air!" (3). Thus was the light unto the nations consumed. Or is it hidden among the ashes? Indeed, it is among the ashes that the authors before us seek what was lost.

What, exactly, was lost? Elie Wiesel has one response to this question. "At Auschwitz," he asserts, "not only man died, but also the idea of man. It was its own heart that the world incinerated at Auschwitz" (*Legends* 230). Through those forms called Holocaust literature, the poets seek the lost soul and self of human being. Through words they seek the lost word that constitutes human being. The concern before us, therefore, is not primarily historical or aesthetic or even literary, in the strict sense of those terms; rather, as we shall see, it is existential, phenomenological, ontological, metaphysical—in short, it is fundamentally religious. Alvin Rosenfeld has indicated as much, correctly arguing that the position of the Holocaust writer is

analogous to that of the man of faith, who is likewise beset by frustration and anguish and, in just those moments when his spirit may yearn for the fullness of Presence, is forced to acknowledge the emptiness and silence of an imposed Absence. The life centers of the self—intelligence, imagination, assertiveness—undergo paralysis in such moments, which, if prolonged, have the effect of a total detachment or the profoundest despair. Yet to indulge in silence is to court madness or death. At just those points where, through some abiding and still operative reflex of language, silence converts once more into words— even into words about silence—Holocaust literature is born. Its birth must be seen as a miracle of some sort, not only an overcoming of mute despair but an assertion and affirmation of faith. [14-15]

In the creation of the Holocaust novel, then, religious concern is a concern for the word; as Kenneth Burke has put it, "Statements that great theologians have made about the nature of 'God' might be adapted *mutatis mutandis* for use as purely secular observations of the nature of *words*" (1-2). Drawing a connection between man, word, and God, Wiesel cites what he calls "the most beautiful words" of Rebbe Menahem-Mendl of Vitebsk, saying, "Man is the language of God" (*Souls* 86). When man or the idea of man is lost, so is the language of God, so is the word. Hence Auschwitz represents a profound loss of the word. As André Neher expresses it, "Auschwitz is, above all, silence" (141), the silence of the word torn from its place and cast into exile among the ashes. "If I know that the place of the word is here in the meaning," Wiesel once said, "it would mean that at least I know the meaning. That's what I would call faith. The faith is not that one day it will come but that one day it was there" (see Patterson, *In Dialogue* 171). The movement of the word in the Holocaust novel is a turning back, a *teshuvah*, a movement of return, response, and redemption. Yet it is also a movement forward, toward the yet-to-be.

Let it be said, then, at the outset, that the Holocaust novel is not primarily an attempt to recount the details of a particular occurrence, to depict a reality that transcends the imagination, or to describe a horror inaccessible to a limited language. It is, rather, an event and an endeavor to fetch the word from the silence of exile and restore it to its meaning; it is an attempt to resurrect the dead soul or self of the human being. Commenting on the relation between silence and the author's sense of self, Jerzy Kosinski said, "Perhaps this silence is also a metaphor for dissociation from the community and from something greater. This feeling of alienation floats on the surface of the work and manifests the author's awareness, perhaps unconscious, of his break with the wholeness of self (*Notes* 17). In a similar vein Wiesel remarked, "You write about what you do not have. It is absence that makes literature. It is what you miss that becomes present" (*Against Silence* 3:286). The absence that characterizes this break with the self, the absence that makes literature, consists of silence; it is the absence of the word. "Before I write," Wiesel tells us, "I must endure the silence, then the silence breaks out. In the beginning there was silence—no words. The word itself is a breaking out. . . . it breaks the silence. We cannot avoid the silence, we must not. What we can do is somehow charge words with silence" (*Against Silence* 2:119). Charging words with silence, the novelist struggles to impart a voice to silence—and to hear a voice from within that silence. In the Holocaust novel silence is always a character, and the word is always its subject matter.

The Holocaust novel, therefore, is not simply about a historical event, nor is its interest only in historical memory. Much more than that, it is about the conflict—it *is* the conflict—betwen word and silence in the restoration of presence of all levels: presence between the self and God, between the self and other, between the self and itself. "The storyteller," in Wiesel's words, "is no more than a messenger whose role is to create links between word and being, man and himself, shadow and the memory of that shadow" (*Against Silence* 2:57). Such links are created through dialogic encounter, so that the Holocaust novel is not set in one period or another but in the space between the voices of encounter, in the dialogue between word and word, word and silence, silence and silence. The form of the novel is the form of this between-space as it takes shape in the dialogic relation that ties the author to character, to reader, and to his own soul. Passing through these levels of relation, word and meaning may once again find their intersection and their resurrection—in the shriek of silence.

The Critical Contexts for the Investigation

Considering the vastness of the literature in question, relatively few book-length studies treat the topic, and all of them can be viewed to varying degrees as pioneer efforts. To be sure, the literature continues to be produced, each new work shedding its own light on all the rest.

The court of scholarship, therefore, is still in session; the chief witnesses—Elie Wiesel, Aharon Appelfeld, Arnost Lustig, Ka-tzetnik 135633, and others—continue their literary testimony. Although the investigation at hand takes issue with all previous attempts to penetrate the literary response to the Holocaust, it could not have been undertaken without those attempts, and it owes a great deal to them. The criticisms that follow, then, are made much more in a spirit of gratitude and respect than in the complacency of casual dismissal.

Among the earliest books to explore Holocaust literature was Irving Halperin's *Messengers from the Dead: Literature of the Holocaust* (1970). Viewing the authors of Holocaust literature "essentially as moral teachers," Halperin argues that the chief intention of such authors "is to teach the reader by interrogating him. The messengers, in effect, ask the reader to rigorously examine his knowledge of and relationship to the Holocaust" (13-14). In this study of selected fiction, diaries, and memoirs, Halperin regards the main task of author and reader as the remembrance of a historical event and the examination of the moral implications of that event. There is no denying the urgency of bearing witness and assessing one's relation to history. What remains to be studied, however, is the more essential matter of the resurrection or redemption of the soul that arises in the dialogic exchange between author and reader via character. In responding to the novel, the reader must gain not so much factual knowledge as self-definition; it is a matter of declaring, "Here I am," not "Now I know." Thus Halperin turns to the message without stopping to consider the difficulties peculiar to the medium, the word wrenched from the void. He hears the shriek but not the silence.

In *Escape into Siege: A Survey of Israeli Literature Today* (1974) Leon Yudkin regards the task of the novelist as an effort to become an individual, not through dialogic interaction within the text but through a flight from the crowd. "The individual," he argues, "has to escape group pressure through flight to establish himself truly as an individual. Once he has become an individual, he can then begin to ponder in an uncluttered fashion the truly central issues. And this sort of metaphysic is the concern not only of the man in his private life or in his relationship to God, but also of the novelist in his written work" (171). Yudkin's main shortcoming is that in his discussion of the tension between group and individual he fails to address language, which is the novelist's medium and subject matter. The word implies the presence of three—speaker, listener, and witness—and no life steeped in language (as all life is) can be lived in isolation. The individual can "establish himself truly as an individual" only through a dialogical relationship with others, both before him and above him.

In 1975 Lawrence Langer published his book *The Holocaust and the*

Literary Imagination, in which he focuses on the conflict between "historical fact and imaginative truth" (8). He writes, "I have organized my study around a number of recurrent themes that illustrate the aesthetic problem of reconciling normalcy with horror: the displacement of the consciousness of life by the imminence and pervasiveness of death; the violation of the coherence of childhood; the assault on physical reality; the disintegration of the rational intelligence; and the disruption of chronological time" (xii). While the Holocaust novel indeed addresses all of these themes, Langer never probes the existential encounters between life and death, word and silence, and self and other that generate such themes. Focusing on aesthetics, he isolates the work of art from the human being who speaks it and thus approaches it as an object for examination rather than an event of human existence. "Image collides with concept," as he correctly observes (149), but so does the soul collide with the void, and this deeper collision Langer tends to overlook.

Edward Alexander's *The Resonance of Dust: Essays on Holocaust Literature and Jewish Fate* (1979) is similar to Langer's study but is less analytical, offering little more than a series of plot descriptions. Like Langer, Alexander addresses the surface issue of how literature voices history, without considering the metaphysical problem of the soul's resurrection to life or the word's restoration to meaning. To his credit, however, Alexander does understand that the Jewish essence of the Shoah and of the literary response to it is precisely what takes us to the core of human being. Quoting Piotr Rawicz, he argues that "the fate and condition of the Jewish people are the very essence of the human condition—the furthest borders of human destiny. And the fate of the 'Holocaust Jew,' . . . is . . . the ontological essence of that ontological essence" (223-24). Alexander's touchstone is history, however, not the existential or phenomenological aspects of giving voice to the novel.

In her long essay that appears in *Encountering the Holocaust: An Interdisciplinary Survey* (1979) Josephine Knopp, like many others, makes the merely half-accurate claim that "the Holocaust writer—virtually alone among writers—faces the difficulty of making a factual subject believable" (270). Such a difficulty bespeaks a much deeper problem involving the life-and-death encounter between the author and the blank page. Addressing the chief difficulty confronting the critic, Knopp is again only half right, maintaining that the critic faces the problem of "applying a number of criteria extraneous to the traditional frame of reference of literary criticism" (267). We shall find that the Holocaust writer implicates the Holocaust reader, whose task is not the application of new criteria but the generation of a language of the self that would establish a responsive dialogic presence in relation to the textual voice. Adding insight to Knopp's remarks, Arnost Lustig, in an appendix to Knopp's essay, states, "While history, philosophy, psychology or sociology each stands alone, literature includes all of them and re-creates all elements into its own literary amalgam, out of which comes something that exists nowhere but in literature" (311). That "something" is the rebirth of the word and, with it, the soul.

Like Knopp, Sidra DeKoven Ezrahi raises the issue of the critical approach to Holocaust literature in her book *By Words Alone: The Holocaust in Literature* (1980). "Traditional perimeters of mimetic art," she asserts, do not apply, "because although Holocaust literature is a reflection of recent history, it cannot draw upon timeless archetypes of human experience and human behavior which can render unlived events familiar through the medium of the imagination. . . . Precisely where it is most confined to the unimaginable facts of violence and horror, the creative literature that has developed is the least consistent with traditional moral and artistic convention" (2-3). Once she outlines the difficulties involving conventional generic categories, Ezrahi proposes new labels for the varieties of Holocaust literature and then discusses works representing those new categories. Although many of her observations are quite astute, her premise is wrongheaded. First of all, Holocaust literature is not a reflection of history but an interaction between human being and human nothingness, a dialogic encounter on all levels. The matter of its confinement, moreover, involves not so much unimaginable facts as unbreachable silence. Like Langer's thematic approach, Ezrahi's formal treatment of Holocaust literature reduces it to an object of observation, denying its existence as an event in the life of a living subject.

Alvin Rosenfeld takes the issues surrounding Holocaust literature to a more profound philosophical level. In *A Double Dying: Reflections on Holocaust Literature* (1980), for example, he shows that "if one can talk about such a thing as a phenomenology of Holocaust literature, it would have to be in terms of this contradiction between the impossibility but also the necessity of writing about the death of the idea of man in order to sustain that idea" (8). Rosenfeld's "principal interest," he explains, "is less in the 'art of atrocity' than it is in other issues, most especially in trying to define the kind of knowledge that we acquire in reading the literature of the Holocaust and in weighing the consequent gains and losses that are ours in its aftermath" (8-9). While Rosenfeld astutely examines these important questions in his analysis of various works of Holocaust literature, he does not always pursue his phenomenological concern to its existential depths. Before sustaining any idea of man, the novelist must go through the tribulation of resurrecting a presence of self through an encounter between self and other, between word and silence. The reader who becomes a witness to this interaction comes up against the human voice that speaks through the text and is implicated by it; Rosenfeld does not address this issue. Here the truth is not something we know but something we might become through the process of dialogic response. What is gained or lost is not simply a concept or idea but the very life of the soul.

The Holocaust in Hebrew Literature: From Genocide to Rebirth (1983), by Alan Yutler, provides an overview of Israeli literature dealing with the Shoah. "The striking consistency," Yutler observes, "in all the works of Israeli literature bearing on the Holocaust and the destruction of the European Jewish people is their concern for the redemptive possibilities of the aftermath" (121). Like most treatments of Holocaust literature, however, Yutler's slips into the shortcoming of what Mikhail Bakhtin calls impressive aesthetics. Bakhtin says, "The problem with *impressive* aesthetics is that here the artistic event as an event between two consciousnesses does not exist; here art is preceived as a one-sided act concerned not with another, with a subject, but strictly with an object, with material" (*Estetika* 82). Containing little more than summaries of plots and poetry, Yutler's work examines "redemptive possibilities" only in the literature's theme and content, without regard to language and meaning or the relationships between author and character, character and reader, author and reader. It is precisely within these relationships and through the word that redemptive possibilities must be hammered out. More descriptive than analytical, Yutler's study maintains a safe distance from the real collisions that distinguish Holocaust literature.

In contrast with scholars such as Ezrahi and Rosenfeld, who perceive generic and epistemological difficulties peculiar to Holocaust literature, Alan Mintz argues that this literature belongs to a standing generic tradition in Hebrew literature. "The impetus for this study," he explains in the preface to *Hurban: Responses to Catastrophe in Hebrew Literature* (1984), "was a dissatisfaction with the conception in literary studies of Holocaust literature as a distinct genre." This literature, he claims, belongs "to a vertical axis of literary tradition, which extended back to the Middle Ages and the Bible," and its meaning "depends on the interpretative tradition of the community or culture seeking that meaning" (ix). While Mintz's approach is useful from the standpoint of cultural or literary history, it sheds little light on the existential event that occurs on the page between author and word, between word and reader. Just as the strictly thematic approach protects the critic from self-examination, so the appeal to generic tradition provides an illusion of explanation that veils human questions of meaning that have no answers. Mintz does, nonetheless, make a very discerning observation with respect to an essential difference between those authors who are survivors and those who are not: "When the survivor writes about the

Holocaust it has the effect of an evasion interrupted or curtailed rather than an experience encountered or investigated; and when he writes of other things, the Holocaust seems to hover as an ontologial condition" (259). The evasion curtailed is the evasion of silence in the flight to the noise of the world. The ontological condition is a condition of silence—not just the silence of the infinite spaces that terrified Pascal but the silence that replaces the word when nothingness displaces being, as it does when reality allows no place for the word. "The word always dies," Jean Améry has noted, "where the claim of some reality is total" (20).

A piece that Mintz regards as a companion to his own work (xii), David Roskies's *Against the Apocalypse: Responses to Catastrophe in Modern Jewish Culture* (1984), also attempts to make sense of Holocaust literature by placing it in a generically traditional context. Roskies's study, therefore, contains the same basic weaknesses as does Mintz's book. To his credit, however, Roskies recognizes at least one critical issue in the life of the self with respect to its literary endeavor:

Ever since the first Jew tried to remove himself from the crowd of exiles mourning by the waters of Babylon, the presence of the one still implied the presence of the many. For if the self desired to bear witness to the destruction, it then became the symbolic survivor of the community (and thus, the community in miniature); or if, as a result of ideology or devastation, it wished to detail its willing or unwilling departure from the community, the rejected group loomed just as large as the self; and if, despite all odds, the self succeeded in negating the group, the self was invariably lost as well. [133]

What Roskies does not emphasize is that when every distinguishing feature of the community is reduced to ashes, so is the self. In the literary response to the Holocaust the self does not negate the group but rather finds itself negated by reality's negation of the group. When the group is deemed guilty of being and is swallowed up by nothingness, nothingness invades the self. Tradition is made of language, but Auschwitz, in its very confusion of tongues, is made of silence, so that an insurmountable void stands between the novelist and tradition. Perhaps what Primo Levi said is true: "If the Lagers had lasted longer a new, harsh language would have been born" (*Man* 144). But it was not born. Here tradition and the group are not what is present as context but what is absent within the text.

Charlotte Wardi makes a similar point about language in her book *Le génocide dans la fiction romanesque* (1986) when she says, "The SS who calls a dog 'man' and a Jew 'dog' latches onto this divided consciousness in order to achieve his goal: the psychological destruction of the Other" (51). The other who is destroyed in this undermining of language is not only the victim but also anyone—person or God—who is the victim's other. The word, again, implies the presence of three (speaker, listener, and witness), and when the word is lost or perverted, so are all the parties whom it might join together. It is not simply the event but the bankruptcy of language itself that robs the writer and reader of all reference points and of all substance. Wardi does not pursue this fundamental issue of language and silence, of self and word. "If, for the survivor," she asserts, "the act of writing answers an urgent need to speak the truth, a duty to testify, it constitutes for him, as for every genocide writer, an interrogation of atrocity, a search for the meaning of a terrible venture, and requires the invention of a form susceptible to the transmission of an 'unimaginable' reality, a logic of horror, and to the communication of a message to a reader incapable of referring to anything known" (39). Rejecting claims (such as those of Mintz and Roskies) that Holocaust literature refers to tradition, Wardi makes a valid point, but she stops short of the more fundamental issue of the exile of the word.

The problem of transmitting experience also forms the basis of James Young's *Writing and Rewriting the Holocaust: Narrative and the Consequences of Interpretation* (1988). "This study," he writes, "asks precisely how historical memory, understanding, and meaning are constituted in Holocaust narrative" (vii). Accenting the historical, Young omits the existential; focusing on what belongs to a faceless collective, he disregards the collision of the living individual who comes before the face of the human being. This complaint is basically the same as Kierkegaard's objection to the Hegelian system in *Concluding Unscientific Postscript*, where he declares, "It may be seen, from a purely abstract point of view, that system and existence are incapable of being thought together, because in order to think existence at all, systematic thought must think it as abrogated" (107). The system that interests Young is the system of metaphors by which history is transmitted through narrative; his concern, therefore, is both thematic and structural. Yet he is aware of the conflict between the existential and the systematic, pointing out that "the Holocaust writer faces an especially powerful quandary: on the one hand, the survivor-scribe would write both himself and his experience into existence after the fact, giving them both expression and textual actuality; but on the other hand, in order to make his testimony seem true, he would simultaneously efface himself from his text" (10). Young nevertheless makes the error of identifying what is true with what is factual, claiming that "the transmission of facts in Holocaust writing still dominates this literature's function for so many writers" (91). This may be the case for some, but it is not the case for novelists such as Wiesel, Rawicz, Katzetnik, Lustig, Appelfeld, and others with whom we are here concerned. As Wiesel put it, "Some events do take place but are not true; others are—although they never occured" (*Legends* viii). The truth that we shall examine is the truth that the soul struggles to become, not a fact or occurrence that one can document. When Oedipus answered the riddle of the Sphinx—what walks on four legs in the morning, two in the afternoon, and three in the evening—he did not simply cite a fact about the world. He was himself the answer.

In all fairness, the scholars discussed above merit a more thorough treatment than space here allows. It is time, however, to penetrate their critical groundwork and delve deeper into the recesses of human being from which the literature in question is born. Whether treating Holocaust literature from the persepctive of genre, tradition, theme, or form, the studies we have considered all operate within the framework of objective thought. "While objective thought," Kierkegaard explains, "is indifferent to the thinking subject and his existence, the subjective thinker is as an existing individual essentially interested in his own thinking, existing as he does in his thought. . . . While objective thought translates everything into results, . . . subjective thought puts everything into process and omits the result (*Postscript* 67-68). In the pages that follow the Holocaust novel is viewed not as a result—that is, not as an object of critical scrutiny—but as a force or a process in the life of the living subject. As Bakhtin has shown, "the text as such never appears as a dead thing; beginning with any text, . . . we always arrive, in the final analysis, at the human voice, which is to say we come up against the human being" (*Dialogic* 252-53). Adopting this Bakhtinian approach, we shall interact with the Holocaust novel from an existential, phenomenological perspective in an effort to apprehend human being through the human voice.

The Philosophical Foundations for the Investigation

Franz Rosenzweig and his ideas regarding the conceptual links between man, God, and world provide the first of our philosophical reference points. In a letter to Mawrik Kahn dated 18 August 1918, Rosenzweig wrote, "The world was created as a fact, and it must be redeemed into personality . . . (see Joel 3:1-2). Therefore each step, each action—consciously for the knowing, naively for the naive—is a step toward the personalization of the factual, the humanization of 'things'" (Glatzer 81). In the redemption of fact into personality the thing, no longer mute, assumes a voice. That which is human is that which speaks. The process of dehumanization, on the other hand, is a process of rendering silent by divorcing word from thing, *davar* from *davar*, dividing the self over against itself. The Holocaust novel addresses this division and struggles to work out some kind of redemption. The man who is called a dog (as in Yoram Kaniuk's *Adam Resurrected*) loses not only his form but his voice as well. The lost self is a self drained of voice, and the process of redemption—what Rosenzweig calls personalization or humanization—is a process of regaining a voice. It is in the voice and through the voice that the word is returned to its meaning.

The Scripture Rosenzweig cites in parentheses reads, "And it shall come to pass afterward that I shall pour out my spirit upon all flesh." The outpouring of the word in the Holocaust novel is an outpouring of spirit upon flesh, of speech upon silence, of life upon death; it is the mad struggle of what has been made into an It to be reborn into a Thou. The author attempts to utter the word of creation in order to receive the word of revelation, which is, says Rosenzweig, "at once revelation of creation and of redemption. And language as the organon of revelation is at the same time the thread running through everything human" (*Star* 110). The three things at work in the Holocaust novel, to use Rosenzweig's terminology, are creation, revelation, and redemption, and the ties that bind them are those that link man, world, and God. If language is the thread that runs through everything human, then in the Holocaust it becomes a broken thread. The word of revelation in the Holocaust novel is drawn not from language but from silence, so that redemption is forever relegated to the realm of the afterward, of what is not yet.

Language forms the basis for what Rosenzweig calls the new thinking, a concept developed in his supplementary notes to *The Star of Redemption* (2d ed., 1930). "In the new thinking," he explains, "the method of speech replaces the method of thinking maintained in all earlier philosophies. Thinking is timeless and wants to be timeless. . . . Speech is bound to time and nourished by time, and it neither can nor wants to abandon this element. It does not know in advance just where it will end. It takes its cue from others. In fact, it lives by virtue of another's life" (Glatzer 198-99). He continues, "I use the term 'speaking thinker' for the new thinking. . . . The difference between the old man and the new, the 'logical' and the 'grammatical' thinking, does not lie in the fact that one is silent while the other is audible, but in the fact that the latter needs another person and takes time seriously—actually, these two things are identical" (Glatzer 199-200). Rosenzweig's new thinking is counterposed to what Kierkegaard calls objective thought, thought ruled by logic and law of contradiction, the mode of thought that characterizes speculative philosophy. With the introduction of the new thinking, Rosenzweig removes the position of truth and meaning from the intellectual solipsism of speculation and places it in the dialogic space between an I and a Thou. He situates truth in an ongoing process rather than in some "logical" outcome. For the "speaking thinker," truth is not a dead datum but unfolds in the transformation of the one who seeks it through the word.

If truth ever emerges in the Holocaust novel, it does so in the dialogic between-space that Rosenzweig posits. Yet with the Holocaust novel a third shift occurs; while the method of speech may not be eliminated, it is at least momentarily eclipsed. Here the method is a method of silence, or of the shriek of silence, which arises by virtue not of another's life but of another's death. Here the "speaking thinker" bespeaks the silence of what Rosenfeld termed "an imposed Absence" (see 14-15) in a collapse of both speech and thought. While speech is bound to time, silence in this instance is bound to eternity as the thing absent, where the Eternal One is the Silent One. Speech takes time and takes it seriously; silence addresses eternity and is the address of the eternal. One thing the two have in common is their need for another. In the case of the Holocaust novel, this is where the reader enters, and what Rosenzweig says of man in *The Star of Redemption* also applies to the reader: "The word itself must take man to the point of learning how to share silence. His preparation begins with learning to hear" (309). It begins with learning how to hear the silence in the word, sharing with the author both word and silence, as two would share a piece of bread. The silence of the imposed Absence—absence of God, self, and other—is in turn imposed upon the reader. All the ideological, formal, thematic, generic, and other critical methods belong to what Rosenzweig calls the thinking method and serve only to veil the face of the one who speaks in a veiling of the critic's own face. Treating the text as an object of investigation and not as a living voice, these methods reduce both author and reader to an It.

Rosenzweig's close friend Martin Buber also places his accent on the dialogic space between two, between an I and a Thou. Since this is the realm in which that event known as the novel occurs, Buber's ideas may shed important light on the existential concerns at hand. For our purposes, one of the most important of Buber's work is *I and Thou* (1923), in which, for example, we read, "I require a You to become; becoming I, I say You" (62). One way to decribe the task of the author is to say that it is an endeavor to become I; this the author sets out to accomplish through a relation to the Thou that is the character, which is, in turn, a relation to the reader. The silence of an imposed Absence is felt in the yearning for "the fullness of Presence" (see Rosenfeld 14-15), and "only as the You becomes present," says Buber, "does presence come into being" (63)—the presence of God, self, and other. Just as absence is associated with silence, so is presence associated with the word. When the word is in exile, torn from its meaning, the I is torn from its Thou. The regeneration of presence, the resurrection of the self, lies in the re-creation of this relation through the word. In the

Holocaust novel neither author nor character speaks; rather, the relation speaks from all levels of relationship—author to character, character to character, author to reader.

These levels of relationship, moreover, take on significance in the light of a higher relation, from which every Holocaust novel draws its life. The Silent One, the one who bears witness to the event of the novel, is the Eternal One. The Eternal One, in Buber's language, is the Eternal Thou, who, as Bakhtin puts it, "is invisibly present, standing above all the participants in the dialogue" (*Estetika* 306). In *Between Man and Man* (1932) Buber explains this presence, which is the substance of all presence: "In the most powerful moments of dialogic, where in truth 'deep calls unto deep,' it becomes unmistakably clear that it is not the wand of the individual or of the social, but of a third, which draws the circle round the happening. On the far side of the subjective, on this side of the objective, on the narrow ridge, where *I* and *Thou* meet, there is the realm of 'between' " (204). In that moment—when the point of the pen descends to the page, when the character is about to speak, when the reader is ready to answer—deep calls unto deep. In this meeting of I and Thou we encounter a Third. "Extended," Buber declares, "the lines of relationships intersect in the eternal You. Every single You is a glimpse of that. Through every single You the basic word addresses the eternal You" (*I and Thou* 123). The Holocaust novel is just such an extension of the lines of relationships. The novel may affirm the Eternal Thou or it may accuse the Eternal Thou, but it cannot ignore Him. If it did it would be neither a novel nor of the Holocaust.

The extension of the lines of relationships in the Holocaust novel takes us to the place where the novel begins—to the silence whose shriek lies at the beginning and at the end of the novel. The novel turns back on itself like a word received and then returned. Response constitutes both the writing and the reading of the novel. Yet the end is not precisely the same as the beginning, and there is a difference between the response of the writer and the response of the reader. When the word of the author is received—when the novel "works"—silence, in the end, may itself become a response, the response of spirit. Buber's assertion in *I and Thou* implies this:

Spirit is not in the I but between I and You. It is not like the blood that circulates in you but like the air in which you breathe. Man lives in the spirit when he is able to respond to his You. He is able to do that when he enters into this relation with his whole being. It is solely by virtue of his power to relate that man is able to live in the spirit. . . . Only silence toward the You, the silence of *all* tongues, the taciturn waiting in the unformed, undifferentiated, prelinguistic word leaves the You free and stands together with it in reserve where the spirit does not manifest itself but is. [89]

Because silence is an issue in the Holocaust novel, spirit is also an issue. The novel's dialogic dimensions, born out of silence, are its spiritual dimensions. This makes the existential concern with the novel, on the part of both author and reader, a matter of life and death. When we fail to respond to the voice coming from within and from beyond the witness, not only do we die spiritually, but the children around us also die, quite literally. For the way of the spirit is the way of the flesh. When the spirit dies, so does the body. And the children are the first to go.

Central to an existential treatment of the Holocaust novel, then, is the problem of response, which is a problem of response ability, that is, responsibility. Here too Buber makes an important point, and where he writes "living situation" in the following passage from *Between Man and Man* we can read "Holocaust novel." For the novel viewed as an event, not as an object, is a living situation. "In spite of all similarities every living situation has, like a new-born child, a new face, that has never been before and will never come again. It demands of you a reaction which cannot be prepared beforehand. It demands nothing of what is past. It demands presence, responsibility; it demands you" (114). There is a definitive link between subjectivity and responsibility. The author, in an effort to redeem or resurrect the self, holds no mirror up to history but engages the other, above and below, in a responsive interchange. Similarly, the reader must allow no critical *isms* to eclipse the author's voice but must answer the text with life, making a response into one that calls for a response. Just as the author in relation to character and to reader is for-the-other, so must the reader become for-the-other, grounding presence in the capacity for response.

Rosenzweig's "new thinking" and Buber's "dialogic" thus bring us to a connection between responsibility and subjectivity as the basis of meaning in the I-Thou relation where human life unfolds. The philosophical insight most helpful in this regard comes from the French-Lithuanian thinker Emmanuel Levinas, a survivor of the Holocaust. In *Otherwise Than Being; or, Beyond Essence* (1980), a work dedicated to the six million, Levinas makes a statement about "saying" that we can apply to the Holocaust novel. "Saying," he explains, is "already a sign made to another, a sign of this giving of signs, that is, of this non-indifference, a sign of this impossibility of slipping away and being replaced, of this identity, this uniqueness: here I am" (145). Inasmuch as the task of the Holocaust novelist is to re-create presence through response, the author becomes, in the novel and through the novel, a sign of this giving of signs. This is how the novel turns back on itself; this is how the novel implicates the reader. The sign of the giving of signs is a sign of responsibility. The novelist, becoming accountable for presence or absence before the truth, makes the reader accountable. The assertion "Here I am" is therefore transformed into a question put to the reader: Where are you? Before the text, the absolute difference between I and Thou—between author and character, author and reader—becomes an absolute nonindifference that cannot be abrogated. The self is redeemed and resurrected through responsibility couched in an absolute nonindifference.

To engage in dialogue, then, is to assume responsibility to and for the other, going out to the other in order to return with a self. This is what leads Levinas to assert, "Subjectivity is the other in the same. . . . The other in the same determinative of subjectivity is the restlessness of the same disturbed by the other" (*Otherwise* 25). Holocaust novels disturb not simply because they deal with horror and atrocity or even because such heinous events actually took place; it is rather because they draw the reader into a position of responsibility, a position of vulnerability. "The other calls upon that sensitivity with a vocation that wounds," says Levinas, "calls upon an irrevocable responsibility, and thus the very identity of the subject" (*Otherwise* 77-78). In more graphic terms, he explains,

> There is a non-coinciding of the ego with itself, restlessness, insomnia, beyond what is found again in the present. There is the pain which confounds the ego or in vertigo draws it like an abyss, and prevents it from assuming the other that wounds it in an intentional movement when it posits itself in itself and for itself. Then there is produced in this vulnerability the reversal whereby the other inspires the same, pain, an overflowing of meaning by nonsense. Then sense bypasses nonsense—that sense which is the same-for-the-other. The passivity or patience of vulnerability has to go that far! In it sensibility is sense; it is by the other and for the other, for another. Not in elevated feelings, in "belles lettres," but as in a tearing away of bread from the mouth that tastes it, to give it to the other. [*Otherwise* 64]

The character puts a question to the author; the author puts a question to the reader; the other asks, "Where are you?" And we must answer with our wounds, out of which we are reborn. This is what it means when we say that a novel is written in blood.

Levinas imparts an unsettling depth to Rosenzweig's insistence on the need for another; he brings out an aspect of the I-Thou relation that is often veiled in Buber's poetic language. The other is the one who summons our presence, the Thou before whom the I becomes I. The author becomes author in the face of the character; as the character is born from the wounds of the creator, the author is reborn. Similarly, the reader becomes reader in the face of the voice encountered in the novel, and the dialogic penetration of the text is also a penetration of self on the part of the reader. "I must experience—must see and discover—what he experiences," Bakhtin contends. "I must take up his position as though I were coincident with him" (*Estetika* 24-25).

Such is the imperative of responsibility, the noncoinciding of the ego with itself. The self is the opposite of its identity, if identity is rendered as those marks of distinction that isolate the self from the other. Regarding the relation between author and reader, Wiesel says, "I write to explore my own self as much as I write in order to help you explore yourself. I believe that basically, and ontologically, there is only one person in the world. That is the beauty, really, of our teaching: there is only one person. That means the 'I' in me and the 'I' in you is the same 'I.' Between our deepest zones there is a bridge" (*Against Silence* 3:230-31). That bridge is reponsibility. In the realm of responsibility, the realm of the Holocaust novel, the other distinguishes the self.

The thing at stake in the Holocaust novel, therefore, is the life of the self or soul. "The soul," Levinas writes, "would live only for the disclosure of being which arouses it or provokes it; it would be a moment in the life of the Spirit, that is, of Being-totality, leaving nothing outside of itself, the same finding again the same" (*Otherwise* 28). The effort in the Holocaust novel to re-create a world or a totality is an effort to become a moment in the life of that which is the source of life. Any meaning, any truth, that may give substance to the relation between author and character or author and reader lies in this relation to a Third, to the Spirit. Levinas suggests this when he says that responsibility "is troubled and becomes a problem when a third party enters" (*Otherwise* 157). The soul is the event that occurs when, in answering for the other, I answer to the Spirit. Buber asserts, "Responsibility presupposes one who addresses me primarily, that is, from a realm independent of myself, and to whom I am answerable. He addresses me about something that he has entrusted to me that I am bound to take care of loyally" (*Between* 45). I am entrusted with a soul, and I care for it through my responsibility to another and for another. Such is the nature of the witness born in the novel and the one born in response to the novel. The insomnia of the soul in its movement toward the other underscores a higher relation; the Infinite, the *Eyn Sof,* bursts forth in the offering of the self to and for the other. In the wake of the offering the waters of the self are once again disturbed. In the Holocaust novel nothing is settled; rather everything is unsettled and called into question, so that the debt to the dead and to the living, the need to respond, increases in the measure that it is paid. For we hear inasmuch as we answer; in the literary response to the Holocaust the answer to the summons to respond deepens the urgency to answer. Always one response behind, I am forever faced with one responsibility more, implicated and accused.

Thus to say "*Hinehni,* here I am" is to say "I hear." Levinas writes, "When in the presence of the Other I say 'Here I am!', this 'Here I am!' is the place through which the Infinite enters into language" (*Ethics*

106). He goes on to explain, "The witness testifies to what was said by himself. For he has said 'Here I am!' before the Other, and from the fact that before the Other he recognizes the responsibility which is incumbent on himself, he has manifested what the face of the Other signified for him. The glory of the Infinite reveals itself through what it is capable of doing in the witness" (109). The Holocaust novel is just such a saying of "Here I am" on the part of the author in relation to character, to reader, and to Hashem. Because the Infinite reveals itself through its disturbance of the witness, the Infinite speaks—not through author, character, or reader but through the dialogic interaction between them. It speaks silently, between the words, in the margins, on the breath about to bear the next utterance. What is beyond speech and imagination is not simply the horridness of the horror but, above all, this invisible, ineffable presence of the divine Third Party.

Hence, face to face with the other, we encounter that which is beyond representation: in the confinement of the name that calls forth the character, we confront the silent murmuring of the Nameless, of the invisible One. "The 'invisible God,'" Levinas points out, "is not to be understood as God invisible to the senses, but as God nonthematizable in thought, and nonetheless as non-indifferent to the thought which is not thematization" (*Ethics* 106). In the Holocaust novel the invisibility of the nonthematizable God takes the form of silence. To the extent that the novel deals with silence, it deals with God. The nonindifference to the thought that is not thematization is the shriek of silence. We discover once again that those studies couched in standard concerns of criticism cannot help but ignore this definitive feature of the event we refer to here as the Holocaust novel. "If I use words," says Wiesel, "it is not to change silence but to complete it" (*Against Silence* 3:267). Thus authors like Wiesel make heard that which is beyond representation.

Preeminent among those philosophers who address the metaphysics of silence is André Neher. In his book *The Exile of the Word: From the Silence of the Bible to the Silence of Auschwitz* (1970), Neher identifies Auschwitz with silence (141) and argues, "The first step after Auschwitz then seems to be the one which would place us at the exact moment when nothing any longer exists but when all may be again. It is the moment of Silence, of that Silence which once, at the beginning of the world, held back the Word while also being its womb; of that Silence which at Auschwitz but a short while ago was identified with the history of the world" (143). Thus we can see that to view the Holocaust novel within the framework of history or tradition is to miss an essential feature of the novel, namely that it comes into being when all has been turned over to nothingness. The "moment of Silence" that Neher invokes is the moment of the Holocaust novel, when the author becomes author, becomes the midwife to the word through which the self may be reborn. Any rebirth that may take place in and through the Holocaust novel occurs from the womb of silence. In Levinas's terms this silence is the utter indifference—the "horrible neutrality of the *there is*" ("Signature" 181)—against which the nonindifference essential to the self arises. The self confronted with the project of rebirth, moreover, is not so much a dead self as one that has been made into nothing, into a silenced self. In the Holocaust novel, "Silence—the 'inert' silence, great and solemn—comes forward not as a temporary suspension of the Word but as a spokesman for the invincible Nothingness. Thus Silence replaces the Word because Nothingness takes the place of Being" (Neher 63). The process of rebirth in the novel, then, is a process of reversal, a process of return. From the muted rumbling of the *there is* arises the utterance of "Here I am." For the author this occurs in an "inverse movement," as Tzvetan Todorov describes it in his book on Bakhtin, "whereby the novelist reintegrates his own position." Bakhtin refers to this movement, Todorov explains, as *vnenakhodimost'*, "or finding oneself within" (153).

Neher draws a connection between the act of reversal and the rebirth of the self out of silence in his discussion of silence in the works of Elie Wiesel. There, he argues, silence has three functions. First, it is "phenomenological: the silence serves as a kind of counterpoint to the thought which it clarifies, explains, criticizes, and challenges." Second, it is "scenic: the silence is a backdrop, an indispensable accompaniment to the action." Finally, it is "theological: bringing the silence of God into the general domain of silence has the effect of reversing all religiously established values. Now it is no longer the words of men which are submitted to the test of truth, but the Word of God" (211). What Neher ascribes specifically to Wiesel's novels definitively characterizes the Holocaust novel. Here silence is a counterpoint to thought because the word that shapes thought is drawn from silence. Silence is a backdrop to the action because Auschwitz pervades the Holocaust novel regardless of the peculiarities of its time and place. Silence in the novel has certain theological aspects because the one who is silent is God; or rather, God is silence, present by His absence, the truth of His Word measured by the withdrawal of His Word. Truth in this instance, again, lies not in the facts that constitute an event but in what the self is in the process of becoming in relation to the silence that is God.

Hence, Neher insists, "a man's true self can be discovered only in one or another of these silences, and the revelation of this ontological potential of silence is undoubtedly the major achievement of the phenomenology of silence in Elie Wiesel" (212). Once more, Neher's assertion extends to the Holocaust novel, and our interest in the phenomenological aspects of the novel concerns the phenomenology of silence. It is an interest in what occurs when the novel—and with it the self—is born from silence into a word that creates a relation between I and Thou. Neher explains the "revelation of this ontological potential of silence": "At the beginning, God is silence, night, death. He is no less so at the end, for 'God himself has not changed,' but what has changed is men, the ontological vibration of their silence which has ceased to be solitary and egotistical. The chord of human silence sets another chord vibrating, and men suddenly learn that 'the silence of two people is deeper than the silence of one'" (221). The act of utterance, the writing and reading of the novel change the human being. We see changes occur between characters in the novel, yet they also transpire between author and character, between author and reader. The author cannot write, nor can the reader read, without undergoing transformation. The thing that summons the reader's response is not just the word but the silence conveyed by the word. Here it may help to recall Bakhtin's distinction between stillness (*tishina*) and silence (*molchanie*): "In stillness there is no sound (or nothing makes a sound); in silence no one says anything (no one speaks). Silence is possible only in the human realm" (*Estetika* 338). Silence is possible only when something must be said, when a witness must be born—else the soul would die.

Thus, if the soul is to live, it must voice its yes "from within the void," as Neher puts it, "from the depths of absence, from the heart of 'no'" (207). The yea-saying that distinguishes the Holocaust novel comes about when there is every reason that one should say no; such is the "overflowing of meaning by nonsense," as Levinas expresses it. The dialogic interaction within the novel and beyond the novel affirms what there is to hold dear, to love, when one has been robbed of what is most precious. "Every dialogue," Neher tells us, "implies an aggression, a renunciation, a death to oneself, and an absolute silence, which are attitudes preliminary to opening up, to communication, to life-within-dialogue, and to love" (48). The shriek of silence by which the soul comes to life in the Holocaust novel is a cry of love, a cry uttered "despite-me, for-another." Levinas writes, "It is the very fact of finding oneself while losing oneself" (*Otherwise* 11). Elsewhere he explains, "To escape the 'there is' one must not be posed but deposed. . . . The responsibility for the Other, being-for-the-other, seemed to me, . . . to stop the anonymous and senseless rumbling of being" (*Ethics* 52). The author's task in writing the novel, as well as the reader's task in reading it, is not simply to be reborn but to die and be reborn in dialogue, to die away from isolation and be reborn into relation—through love. For love redeems and reestablishes the presence of the one who is absent, the one who is the *kol demamah dakah*, the "thin voice of silence" (1 Kings

19:12; cf. Neher 84-85). Love is the stuff of presence and the essence of the Holocaust novel.

Introducing these philosophical considerations in order to identify the premises of an existential, phenomenological treatment of the novel, we bring to the investigation a dimension generally absent from the other studies. Rosenzweig's counterposition of speech to thought, Buber's relation between I and Thou, Levinas's connection between subjectivity and responsibility, Neher's phenomenology of silence—all combine to take us from the periphery of the novel as object to the inside of the novel as event. It is as though we no longer sit and describe the nature of Jacob's injury but rather join him (to the extent that it is possible) in his wrestling match at Peniel, coming face to face with the one whose name he seeks and by whom his name is changed.

The Theoretical Basis for the Investigation

Mikhail Bakhtin provides the primary source for our theoretical approach. Katerina Clark and Michael Holquist have said, "Bakhtin's distinctiveness consists in his invention of a philosophy of language that has immediate application not only to linguistics and stylistics but also to the most urgent concerns of everyday life. It is, in effect, an Existentialist philology" (9). Unsurprisingly, then, several connections exist between the philosophical background for this study and the theoretical approach behind it. The neo-Kantian thinker Hermann Cohen, for example, greatly influenced both Rosenzweig and Bakhtin. Bakhtin's emphasis on the dialogic relation between self and other has led to studies comparing his ideas with those of Buber (see Nina Perlina), and his concern for the definitive links between responsibility and spiritual life has suggested comparison with Levinas (see Patterson, *Literature and Spirit* 98-127). These philosophical overtones in Bakhtin's literary theory lie behind his view of the novel as a force of discourse rather than a particular genre or form. The novel, as Bakhtin regards it, is a process of dialogic interaction, an event of creation, a process of seeking truth. Wiesel has said about the Holocaust novel that "a novel about Treblinka is either not a novel or nor about Treblinka" (*Dimensions* 7). As Bakhtin might point out, a novel is not subject to generic classification, and it is always about itself, that is, about the life and the world that bring it into being.

The word, or discourse, in the novel (both terms are couched in the Russian word *slovo*) is inextricably linked to the life that it utters and that gives it utterance. "Discourse in the novel," Bakhtin argues, "is structured on an uninterrupted mutual interaction with the discourse of life" (*Dialogic* 383). Novelistic discourse emerges from meeting and encounter, from coexistence and dialogic exchange; in the novel being there means being with. The idea at work in the novel, Bakhtin explains, "begins to live only when it enters into genuine dialogic relationships with other ideas. . . . The idea is a *live event*, played out at the point of dialogic meeting between two or more consciousnesses" (*Problems* 88). This meeting of ideas is a meeting of voices, and it begins in the encounter between author and character throughout what Bakhtin calls the "aesthetic event." He says, "In the aesthetic event we have an encounter between two consciousnesses, . . . where the consciousness of the author stands in a relation to the consciousness of the hero—not from the standpoint of his thematic composition or thematically objective significance but from the standpoint of his living subjectivity" (*Estetika* 79-80). Assuming a name, the character assumes the task of becoming a self; becoming a self, the character generates a word, a voice with which the author can interact. Hence, says Bakhtin, "the novel always includes in itself the activity of coming to know another's word" (*Dialogic* 353). This is true of the self-to-other relation not only between author and character but between character and character and between author and reader as well. If discourse in the novel is dialogic, then it entails the transformation of discourse—and of the self, since the self lives, dies, and is reborn through the word it offers or withholds.

Because encounter in the novel is encounter between discourses, "language in the novel," Bakhtin points out, "not only represents, but itself serves as the object of representation" (*Dialogic* 49). This insight may help us to see why the subject of the Holocaust novel is the word, particularly as it interacts with an alien word or discourse. In this connection Bakhtin introduces his notion of polyglossia or the multiplicity of languages, which, he argues, is essential to the novel's examination of language (see *Dialogic* 50-51), since it is the multiplicity of languages that makes possible the encounter between the familiar and the foreign. Polyglossia draws language into a self-reflective process of speaking and response and makes the discourse of one responsive to the discourse of another. This interaction especially applies to the Holocaust novel, for the concentrationary universe from which its authors arise comprises a multiplicity of languages. Primo Levi expresses this point quite well in describing the concentration camp: "The confusion of languages is a fundamental component of the manner of living here: one is surrounded by a perpetual Babel" (*Man* 36). He bitterly describes the Carbide Tower at Buna as the Tower of Babel, exclaiming, "Its bricks were called *Ziegel, briques, tegula, cegli, kamenny, mattoni, téglak*" (*Man* 81). Indeed, many authors of Holocaust novels—Wiesel, Rawicz, Appelfeld, and Ka-tzetnik, for example—write in languages other than their native tongues.

A person torn from a native tongue is also torn from the self, and this linguistic division indicates the existential division addressed in the Holocaust novel, both in its content and in its creation. Yet this multiplicity and conflict of languages may, in Bakhtin's words, "open up the possibility of never having to define oneself in language, the possibility of translating one's own intentions from one linguistic system to another, of fusing 'the language of truth' with 'the language of the everyday,' of saying 'I am me' in someone else's language, and in my own language, 'I am other'" (*Dialogic* 315). Thus the collision between languages, with all its existential difficulties, assists the author in the effort to become other, in order to create character. The author, Bakhtin asserts, "must become *other* to himself, must look upon himself through the eyes of another" (*Estetika* 16). To be sure, the interaction of languages that places one in a position of being other to oneself often arises in the Holocaust novel through encounters between German and Pole, Czech and Hungarian, Russian and Italian, and so on. The reader also comes before the novels of the Holocaust in a multitude of languages, including Hebrew, French, English, German, Czech, Italian, Yiddish, and Russian. The frustrations of communication and translation underscore the urgency to speak and fuel the struggle for a voice.

Thus polyglossia accentuates the need for dialogic interchange and promotes the novel's endeavor to create meaning. Bakhtin points out that "creation is always accompanied by new meaning" (*Estetika* 342); the novel constitutes a movement toward meaning undertaken as a result of a loss of meaning in the breakdown of the word. In the initial silence of this breakdown, one discovers a certain freedom, for, as Neher noted, freedom "is dialectically connected with silence" (168). For the author, this is a freedom to be other, born from the encounter or collision of one discourse with another. New meaning is always alien meaning, and the confrontation with an alien discourse launches the author into the creative act. Those who open up such freedom, according to Bakhtin, are the rogue, the clown, and the fool (see *Dialogic* 159). These figures, to be sure, are found in Holocaust literature—Gauthier Bachmann, for example, in Jakov Lind's *Landscape in Concrete* and the title character in Romain Gary's *The Dance of Genghis Cohn*. Such characters, in Bakhtin's view, introduce laughter to discourse and thus free "consciousness from the power of the direct word" and destroy "the thick walls that had imprisoned consciousness within its own discourse" (*Dialogic* 60). Further, Bakhtin argues in *Rabelais and His World*, "laughter has a deep philosophical meaning, it is one of the essential forms of the truth concerning the world as a whole, concerning history and man; it is a peculiar point of view relative to the world; the world is seen anew, no less (and perhaps more) profoundly than when seen from the serious standpoint" (66). Wiesel suggests the importance of laughter in the Holocaust novel when he says, "Revolt is not a solution, neither is submission. Remains laughter, metaphysical laughter" (*Souls* 199).

In the Holocaust novel, however, the one who most often seizes the freedom to be other is not the clown but the madman; it is he who "lifts the barriers and opens the way to freedom" (Bakhtin, *Estetika* 339). His is the most alien of discourses and the most disturbing of silences, since, as Michel Foucault points out, "madness begins where the relation of man to truth is disturbed and darkened" (*Madness* 104). Bakhtin similarly notes that "the theme of madness is inherent to all grotesque forms, because madness makes men look at the world with different eyes, not dimmed by 'normal,' that is by commonplace ideas and judgments" (*Rabelais* 39). The dying away of the self in its effort to be reborn requires this collision with madness, for in this collision with the radical otherness of madness the author perceives the self as radically other. The result is the creation of a character through whom the author may regain a self. As Foucault has indicated, the discourse of the madman is "credited with strange powers, with revealing some hidden truth" (*Archaeology* 217). Since, from an existential viewpoint, truth lies in what one is and not in what one knows, the creation of self and the generation of truth are of a piece. "For this theme," says Wiesel, "I need the madman" (see Patterson, *In Dialogue* 48), because the madman is an essential mediator in the rejoining of word to meaning, of the self to itself.

Because the author arrives at the self by way of the character, Bakhtin insists that "the artist's struggle for a stable, well-defined image of the hero is largely his struggle with himself" (*Estetika* 8). In this view, consciousness of self is achieved in the movement toward the discourse of the other, whereby the author lends an ear to his own discourse through the resonance of the other's discourse. Yet as soon as this shift occurs, the image of the self as other, says Bakhtin, "immediately becomes a feature of the inwardness (experienced) of my own life" (*Estetika* 77). This is how the author approaches the "man in man" within the self as well as within the character (see Bakhtin, *Problems* 57-58). Because "every understanding of living speech, of living expression, is of an actively responsive nature" (Bakhtin, *Estetika* 247), the readers who would make the novel part of their own inner lives face a similar task of becoming other to themselves. The relation between reader and text, like the relation between self and world, Clark and Holquist explain, is grounded in this act of response, "where the responding aspect of the word, the *otvet* of *otvetstvennost'*, is given its fullest weight. Responsibility is conceived as the action of responding to the world's need, and is accomplished through the activity of the self's responding to its own need for an other" (77). The dialogic event, the voicing of a world, that the reader encounters in the text summons response, so that the reader too may be reborn by bearing witness. This capacity to respond, this responsibility, draws the reader into a relation to truth.

Bakhtin describes the novel's concept of truth: "At the base of this genre lies the Socratic notion of the dialogic nature of truth, and the dialogic nature of human thinking about truth. The dialogic means of seeking truth is counterposed to *official* monologism, which pretends to *possess a ready-made truth*. . . . Truth is not born nor is it to be found inside the head of an individual person, it is born *between people* collectively searching for truth, in the process of their dialogic interaction" (*Problems* 110). This understanding of truth takes it out of the realm of fact and places it in a third position between an I and a Thou. The truth of what happened in the Holocaust is not buried in the past but remains in an open-ended, unfinished future, in the silence harbored by the dialogic word. Neher points out, "The radiations of the future are totally silent. Indeed, of the three dimensions of time—past, present, and future—the future alone is completely identified with silence, and its plenitude but also in its remarkable ambivalence" (168-69). The Holocaust novel's concern with silence is a concern with a truth that belongs to the yet-to-be. Always situated in a third position between the participants in the dialogic exchange, truth is that which is yet to be revealed, the name yet to be uttered, the meaning yet to be rejoined with the word.

Hence Bakhtin maintains that "every dialogue proceeds . . . against the background of a third who is invisibly present, standing above all the participants in the dialogue. . . . The third referred to here has nothing to do with metaphysics; . . . it is a constitutive feature of the whole expression" (*Estetika* 306). We recall Levinas's remarks on the invisibility of God (*Ethics* 106); the one invisibly present is present by a silence that, in Neher's words, is the "supreme experience of the possible" (40). The Third represents the silent horizon of possibility for response within the dialogue. As possibility—or the one for whom all things are possible—the Third sustains the movement of dialogue, witnessing and judging its truth. Thus the Third introduces to dialogue what Bakhtin calls a special responsibility. He writes, "Whenever alibi becomes a prerequisite for creation and expression there can be no responsibility, no seriousness, no meaning. A special responsibility is required. . . . But this responsibility can be founded only on a profound belief in a higher truth, . . . the belief that another, higher being respnds to my special responsibility, that I do not act in an utter void. Apart from this belief there can be only empty pretense" (*Estetika* 179). The Holocaust author has a reader, but the dialogic interaction with the reader, as well as with the character, has its higher witness.

Wiesel remarks: "The writer must think for himself; he must be alone. In my case, he must be alone always. Yet when I write I have a distinct feeling of a presence" (*Against Silence* 1:187). Here Wiesel invokes, perhaps, what Bakhtin calls the "over-*I*": "The overman, the over-*I*— that is, the witness and judge of every man (of every *I*)—is not a person but the *other*" (*Estetika* 342). Without this other, this higher witness, this presence present by its absence, any issues involving word and silence, word and meaning, word and self are empty pretense.

The silence of this witness, again, places everything in an open-ended future. Neher says, "Abraham's 'Yes, me!' [*hinehni*] is the acceptance of the silence which Abraham faces at the moment of the *Akedah*: the silence of the future, what I shall call the 'horizon-silence.'. . . The horizon-silence is the meeting point between the relative and the absolute, between the immanent and the transcendent" (176). The silence that shrieks in the Holocaust novel is not the silence of the inability to describe events that elude language; nor is it the silence of the gap beween the familiar and the absolutely alien. Rather, it is the silence of meaning lost and yet to be regained, the silence of a soul lost and yet to be reborn in a future forever yet to be. Bakhtin observes, "The definition given to me lies not in the categories of temporal being but in the categories of the *not-yet-existing*, in the meaningful future, which is at odds with anything I have at hand in the past or present. To be myself for myself means yet becoming myself *(to cease becoming myself. . . . means spiritual death)*" (*Estetika* 109). He goes on to assert, "For the 'I,' memory is memory of the future" (*Estetika* 110). This memory of the future is a mindfulness of what I shall have been, in the light of what I am in the process of becoming through my relation to the other. It is an orientation toward the horizon-silence, where, Neher says, God "reveals Himself in His entirety, . . . in the features of His unknowble Face" (176). Like all Holocaust witnesses, those summoned to remember are summoned toward the silence of the future.

Steeped in the not-yet-existing, the life sought through the Holocaust novel is a life made of questions, of the yet-to-be-resolved. As Wiesel expresses it in *The Town beyond the Wall*, "The essence of man is to be a question, and the essence of the question to be without answer. . . . The depth, the meaning, the very salt of man is his constant desire to ask the question ever deeper within himself, to feel ever more intimately the existence of an unknowable answer" (187). What is rendered here as "desire" is much more actively expressed in the French text by the word *chercher*, which is "to seek, to search," forever sustaining the movement of penetration inward, *toujours plus intérieurement, . . . toujours plus intimement* (202). The question that resounds in the increasing depths of the soul comes both from within and from beyond the human being: Where are you? Author, character, and reader are faced with the task of responding, "*Hinehni*, here I am." In the shriek of silence, at the threshold of response, question and response collide. The dialogic event known as the Holocaust novel occurs in this collision and opens up the dialogic dimensions of life in the post-Holocaust era. As a reader of the novel, "I must respond with my life for what I have experienced and understood in the art," to borrow a statement from Bakhtin. "Art and life are not one and the same, but they must become one within me, in the wholeness of my responsibility" (*Estetika* 5-6). The Holocaust novel, far more than other novels, transforms me into a witness and a messenger, calling me forth from a position of death and indifference into an absolute nonindifference by which I may live. There is no slipping away. If the Holocaust novel is about the word, if it is an endeavor to fetch the word from silence and rejoin it with its meaning, if it is about the desperate struggle for the redemption and the resurrection of the soul—then it is about me. "Listening creatively," Wiesel points out, "is in French *comprendre* or *prendre avec*. This means to be part of, to be taken with the teller of the tale, to become part of the tale" (*Against Silence* 1:187). To listen creatively is to engage in response; to become part of the tale is to become who I am. There is no slipping away. Those of us who were not there can never cross over into the Kingdom of Night, but, through the event of the Holocaust novel, it crosses over into us.

2
The Word in Exile

"At grief so deep the tongue must wag in vain; / the language of our sense and memory / lacks the vocabulary of such pain." Thus wrote Dante in his *Inferno* (235). But, as we shall see, the problem of language in the Holocaust novel is not a matter of insufficient vocabulary. Those who pursue the word in exile enter realms undreamt of even by Dante.

Casting the word into exile inaugurates the reign of silence and initiates the human struggle for presence through redemption. Yet within the silence that occludes the voice is hidden a remnant, a seed, of what was lost. This is indeed the Jewish condition, ever the human condition. "In Judaism," says Franz Rosenzweig, "man is always somehow a remnant. He is always somehow a survivor, an inner something, whose exterior was seized by the current of the world and carried off while he himself, what is left of him, remains standing on the shore. Something within him is waiting. And he has something within himself. . . . And this is just that feeling of the 'remnant' which has the revelation and awaits the salvation" (405). In silence the surviving shred of what was swallowed up intensifies, until it bursts forth into words that seek to bring the living word out of exile. When the word is in exile, therefore, words need the very silence they would overcome. For when the word realizes the fulfillment of its utterance, it is uttered silently, heard through the flux and flow of silence, on "the other side of speaking," as Paul Tillich put it, where silence "becomes itself a kind of speaking" (*Eternal* 99)—like the "thin voice of silence," the *kol demamah dakah*, of 1 Kings 19:12. "They faded into the night, like a slim double shadow," we read of Danny and Manny in a work by Arnost Lustig. Yet "the stillness was not silenced," for it broke through the silence in a novel called *Darkness Casts No Shadow* (173).

What exactly, then, does the author of the Holocaust novel attempt to hear and thus make heard? Whose voice, whose silence, impels one to speak or to bespeak the word in exile? In *A Jew Today* Elie Wiesel relates a brief tale that suggests one approach to these questions, bringing out not only what is exiled but also the place of exile. It is the story of a child named Joel the Redhead. A mere five years of age, little Joel was forced to hide with his family in the silence and darkness of a cave, lest the enemy should find them and cast them into a more terrible darkness. Hidden in the cave, he never knew whether it was day or night; thus are distinctions erased or overturned when the word goes into exile. He also had to learn to communicate silently; thus is the voice paralyzed. One day his father ventured out of the cave and was killed. "And in the shelter," we read, "Joel succeeded in crying without crying." Then his mother went out, never to return, and his Uncle Zanvel had to clasp his hand over the little one's mouth. "Zanvel, too, disappeared," Wiesel goes on. "And Joel was left alone in the darkness. His hand covering his mouth, he began to sob without a sound, scream without a sound, survive without a sound" (132). So the Holocaust author moves one hand across the silence of the blank page, leaving a trail of words on the track of the word. And the other hand he holds over his mouth.

To the extent that a figure such as Joel the Redhead can become a character in a tale or novel, silence can also become a character in a novel that deals with the word in exile. Wiesel's *The Town beyond the Wall* conveys this point explicitly: "'The hero of my story,' Michael began, 'is neither fear nor hatred; it is silence. The silence of a five-year-old Jew'" (119). Silence is the hero not only of the tale Michael relates but also of his own tale. The Silent One ultimately enables Michael to work out some form of salvation by bringing salvation to another, to the Silent One. "Later," Michael says to the Silent One, "in another prison, someone will ask your name and you'll say, 'I'm Michael.' And then you will know the taste of the most genuine of victories" (188-89). The most genuine of victories is the victory of the self over itself in the offering of itself to and for another both in word and in deed. This offering brings the word out of exile, if only for a moment. In *The Town beyond the Wall* the character's task is the same as the author's: to impart a voice and with it a name to another. Michael seeks the name of the Silent One because, in the words of Miguel de Unamuno, "Tell me thy name! is essentially the same as Save my soul!" (181). Conferring a name upon the character, the author offers up his voice for the sake of the character, until he himself becomes the "silent one." Here we recall a curious incident related by Wiesel. "I had a psychosomatic experience," he tells us, "while writing *A Beggar in Jerusalem*: I lost my voice. Everything had gone into the book" (*Against Silence* 3:281). Losing his voice, he perhaps found himself or regenerated a self that had been lost in the exile of the word. For a moment, perhaps, the word was drawn out of exile as the voice was drawn out of the author.

The exile of the word is revealed through the novelist's attempt to bring the word out of exile; what is lost is felt in the effort to regain it. Michel Foucault suggests such a view of language in general: "Language always seems to be inhabited by the other, the elsewhere, the distant; it is hollowed by absence. Is it not the locus in which something other than itself appears?" (*Archaeology* 111). The Holocaust novel, however, is not hollowed by absence but is instilled with it. Something other than itself indeed appears, for the Holocaust novel includes what precedes it, not just the historical circumstances from which it arises, but, more essentially, the phenomenological and existential condition out of which it is born. The work moves forward by turning back on itself, so that the thematic features of the novel reveal the phenomenological encounters and collisions that create it. Written in a time of exile, the novel addresses and summons the word in exile. Words invoke this loss of the word, this primal event, that launches the human being into authorship, into the collision with silence that announces the exile of the word.

The Collision with Silence

The silence of the word in exile is not a blank emptiness but an oppressive, stifling substance, a "rumbling," as Levinas characterizes it (*Ethics* 48), that rattles the soul and seizes the breath. Here silence emerges "as a spokesman for the invincible Nothingness. Thus Silence replaces the Word because Nothingness takes the place of Being" (Neher 63). Because nothingness overtakes being, the collision with silence belongs to no specific time; the Holocaust novel erases the distinctions of before, during, and after. Aharon Appelfeld's *Badenheim 1939*, for instance, is set outside the Kingdom of Night; yet Appelfeld writes, "The silence was dense, and from day to day it grew denser" (70). The word here translated as "dense" is the Hebrew word *samikh* (40), which also means "thick" or "clogged," as if the silence were impenetrable. The measure of time is not the passing of days but the thickening of silence. The word in exile is isolated not in time or space but in silence.

This point is made even more strikingly in Ka-tzetnik's *Sunrise over Hell*, in which darkness descends over the town of Metropoli and the Jews are gathered into a stadium to await deportation. "Gripped by the fear of death, a cry arose from the multitude. . . . The outcry engulfed the stadium and split the heavens, but Heaven remained lofty and silent as though God had deserted its temples. . . . Time didn't exist. Only darkness" (78-79). Once again, the author's tongue voices much more than its translation and reveals far more about the inner event of the novel. Where the English translation reads "heavens," for example, the Hebrew text has the word *shmei-hashamayim* (78); full of biblical overtones (see Psalms 148:4), this term means "the Heaven of heavens" or "the Most High," God's Holy Name as heaven itself. When these heavens split, so does God. The phrase "as though God had deserted its temples," moreover, is *k'mo nitrokanu v'eyn Elohim b'm'romim*, literally "as though they were emptied and there were no God in the heights" (78). From within the human outcry resounds God's silence, distant and elsewhere. When the word is in its place, joined with its meaning, man is the language of God; when the word is in exile and language is lost, man is the shriek of silence, filled with the emptiness of the emptied heavens and forever in collision with the silence of God. Thus the collision continues, as we see in I.B. Singer's *Enemies: A Love Story*, set in New York years after the Shoah: "They were all silent: God, the stars, the dead" (115).

Among the best descriptions of the tangibility and substantiality of silence is the following passage from *The Terezin Requiem* by Josef Bor:

The silence had penetrated here, Schächter realized, from outside, from above, from everywhere, and now it spread throughout the room, strident and imperative, it overwhelmed everything, froze the walls into dumbness, maimed the people; not even a quiver of air moved here now. The murmur is silenced, the hum of everyday life, which at other times flows everywhere, in the streets, in the house, even in you yourself, though solitary. The walls receive it and return an echo, the air is tremulous and warm with it, there is so much of it everywhere, and yet you never notice it. As you never feel the air you breathe. And suddenly the hum has ceased. At first you don't even realize that something has happened. There is only a chill somewhere in the marrow of your bones, as though the coldness of the dark night had touched you. As though the breath of death itself had wafted over you. . . . Then suddenly you are aware of the silence. [41-42]

Where the translation reads "strident," we find in Bor's Czech text the word *křičí*, which means "screaming" or "shrieking," a shriek of silence raining down from above and cutting through the solitude of the self, *tobě samotném* (27-28). The word translated as "overwhelmed" is *zmocnilo*, meaning "seized" or "took possession"; when the word takes leave of the world, silence becomes the place of the world. The silence with which the author collides—and by which character and reader are drawn into collision—is both inert and dynamic, within and without, something and nothing. As Bor suggests, it has the existential features of a death that not only befalls the man but also lays claim to him. When the word is in exile, the reign of silence is inaugurated. Its emblem is the death's head emblazoned as a frontlet between the eyes of the SS.

The collision with silence, as Bor implies, is a collision with death; the struggle with the word in exile is a struggle with death, which is as palpable as silence. "Death is truly not what it seems," Rosenzweig points out, "not *nothing* but an inexorable *something* that can't be got rid of. Its harsh cry sounds unabated even out of the fog with which philosophy surrounds it" (Glatzer 182). Neher notes that "death is silence—abrupt at first, in the silent plunge which immediately follows the last word of life, and then afterward deep, in the irrevocable expanse of silence which death weaves, as it slips further away, between itself and life. The moment of death is silence overtaking life. The duration of death is silence becoming infinitely removed from life" (37). What is made "real" in the Holocaust novel is not just the death camp but death itself; words that transmit silence transmit death. Death is not only, however, a force that overtakes life but also the thing that life struggles to overtake through the return of the word from its exile. The harsh cry of death that splits the heavens pours from the mouth of life. The author cries out to make heard the outcry of those who have been silenced. In that hearing he finds his own voice, and through that voice he regains life.

Elie Wiesel explores the inimical aspects of silence in its relation to death. He most thoroughly pursues that relation in *The Testament*. There his main character, Paltiel Kossover, an author, is locked into the solitary confinement of a Soviet jail, where he writes his testament. In his cell he discovers that "silence acts on both the senses and the nerves; it unsettles them. It acts on the imagination and sets it on fire. It acts on the soul and fills it with night and death. The philosophers are wrong: it is not words that kill, it is silence. It kills impulse and passion, it kills desire and the memory of desire. It invades, dominates and reduces man to slavery. And once a slave of silence, you are no longer a man" (209). The phrase "it invades . . . man" is a translation of *il envahit l'être* (173), where the term *l'être* or "being" places a greater existential accent on the problem of silence. Wiesel posits silence, death, and slavery against word, life, and freedom, underscoring the dialectical connection between silence and freedom. Situating his character in this dialectic, the author reveals his own life-and-death, word-and-silence, freedom-and-slavery situation, which, of course, has existential implications for the reader's position. Freedom—for author, character, and reader—is born from a response capacity, from responsibility, the one thing that can bring the word out of exile and overcome the silence that kills. One recalls that for Levinas, only responsibility could "stop the anonymous and senseless rumbling of being" (*Ethics* 52). In response ability the human being is no longer enslaved by silence or threatened by death; rather, the person becomes free for death through a responsibility for the other, like a mother liberated in her readiness to die for her child.

In the collision with silence, however, it is the silence of the other with which one collides. In its association with death, the silence of the other finds its expression in the silence of the victims, as Wiesel suggests in *Somewhere a Master*. "More than the hunger of the hungry," he writes, "more than the agony of the tormented, more than the flames over the mass graves, it is the silence of the victims that is haunting us—and will haunt us forever" (201). What do we hear through the silence of the victims? In *The Six Days of Destruction* Wiesel tells us: "And there was darkness and there was light, a light filled with darkness. A cry tore through the silence. No one asked who had called out. They knew: it was Death" (33). The word in exile reverberates in the howl of death; the Holocaust novelist confronts the task of transforming that howl, that shriek of silence, into words and tales. The author is haunted by stifled voices that eclipse the voice. In stillness, as Bakhtin has said, there is no noise, while in silence there is a voice that does not speak (*Estetika* 338). In the silence of a Holocaust novel, it is a murdered voice. This silence is quite different from the silence of infinite spaces that frightened Pascal or the silence of a cosmic refusal in Kafka's works. "Silence," Bakhtin asserts, "is possible only in the human realm" (*Estetika* 338), because death in the form of murder belongs only to the human realm; indeed, human death began with Cain's act of murder. While death may eliminate the victim, it cannot eliminate the silence of the victim. This silence both informs and implicates the author, as well as the character and the reader.

"Why are we silent?" the victims ask in Wiesel's *Dawn*. "Because silence is not only our dwellingplace but our very being as well. We *are* silence. And your silence is us. You carry us with you. Occasionally you may see us, but most of the time we are invisible to you. When you see us you imagine that we are sitting in judgment upon you. You are wrong. Your silence is your judge" (68-69). Thus confronting his character with the address of the victims, Wiesel himself confronts the silence of the victims, which he makes heard through his character's collision with that silence. As the man—both character and author—collides with silence, he is invaded with silence; those who were robbed of their cemeteries, reduced to smoke and ash, make the survivor into the cemetery of their silence. The more that silence is articulated, the deeper it runs; the more the author bespeaks the silence of the word in exile, the greater becomes his need to speak. The debt increases in the measure that it is paid; thus the silence of the other that cuts into me becomes the judgment I pronounce upon myself. The Holocaust novelist, therefore, lives in an "accusative that derives from no nominative" (Levinas, *Otherwise* 11). The author is accused not of survival but of silence; the author's responsibility for the exile of the word demands response. The sentence for the failure to respond is the death that lurks in the silence.

In Jakov Lind's *Landscape in Concrete*, Bachmann, the hero, cries out, "If you don't talk, you die. . . . The dead are speechless, doesn't that prove it?" (141). *Ist das kein Beweis*, reads the German text, "is that not proof." Yet *Beweis* also means "mark" or "sign"; death is the sign of silence, the sign that engages the author in the struggle with signs. Once again, the character's outcry belies the author's existential concern. The author who dies as an author dies of silence, as Paltiel discovers in Wiesel's *The Testament:* "I didn't know that it was possible to die of silence, as one dies of pain, of sorrow, or hunger, of fatigue, of illness or of love. And I understand why God created heaven and earth, why He fashioned man in His image by conferring on him the right and the ability to speak his joy, to express his anguish. God too, God Himself was afraid of silence" (210). The voice lives by the word, and the self lives by its voice. To live is to be present, and to be present is to have a voice. The word calls forth the voice, and the self comes to life through its response of "Here I am." When the word goes into exile, the self goes with it, so that the Holocaust novelist who strives to transform the sign of death into an affirmation of life struggles also to regain the voice that might restore life. The author brings the character to life by imparting a voice to that character, a voice by which the author's own voice may be regained. If God fashions man in His image because He is afraid of silence, so does the author fashion the character, laboring to regenerate the word lost in the wake of the collision with silence.

The sign of death thus proclaims the collision with silence and snatches away the sign of life, the voice of the self. The survivor is rendered voiceless by the voicelessness of the victims. The years of silence that followed the Shoah reflected this. One also sees the loss of voice that signals the exile of the word among many characters in Holocaust novels, especially those written by Elie Wiesel. The silence of the Silent One, who shares Michael's cell in *The Town beyond the Wall*, for example, not only reveals to Michael a silence within himself but also offers him the opportunity of redemption, whereby he imparts his own voice, and with it his own name, to the Silent One. Offering his name to the Silent One, Michael receives the Silent One's name. "The other bore the Biblical name of Eliezer, which means *God has granted my prayer*" (189). It is also the name of Michael's author. Here we see quite clearly how the interaction between characters expresses the interaction between author and character. The articulation of the loss of voice in the collision with silence lies in the effort to get the Silent One to speak. Just as the Silent One is positioned opposite Michael, so is Michael positioned opposite his author.

In Wiesel's *The Gates of the Forest*, Maria endeavors to save Gregor by making him pose as a mute. "And so by the grace and will of Maria, Gregor gave up speech. This was no sacrifice at all. Already in the cave he had become used to silence and loved it" (63). Yet in the cave of isolation Gregor's self splits in two, into Gregor and Gavriel. The silence that at first appears to be a refuge, the silence of the cave, turns out to be the silence of a tomb in which the voice and the self are lost. Outside the forest Gavriel/Gregor ultimately discovers that "too many roads are open, too many voices call and your own is so easily lost. The self crumbles" (221). In the end the self that was lost with the loss of the voice is redeemed when the voice is regained through the utterance of the Kaddish, the prayer for the dead. "He recited it slowly," Wiesel relates, "concentrating on every sentence, every word, every syllable of praise. His voice trembled, timid, like that of the orphan suddenly made aware of the relationship between death and eternity, between eternity and the word" (225-26). The word that restores the voice, the word drawn out of exile, is a prayer. "Both prayer and literature," Wiesel notes, "take everyday words and confer upon them another sense; both appeal to the most personal and most elevated needs of a man" (*Paroles* 166). *The Town beyond the Wall* is divided into four prayers; Arnost Lustig's novel *A Prayer for Katerina Horovitzova* itself constitutes the prayer alluded to in its title. These novels confer upon ordinary words not only a new sense but also a lost meaning, in which sense and sensibility merge.

For Grisha, the son of Paltiel in Wiesel's *The Testament*, the exiled word takes the form of his imprisoned father, the poet whose word Grisha feels he must protect—even to the point of biting off his own tongue. "I tried to show the muteness," Wiesel remarked about the novel. "And the fact that the child, the son of Paltiel Kossover, cannot talk . . . and *he* is the one who can save his father's writing—that to me was the ultimate tragedy" (Patterson, *In Dialogue* 39). Grisha is himself a poet, "not like his father" but "in place of his father" (Wiesel, *Testament* 17). The author likewise must become a voice in the place of the victims whose silence invades him; again, the character-to-character relation expresses the author-to-character relation. In the collision with the silence that seizes him, the author loses his own voice, so that the character speaks for him—as Grisha must be a poet for his father—thus enabling him to regenerate a voice via his character. Commenting on Dr. Mozliak, who visits his mother in his father's absence, Grisha notes, "At last I understood: it is me he has come to see, not Mother. His purpose? To steal my father from me. To take him away a second time" (303). This is why Grisha fills his own mouth with blood; this is why he must speak and yet cannot speak. This is also the dilemma facing the author. Similarly, when the first-person narrator of Wiesel's *Dawn* asserts, "I wanted to transfer the lifeblood of my body into my voice" (66), we hear the author's own longing to regain his voice. For in his voice lies not only his own life but also the lives of those who were swallowed up in silence; through his voice these lives penetrate the life of the reader.

Other novelists, of course, pursue their own variations of the loss of voice. In Jerzy Kosinski's *The Painted Bird*, for example, the boy who is the main character loses his voice just past the novel's halfway point

The Word in Exile 37

upon being baptized, as it were, in a pit of excrement. "Suddenly," he relates, "I realized that something had happened to my voice. I tried to cry out, but my tongue flapped helplessly in my open mouth. I had no voice. . . . The last cry I had uttered under the falling missal still echoed in my ears. Was it the last cry I would ever utter? Was my voice escaping with it like a solitary duck call straying over a huge pond? Where was it now? . . . There must have been some cause for the loss of my speech. Some greater force, with which I had not yet managed to communicate, commanded my destiny" (146-47). Not until the end of the novel does the boy regain his voice—or rather, the voice regains the boy. "The voice lost in a faraway village church," he says, "had found me again and filled the whole room. I spoke loudly and incessantly like the peasants and then like the city folk, as fast as I could, enraptured by the sounds that were heavy with meaning" (250-51). Lawrence Langer has observed that "*The Painted Bird* is literally a speechless novel, totally lacking in dialogue and containing less than half a dozen fragments of language presented through direct quotation" (168). This formal aspect of the novel clearly has conceptual significance. The word in exile is the word torn from its meaning, like a tongue torn from a mouth; the collision with silence is a collision with meaninglessness. When the boy is "baptized" in that which defiles, we see meaning overturned, and the voice is lost. When the voice returns, so does meaning, heavy and filled with substance.

Nowhere is the loss of meaning, and with it the loss of voice, more concentrated than in the concentrationary universe itself. Auschwitz is silence, as Neher insists (141), because Auschwitz is voicelessness. Ka-tzetnik's *Atrocity*, for instance, underscored this mute condition. When the boy Moni, the novel's hero, enters the Auschwitz barracks, the prisoners "received him the way the pile behind the block receives a skeleton just dumped by the block orderlies. Here no one utters a word. Here speech is extinct" (92). Not simply speech is extinct but, in the Hebrew, *kal lashon* (67), "every language," every tongue that might give utterance to speech. Death wordlessly receives death; death is precisely this wordlessness. Professor Raphael, the French scholar, knows ten languages, yet "only three words ever break from Professor Raphael's mouth: the names of his wife and two children" (138). Once again the silence of the victim assails and implicates the survivor; the fate that befalls the character is the fate that threatens the author. In an effort to speak silently and thus bespeak the silence with which he collides, Ka-tzetnik relates an episode concerning the inmates Bergson and Hayim-Idl, two singers who go to offer their voices for a play being produced in the camp. The director of the production informs them, however, that the play is to be a mime (154). Like five-year-old Joel the Redhead, and like their author, these characters confront a silence in which they must scream and sob without a sound.

The loss of voice in the collision with silence belongs to the Holocaust novel, not just to the concentration camp. Consider the fate of the child singer, the yanuka, in Appelfeld's *Badenheim 1939*. Living amid a silence that daily grows more dense, the yanuka in the end "had grown fat, his cheeks had grown pink, and he had learned to understand German. His voice had apparently been lost altogether, and the few things he remembered about his home, his parents, and the orphanage in Vienna were quite gone" (162). One recalls a statement Wiesel makes in *The Gates of the Forest:* "Everything that remains of the past is in your voice, *is* your voice" (54). The silence of the word in exile threatens not only the voice but time and memory as well, casting the human being into a position or a nonposition that is neither here nor there, neither now nor then. When the word goes into exile, it takes time and place—the stuff of memory—with it, fleeing to a realm prior to any beginning and beyond every horizon. In this nonposition the author encounters an inversion of "the *arche* into anarchy," where "there is forsakenness of the other, obsession by him," out of which the author must generate "responsibility and a self" (Levinas, *Otherwise* 117). The silence within which the author undertakes the Holocaust novel, therefore, is anarchic; not only chaotic, the anarchic silence also precedes any *arche* or beginning.

This feature of the silence that is Auschwitz places the Holocaust novel outside the lines of tradition and generic distinction. Elie Wiesel and Albert Friedlander, for example, give their book *The Six Days of Destruction* its title to suggest this "uncreation" of the world. In *A Beggar in Jerusalem* Wiesel's character Katriel explains the difference between two main categories of silence: "There is the silence which preceded the creation; and the one which accompanied the revelation on Mount Sinai. The first contains chaos and solitude, the second suggests presence, fervor, plentitude" (108). Because the loss of voice indicates a loss of presence and plentitude, the silence with which one collides in and through the Holocaust novel is the silence of chaos and solitude; this is one feature that distinguishes it from other novels.

The visual metaphor most commonly used to express this silence before beginnings is, of course, darkness, the darkness over the face of the deep. Ka-tzetnik expresses it eloquently, terrifyingly, in one of his visions from *Shivitti:* "I can touch darkness. Darkness is in my mouth. I can taste it. I sense darkness on my palate as if it were a thing I put in my mouth" (4). Here the metaphor's connection to what it signifies is all too apparent. The light of life draws its brilliance from the utterance of the word; where the word fails, darkness enters. Looking further, we recall the darkness of the night that gives Wiesel's first book its title.

It is akin to the night that Ilse Aichinger personifies in *Herod's Children:* "Night shook with laughter, but she laughed silently, pressing both hands to her eyes and mouth. . . . Under her coat she carried her master's most powerful lamp: darkness" (141). The term "silently" here is translated from the German word *stumm* (136), meaning "mute" or "dumb": the laughter of the night is the laughter of the muted word struck dumb with darkness. When the word flees the world it takes with it the light created by the Word. The master of night is silence, and the Holocaust novelist works by the lamp of this darkness. Cast into an anarchic condition, the novelist works in a nonposition that precedes the cycles of light and darkness that constitute time. The distinctions collapse; time is lost. Yet, like the light that answers the summons to come into being before it exists, the novelist in collision with silence must answer before being called (cf. Isaiah 65:24).

The English title of Ka-tzetnik's *Sunrise over Hell* reveals the inversion of the *arche* into anarchy, for the sunrise that would be a beginning is the descent of darkness that occludes the light of all beginning. This novel portrays the original night and its dreadful silence: "The Site of Silence. Soundlessness was all around, engulfing the outflow of humanity from the cattle trucks. The different laws governing here were instantly tangible; the air was different; the platform lights here shed a different glow. Night here had an essence all its own. Night here was at the beck and call of an omnipotent sovereign, a sovereign supreme over the Planet. Night muffled, stealing inaudibly on tip toes to envelop you, inaudibly, so as to keep from trespassing upon the terrifying silence reigning supreme" (158). Ka-tzetnik enables us to see the anarchic nature of this silence more clearly still in *Atrocity*. In this novel the mime performed by Hayim-Idl, Bergson, and others is acted out in the "primordial space" that constitutes the position of the author: "Two actors emerge, heads facing each other, their eyes conducting a horror-dialogue as their feet climb a staircase of air. Queer, mute gesticulations. Speaking shut-mouthed. Towards them come floating two others, announcing something in an esoteric eye-dialect, not moving lips or hands. Their feet really do not seem to be touching the ground. Everything here is happening as though not in the world of man, and not even in the world of Auschwitz, but somewhere in primordial space between Chaos and Creation" (158). The mime is an effort to articulate Auschwitz, "shut-mouthed." Mirroring the condition of the prisoners, the players are suspended in a void between heaven and earth, in a nothingness between worlds and words, their feet out of touch with the earth just as the exiled word is out of touch with its meaning. This point is even more evident in the Hebrew text, in which the actors climb not a "staircase of air," but *b'halal*, "in the void" (119). The force of this word is then accentuated in the phrase *b'halal-y'kum*, which is translated as "in primordial space" but literally means "in the void universe" or "in a universe of the void"—the concentrationary universe of the author.

When the word goes into exile, time and space, the garments of the world, thus go with it; for the word is not in time or space, but rather time and space are in the word. Timelessness and spacelessness, then, make up the nothingness of which Neher speaks: "Silence replaces the Word because Nothingness takes the place of Being" (63). The collision with silence is a collision with nothingness. As Ka-tzetnik expresses it in *Shivitti*, "Time There, on Planet Auschwitz, was not the same as here. Each moment There revolved around the cogwheels of a different time-sphere" (xi). In the Holocust novel, therefore, the confusion of time and space constitutes not only an experimentation with structure but also an expression of the silence of the word in exile.

The Permutation of Time and Space

"Speech is bound to time and nourished by time," Rosenzweig said (Glatzer 199), but when the word is in exile, detached from time, time itself loses the speech that sustains it. Divorced from the word, time tells nothing, and there is no telling time. The title of Yehuda Amichai's novel *Not of This Time, Not of This Place* might serve as the title of every Holocaust novel. The breakdown of time and place lies not in the length of time passed or in spatial distances; rather, it is an existential breakdown that concerns the self. "This diachrony of time," Levinas explains, "is not due to the length of the interval, which representation would not be able to take in. It is a disjunction of identity where the same does not rejoin the same: there is non-synthesis, lassitude" (*Otherwise* 52). To be sure, Levinas's words quite accurately describe the situation of Amichai's main character, Joel. For him time is so twisted that the self is wrenched from itself to form two Joels. Elie Wiesel makes a similar point concerning time in the chapter titled "The Watch" in *One Generation After* (whose French title, significantly, is *Entre deux soleils*, Between two suns). Wiesel relates the tale of his return to Sighet and his effort to dig up a watch he had buried just before his deportation. "I was laboring to exhume not an object," he writes, "but time itself, the soul and memory of that time" (83). He retrieves the watch from its twenty-year-old grave, yet he is unable to take it with him and returns it to its resting place. The time told by that watch was not of this time. "Since that day," he continues, "the town of my childhood has ceased being just another town. It has become the face of a watch" (86). The lost time belongs to the lost place, and both belie the lost self who is left to the struggle to regain itself by fetching the word from exile.

At the beginning of Primo Levi's *If Not Now, When?* we find that

Mendel, the novel's main character, is a mender of watches who comes from a town known for the broken clock on its church steeple; this image, of course, implies a link between a loss of the word embodied by the church and a breakdown of time. Leonid, a double figure to Mendel, reminds the latter of "some other watches that they had brought to him to mend: perhaps they had had a blow, the coils of the springs had become tangled, they ran a bit slow, then were wildly fast for a bit, and all of them in the end were broken beyond repair" (206). Like his character, Levi, the author on the track of the exiled word, is on the track of time. A kind of mender of time, he seeks something like a *tikun* of word and time. Through his character, he sets out to rejoin the word with its meaning, the time with its place. Those for whom the time is out of joint have no place, no home: "A man enters his house and hangs up his clothes and his memories; where do you hang your memories, Mendel, son of Nachman?" (271). Similarly, in Haim Gouri's *The Chocolate Deal*, Mordi, who "hath not where to lay his head" (61), learns that "just as there are earthquakes, so there are, among men, timequakes" (52). Gouri's novel also has its watchmaker, Mr. Shechter, who in fact owns no watch and is left in the end with the impossible task of locating Rubi, a double figure and companion to Mordi. Rubi also bears the fate of surviving his friend. As always, the character's loss of the other reflects the author's loss of self; like the watchmaker who owns no watch, the author sets out to find the character and thus to attempt to set right the time out of joint, the word out of place, the self out of sync with itself.

The permutation of time entails the undermining of the present and therefore the loss of presence; as the word is cast into exile, presence is thrown into a formless elsewhere or a nameless nowhere. Thus in Aharon Appelfeld's *Badenheim 1939* we read, "The words did not seem to belong to the present. They were the words of the spring which had somehow lingered on, suspended in the void" (117). In the Hebrew text a word omitted in the English translation begins this passge. It is *dumah*, "silence" (67); Dumah is the name of the Guardian Angel of the Dead, as well. The term rendered as "void," *b'liymah*, also has powerful connotations, meaning "nothingness" or "abyss." The exile of the word and the reign of nothingness are announced by such words out of place and out of season. To recall an insight from Elie Wiesel, one must "learn to say the right word at the right time and in the right place" (*Beggar* 84); this dictum sums up the task of the novelist. The author must re-create presence in the face of a terrible absence, striving to emerge from the oblivion of what Anna Langfus calls a "zone of silence." In *The Whole Land Brimstone*, for example, she describes the invasion of silence and the loss of presence that occur when her character's Polish hometown comes under attack: "Then the first bomb fell on the ghetto. It hit me simultaneously and silence and oblivion engulfed me" (117). Langfus's French reads, *je descends dans le silence, l'oubli*, for "silence and oblivion engulfed me," suggesting a movement elsewhere, to a nowhere: "I descend into silence, into oblivion" (119). *L'oubli* is also "forgetfulness"; the function of memory in the Holocaust novel is to reestablish presence. The zone of silence and forgetfulness is the zone of absence, of twisted time and perverted space, the phenomenological zone from which the novel arises and to which the novel bears witness. It enters the Holocust novel as part of its setting because the author sets out to reconstitute or re-member human presence precisely in the realm that is hostile to human presence. The mutated time and place of the novel is the time and place of its creation, and what threatens the character also threatens the author and, ultimately, the reader.

In *Touch the Water, Touch the Wind* by Amos Oz, Elisha Pomeranz closes "himself up in his room and his silence" (77), but he endeavors to penetrate the zone of silence in which he has lost himself. Because the word has gone into exile, Pomeranz attempts to traverse his emptiness through the mute mathematics of infinity. Yet "no one could ever cross this final line without collapsing into contradiction, absurdity, mysticism, ecstasy, or madness. This line marked the final limit of reason and the threshold of silence" (81). The danger is even greater than the translation suggests, since the Hebrew word for "contradiction," *stiyrah* (88), also means "destruction." Working out his dangerous theorem, Pomeranz crosses one threshold of silence only to lose himself in another silence: "Alert man A said to alert man B: 'He's set the whole world buzzing and now he's lost somewhere in this goddam silence.' Alert man B displayed a cautious smile, replaced it and answered: 'As soon as you said silence, goddam silence, I could hear the sound of an animal, barking perhaps, and there's a rhythmic throbbing noise on the other side of this hill'" (82). One recalls Levinas's comments on the silent rumbling of the "there is," a "noise returning after every negation of this noise" (*Ethics* 48). The sound of the animal, who is speechless, robs the man of human presence. Losing the order and structure, the time and space, of reason, he is cast into a place of exile here described as "goddam silence," which in the Hebrew text is *dumiyat Elohim* (89), the silence of God. The loss of presence is the loss of God; the silence of God is the absence of God. It is not the mathematics of infinity but the word uttered in its fullness, at the right time and in the right place, that restores the presence of God and of the self.

"What I lack is words," says Bachmann in Jakov Lind's *Landscape in Concrete*. "I'm afraid of the words I lack" (140). He is afraid because, lacking words, he lacks presence; lacking words, he, like Pomeranz, is left to the "goddam silence" of a God who has followed the word into exile. The Eternal One who is revealed in the word is revealed in time; speech is bound to time, and "what is not to come save in eternity," Rosenzweig has rightly said, "will not come in all eternity" (Glatzer 358). The time and place that are lost upon the loss of the word belong to the here, not the hereafter, for it is here that the eternal is revealed, if it is to be revealed at all. With the loss of presence that results from the permutation of time and space, the present becomes a void, a black hole, that consumes all that was and is yet to be. Herman, the main character in I. B. Singer's *Enemies: A Love Story*, collides with this realization when it strikes him that "everything has already happened.... The creation, the flood, Sodom, the giving of the Torah, the Hitler holocaust. Like the lean cows of Pharaoh's dream, the present had swallowed up eternity, leaving no trace" (143). It leaves no space for the word, for the self, for God. God dwells where He is allowed to enter, as Menahem-Mendl of Kotzk once said (see Wiesel, *Souls* 248), and He enters into time and space through the word spoken at the right time and in the right place, through the presence generated by the capacity for response. Presence, the time and space of the self, is rooted in the voice.

Anything that would obfuscate the voice, such as Pomeranz's mathematical theorem, displaces the self, removing it from the time and space that constitute its here. Such is the fate that befalls the title character in *Mr. Theodore Mundstock* by Ladislav Fuks. Attempting to calculate every contingency with which the Nazis might confront him, Mr. Mundstock has "every sentence . . . carefully arranged and every word accounted for" to such an extent that he cannot respond to a simple "good evening" (147); indeed, the Czech word translated as "accounted for," *vypõtěno*, means "calculated" (124). Mr. Mundstock thus makes himself into an exile in his own home, transforming it into an elsewhere in which he has no place. The formula is the opposite of the word; it is the expression of the silence that signals the exile of the word. The artifice of the formula and its mutation of time and space come out in the false and flimsy structures imposed on the lives of characters in the novels of Aharon Appelfeld as well; *Badenheim 1939*, *The Retreat*, and *The Age of Wonders* readily come to mind. In all of these novels, characters cling to the mirage of a time and place that have no existence in the world. Clutching their fantasy, they ultimately lose themselves to the reality—or the unreality—that invades their lives. "It still seemed," we read in *Badenheim 1939*, "that some other time, from some other place, had invaded the town and was silently establishing itself" (54). Once again the translation omits a critical word that appears in the Hebrew text: it is *dumah*, "silence." What invades the town is the "silence of another time, a time not of this place" (31). In Appelfeld's novels the reader is privy to the lie by which the characters fool themselves, so that the author seeks the truth under the inverted sign of the lie. The truth sought is not so much a particular "reality" as a place in which the word may once more find its meaning. The unity of life, Bakhtin has argued, is "primarily defined by the *unity of place*" (*Dialogic* 225); it lies in a space where the relation of *adam l'makom*, of man to the place, may be reestablished through the relation of *adam l'adam*, of man to man.

Appelfeld's *Tzili: The Story of a Life* treats the loss of place as an absence from home. Because the loss of place is definitively linked to the exile of the word, homelessness is bound to wordlessness. Tzili, for example, lives for a while in the muted space that comprises the small dwelling of an old peasant couple. "Here there were only cows, cows and speechlessness. The man and his wife communicated in grunts" (50). The Hebrew word *elem* is rendered as "speechlessness" (28), but "dumbness" or "muteness" is closer to its meaning, as if the word were snatched from the mouth. The cows and grunts bring to mind the barking of the animal in Oz's novel; when the word is in exile, man loses his likeness to God and takes on the image of the beast, the image of dumbness. The permutation of time and space brings with it the perversion of the human image, a perversion of inner space. Appelfeld accentuates the connection between Tzili's loss of the word and her loss of place when he writes, "She was no longer accustomed to the old words, the words from home. She had never possessed an abundance of words, and the months she spent in the company of the old peasants cut them off at the roots" (62). The original text phrases "no longer accustomed" much more strongly, saying that "she no longer had" the old words, *lo hayu lah 'od* (33). Further, in the Hebrew we see that not only are the words cut off "at the roots," but the roots of words, *shoreshyi ha-miliym*, are themselves cut off (33); the root or *shoresh* of the Hebrew word is the very stuff of its meaning. When the word is in exile, the human being is exiled from the *makom*, from the place, here expressed as home—and so is the word exiled from its home, from it roots. To be sure, exile is by definition exile from home. Nearly all of the authors of the Holocaust novel live in lands other than their homelands and write in languages other than the languages of their homes.

The loss of the word in its association with an exile from home is a major theme in two of Wiesel's novels, *The Town beyond the Wall* and *The Testament*. In the former the town beyond the wall is Michael's hometown, which lies beyond the wall of silence left by the exiled word, the wall at which he struggles to regain a voice through the "prayers" that make up the four sections of the novel itself. The place of the character is tied as much to the novel's structure as to any geographic setting. Once the place of prayer, of the word in its fullness, the town is transformed into a place of indifference inhabited by the spectator who, in his failure to respond, represents the wordlessness of the It (171). Like Michael, Paltiel in *The Testament* is a man cut off from his home and imprisoned in a cell; his condition underscores the loss of place. Any attempt Paltiel makes to return to his home only results in an increased awareness that he is himself out of place. Serving as a medic in the Russian army, for instance, he enters his childhood hometown of Liyanov and finds the house where he and his parents had lived. "A mad idea shoots through me," he relates. "The house is my house, but I . . . I am not I" (288). The loss of place upon the exile of the word entails a loss or split of self. "Some people define themselves in relation to what they do," Paltiel explains. "I define myself in relation to the place where I happen to be" (205). But when the word is in exile, the place is lost and the self is no self: I am not I. Like the self, the word takes on its definition, its meaning, in relation to its time and place. The permutation of time and space, therefore, brings a divorce of the word from meaning.

In *Blood from the Sky* Piotr Rawicz writes, "One by one, words—all the words of the human language—wilt and grow too weak to bear a meaning" (132). The French verb translated as "wilt" is *se fanent* (118), which means "fade," suggesting a waning of presence attached to the loss of meaning. The context for this statement is the flight of Yuri, who has changed his name to Boris, to escape death at the hands of the Nazis. Once the man cannot bear the name—once Boris can no longer be Yuri—the contact between word and meaning breaks down. The condition of the fugitive Boris in this novel reflects the flight of the word from its meaning, bound in turn to the fugitive's loss of place. Like many figures in the Holocaust novel, he lives in the "chronotope," as Bakhtin calls it, of the open road, which is distinguished "by the *reversibility* of moments in a temporal sequence, and by their *interchangeability* in space" (*Dialogic* 100). The character's movement of flight thus may become the author's movement of return; through the word that constitutes the novel, the author articulates the divorce from meaning in an effort to restore meaning. For meaning is to be restored only in a dialectical manner, in a transformation of the silence of its loss into an utterance of its loss. Arnost Lustig voices this inversion in *Darkness Casts No Shadow* through his character Manny, who is also a fugitive and for whom "looking backward was a way of looking forward" (89). He explains, "They stole away the meaning words used to have. It's like learning a whole new language in a strange new world" (90). The new world is the permutated world from which the word has fled; the new language is the language of the divorce from meaning, the language from which the author must free the word. The word is liberated from language when it is no longer a noise that breaks the silence but a response that contains the silence and transforms it into eloquence. The word drawn out of exile does not fill the silence but rather is instilled with silence.

The divorce from meaning is a divorce from life. True to Heinrich Heine's prophecy that when books are burned people follow, when the word goes into exile people go to their deaths. The permutation of time and space in the Holocaust novel, then, expresses life turned into death upon the word's divorce from meaning. In *A Prayer for Katerina Horovitzova*, Lustig writes, "She couldn't get rid of the persistent impression that the smoke wasn't coming from the chimneys over the camp but from Mr. Brenske's mouth" (62). Brenske is the Nazi, the symbol of the mutation of the word, who uses words that promise life to lead Katerina and her company to death. The image of smoke coming from his mouth points up the death that comes with the lie of the word divorced from meaning. Brenske leads the party of victims on a train that goes nowhere, suggesting the mutation of space; he promises an imminent salvation that never comes, underscoring the perversion of time. Both manifest the author's own phenomenological difficulty; proceeding from a space that has no place in the world, he must rejoin the word to its meaning and thus open up time and space for life. Lustig takes up this issue in "White Rabbit," a tale in his book *Diamonds of the Night*, in which the main character, Thomas, maintains a silent relation to a woman locked inside a mental hospital. She is the word in exile, whom he addresses from the outside, through a closed window, even though she cannot hear him. One day he finds that she is gone. When Thomas asks where she is, he is told, "Elsewhere" (74). The Czech word is *jinde* (44), just a letter away from *jindy*, meaning "at another time." This "elsewhere" is the nowhere that inserts itself into life when the word and the life it engenders are divorced from meaning. Through the tale the author reconstructs a place and a time for this "elsewhere," making it here and now. The woman, the word, who has been lost is here, silently and invisibly before us.

The word, Unamuno has said, "gives us reality, and not as a mere vehicle of reality, but as its true flesh" (311). The word is the place of the world, the vessel of time and space in the novel; its divorce from meaning is reflected in the character's divorce from reality, from life. The title character in Lustig's *Dita Saxova*, with the faith of a novelist, clings to the conviction that the word may be returned from exile: " 'I can't agree when people who weren't there say it's impossible to put into words, to give it meaning.' Dita said. She could not give up the hope that everything people have done—even the most perverse things—could be described. 'The sense of a word may shift, but I'm not afraid that reality will evaporate like mist. Every reality—fortunately and unfortunately, as Mr. Goldblat says—can be put into words. And one day not only will words get their meaning back, but things will too' " (129). Reality may not evaporate with the shifting of the word, but it shifts as the word shifts, in earthquakes and timequakes. In Dita's case, it shifts as irrevocably as the time past, shoving her over its edge in that wordless malediction we call suicide. Immediately before taking her own life, Dita has a perverse physical encounter with two brothers, which accentuates the collapse of human relation that accompanies the exile of the word. When reality shifts and space and time twist out of shape, there remains no place for the *between* realm that joins human to human. Once this relation to the other is lost, so is the relation to and the life of the self.

If, as Bakhtin claims, "the author-creator is a constitutive element of the artistic form" (*Esthétique* 70), then so too is the artistic form a constitutive element for the author. The character writes the author as the author writes the character, and the reader's effort to respond is a similar ordeal of authorship. One need only recall the suicides of Tadeusz Borowski, Piotr Rawicz, Jean Améry, and Primo Levi to see that the character's struggle reveals the author's. "For most writers," Wiesel has noted, "their work is a commentary on their life"; for the authors of the Holocaust novels, however, "it is opposite; their lives are commentaries on their work" (*Against Silence* 2:255). Like Dita Saxova, these authors live or die according to the success or failure of the word to overcome its divorce from meaning. The divorce from meaning, in turn, is linked to the divorce of one human being from another; instead of the one-for-the-other relation of signification and meaning, we have the one-from-the-other divorce of meaninglessness.

The Collapse of Relation

Speech, Franz Rosenzweig explains, "does not know in advance just where it will end. It takes its cue from others. In fact, it lives by virtue of another's life" (Glatzer 199). He goes on to add that the "method of speech" or the "speaking thinker . . . needs another person, and takes time seriously—actually, these two are identical" (Glatzer 200). When the *parole* (word or speech) goes into exile, time and space are thrown out of joint; similarly, the exile of the word brings about a collapse of interhuman relation, since the word is the substance of that relation. This collapse underlies not only the author's development of the relation between characters but also the development of the author's relation to a given character. "One *has* to write," as Piotr Rawicz has said (134), because fetching the word from exile is the only way to restore the interhuman relation that sustains human life. In Wiesel's *The Town beyond the Wall* Pedro declares to Michael: "To say 'I suffer, therefore I am' is to become the enemy of man. What you must say is 'I suffer, therefore you are.' Camus wrote somewhere that to protest against a universe of unhappiness you had to create happiness. That's an arrow pointing the way: it leads to another human being" (127). This "I am" that Wiesel invokes through his character is the "I am" of paralysis and isolation; it is mute and unmoved. The "you are" of relation, on the other hand, brings the I into a genuine presence through the word. Buber's lines again come to mind: "I require a You to become; becoming I, I say You" (*I and Thou* 62). Saying You, I move freely into the open.

Wiesel also addresses this point in *The Gates of the Forest*, where Yehuda says to Gregor, "The Talmud tells us that God suffers with man. Why? In order to strengthen the bonds between creation and the creator; God chooses to suffer in order to better understand man and be better understood by him. But you, you insist upon suffering alone. Such suffering shrinks you, diminishes you" (178-79). In these examples from Wiesel's novels we see that the collapse of relation is articulated from within the framework of relation (Pedro-to-Michael, Yehuda-to-Gregor), much as the exile of the word is voiced from within the framework of the novel, where the word might again find a voice. If only for an instant, what is lost is regained. As ever, the task confronting the character—to say "I suffer, therefore you are"—is the task confronting author and reader. The struggle to restore meaning to the word is an effort to recover the relation of an I to a Thou, of one-for-the-other, of "despite-me, for-another" (Levinas, *Otherwise* 11). The restoration of the word has certain messianic aspects, since, in the words of one of Wiesel's characters, "the Messiah is that which makes man more human, . . . which stretches his soul toward others" (*Gates* 33). This idea may lie behind Aboulesia's remark in *The Testament* when he says to Paltiel, "The story of the Messiah is the story of a quest, of a name in search of being" (160). When the I utters the name of the Thou with its whole being, being is restored to the name; the word comes out of exile, and eternity enters time, undoing all mutations of time. "One of the characters who has been present in all my writings," Wiesel has said, "is the character of the Messiah; what is the Messiah, if not the embodiment of eternity in the present, the embodiment of eternity in the future. He is waiting for us as long as we are waiting for him" (*Against Silence* 3:288). For the author, then, the character serves the messianic function of restoring the relation between word and meaning, time and eternity, I and Thou.

Inasmuch as the Holocaust novel deals with the collapse of relation, it deals with the collapse of language, with an overturning of sense, which takes the form of a breakdown in the boundaries of distinction. The word in exile is not the word that has crossed some frontier; rather it is the word that has lost its frontiers. The relation of an I to a Thou is rooted in a difference that is a nonindifference. In the exile of the word, on the other hand, all differences are overturned. "Children were old," Wiesel said, "and old men were as helpless as children, so that there was a confusion, a total confusion, of concepts and virtues and powers. And when the Messiah will come, one of the symptoms that should announce his coming, we are told, will be the restoration of frontiers around some of the confusion that took place. Good will be good, evil evil; children will be children, and old men old men" (Patterson, *In Dialogue* 19). Here too we see some aspects of the messianic elements in the Holocaust novel, insofar as it attempts to redefine the lost distinctions by addressing and responding to them. The author's I-Thou relation to the character, moreover, is the analogue for the character's struggle to restore the differences that make human relation a relation of nonindifference. The substance of the I is grounded in this relation, since, as Levinas has shown, "the self is nonindifference to the others, a sign given to the others" (*Otherwise* 171). The collapse of relation is a collapse of self.

An image in Ka-tzetnik's *House of Dolls* hauntingly echoes Wiesel's statement. Two children, a boy and girl, pull an old man through a Polish ghetto in a baby carriage (44); children are old, and old men are as helpless as children. Soon after, Harry bemoans the overturning of sense, remarking to Daniella, "These days a man has no way of knowing if he's already in the hereafter, or if he still has to wait for death. Everything is mixed up. Life and death in one brew. A hereafter that's not here, not after. Fraud and hoax" (63). For "hereafter" Ka-tzetnik does not use the common *olam-habah*, but *olam-haemet*, literally "the world of truth." "A hereafter that's not here, not after" is a translation of *olam-emet sh'b'sheker*, which means "a world of truth that is a lie" (65). Thus placing the Hebrew original alongside the English translation, we hear echoes of the permutation of time and place brought into a connection with the collapse of distinctions, of truth. The confusion of boundaries that comes with the exile of the word is a confusion of life and death, of truth and lie. "The moment I really exist," Kierkegaard said, "the separation between 'here' and 'hereafter' is there, and the existential consequence of annulling the distinctions is suicide" (*Postscript* 310). The consequence of existential suicide is murder.

Hence we find a group of rabbinical students engaged in prayer and study in Ka-tzetnik's *Sunrise over Hell*, searching for "the borderline separating life from death" (143). As they pray, so their author writes. "I have no fear of dying—nor of living," says Moshe in Wiesel's *The Oath*. "What frightens me is not to be able to distinguish between life and death" (196). In the silence of the exiled word, in the silence that is Auschwitz, life is indistinguishable from death. "Everything is normal here," Ka-tzetnik writes of the death camp in *House of Dolls*. "The wildest absurdity—the soberest reality. Anything goes here, anything is possible, the way anything goes and is possible in insanity. Death and life dwell together here. Blood and wine are drunk from the same flask. The Carrion Shed and the SS rooms are one. Borders erased. Boundaries lost" (212). As words are lost or mutated, spaces merge, leaving no between-space for human relation. This erasure of the borders, this mixing of life and death, constitutes the true enslavement of the soul. Life and death dwell together not just "here," as the translation reads, but *b'kfiyfah ehat*, "in one cage" (218).

"Proximity," Levinas has shown, "is difference which is non-indifference, is responsibility" (*Otherwise* 39). In the loss of relation that occurs upon the exile of the word, the ability to respond is lost. Hence, writes Arnost Lustig, "a new system of human relationships operated in the camp; a different scale of sensibilities and obligations had been established, different from the one in the Five Books of Moses or in the writings of socialist scholars or even in sociology textbooks" (*Prayer* 19). "Human relationships," however, does not appear in the Czech text; it reads *nového lidského řádu*, a "new human order" (19), which is here antithetical to relation. This order leads Katerina to realize that "causes and effects were all mixed up. . . . She mustn't hang onto a word like 'right' or 'wrong'—such words were beside the point now" (15). This is where she begins, and this is where she ends—"a lot of words had been kneaded into different shapes" (151)—in a blurring of distinctions between beginning and ending. Yet to hang onto a word is to hang onto life, for the word joins the human being to life through a relation to the life of another. The shifting in the scale of human sensibilities results from the shifting in the order of sense. The author's task of drawing the word out of exile, therefore, entails the creation of sense out of nonsense through the regeneration of the I-Thou relation, so that the reversal is itself reversed. "Then sense bypasses nonsense," Levinas writes, "that sense which is the same-for-the-other. . . . In it sensibility is sense; it is by the other for the other, for another" (*Otherwise* 64). The character's words articulate the author's difficulty, and from a phenomenological and dialectical standpoint, the articulation of the difficulty is the initial movement toward its resolution, even though that resolution may never be realized. Creating the character, the author becomes for another; through the character's word the author may regain the relation in which sensibility is sense.

In *Dita Saxova*, Lustig, through his narrative voice, explains that the survivors "had their own particular yardstick and rules, but the meaning of words had shifted. They forgave the past for nothing. And there was always someone around who personified the past for them. They spoke one language and heard another beneath it" (117). Here Lustig writes as a survivor about a survivor, using words to give utterance to the shifting of words. His character Dita Saxova, who is made of shifted words, personifies the past for him. This personification distinguishes character from type; as Bakhtin has put it, "character is in the past, type in the present; a character's surroundings are to some extent symbolic, . . . while the type's surroundings are more like an inventory" (*Estetika* 159). Not only through the character but also in the creation of the character, the author invokes one language—the language of exile—so that another—the language of redemption or the longing for redemption—can be heard in the silence that lurks beneath it. Through the creation of the character the author is able to overcome, for however long, the overturning of sense that the character often cannot surmount. "With a smile on her lips, she wondered, Who can feel more alone than children without parents, than parents without children, husbands without wives, and wives without husbands? She continued to smile. She would never be able to say it to anyone" (Lustig, *Dita* 179). Dita loses the human relation by which she might have lived, loses the distinction between here and hereafter, and takes her own life—so that her author does not have to take his. For through the character Lustig has said what the character could not say; in saying it, he restores or at least posits that relation that is needful to life—a relation to a listener, to a reader—via a character who could not speak.

It is possible, therefore, to die of silence, inasmuch as silence leads to isolation and the collapse of relation. The silence of the exiled word is at once paralyzing and isolating, revealing the loss of contact with the word and therefore with others. One character expresses the linkage between silence and paralysis in A. Anatoli's *Babi Yar*: "The utter silence made my head swim. It was like being tied up in a black sack or buried alive deep under the ground, where you couldn't budge and it was no use wriggling about because there was no way out" (356). The Russian word translated as "utter" is in fact *glukhoi*, which renders the silence "deaf" (429), a silence in which there is no appeal and therefore no way out. Having a way out entails not only having a place to go but also having someone with whom to speak, having a dialogic relation that might breach the silence and return the human being to life. "Two voices is the minimum for life, the minimum for existence" (Bakhtin, *Problems* 252). The silence that descends on Kiev in *Babi Yar* is the silence that rises up from the author's blank page; those who write can understand how a page may become a cage, an isolation cell like the one Paltiel describes in Wiesel's *The Testament*: "No master had ever told me that silence could become a prison. You taught me more than my masters, Citizen Magistrate. In this 'isolator'—the word is well chosen: in it one becomes isolated not only from mankind but from oneself—I have attained a level of knowledge I had despaired of reaching" (207). The isolation from the other and the isolation from oneself are of a piece; both are features of a single exile, of the word in exile. "Why does one write," Wiesel asks, "if it is not to break out of this solitude?" (*Against Silence* 3:197).

A distinctive feature of the Holocaust novel, therefore, is its concern with the breakdown of interhuman relation. In a way that bespeaks the condition of the Holocaust novelist, the Holocaust novel consistently includes a character in isolation. The author who is not personally a survivor must move into a realm of isolation similar to that of the survivor, through the character. Thus in *Mr. Sammler's Planet*, for example, Saul Bellow writes, "He was not sorry to have met the facts, however saddening, regrettable the facts. But the effect was that Mr. Sammler did feel somewhat separated from the rest of his species, if not in some fashion severed—severed not so much by age as by preoccupations too different and remote, disproportionate on the side of the spiritual" (43). The Holocaust novel operates on the side of the spiritual, the side of silence and exiled word; in the age of the exiled word, the spirit is always elsewhere. Mr. Sammler has literally risen from a mass grave, and the world into which he rises is not the world from which he fell. His movement was not so much a fall and a return as a crossing of a threshold from one planet to another. His is not the planet Earth but the planet Hell, the planet of isolation that Yoram Kaniuk describes in *Adam Resurrected*: "That's Hell: one man shouts in the ear of another, but nobody hears" (308). It is the planet over which a darkened sun rises in Ka-tzetnik's *Sunrise over Hell*, a novel in which the poet Eliezer loses his voice as he is taken away in a death van (66). Isolated from human life, he is isolated from the word.

In other novels and other contexts the issue of isolation reoccurs. I.B. Singer's character Tamara, for instance, voices her terrible isolation in *Enemies: A Love Story* when she says to Herman, "It used to be that when someone told me something, I knew exactly what he was talking about. Now I hear the words clearly, but they don't seem to get through to me" (126). Once husband and wife, Herman and Tamara have lost the word that made them so; having lost sensibility, they have lost the highest expression of the I-Thou relation, the relation of marriage. When the word is divorced from meaning, human is divorced from human. In *Marksizm i filosofiya yazyka* (Marxism and the philosophy of language), a work attributed to V.N. Voloshinov but probably written by Bakhtin, the author points out that we do not actually "hear the word; rather, we hear truth or lie, good or evil, important or unimportant, pleasant or unpleasant, and so on" (Voloshinov 71). Yet Tamara cannot hear these things, since they are heard only within the realm of human relation. In her isolation sense has been torn from sensibility, and she hears not the word but merely the noise of words, words, words. The most telling indication that ours is the age of silence, the age of the exiled word, is that ours is the age of noise. "I cannot imagine a century noisier than ours," Wiesel once remarked to me. "Conscientiously and consciously for noise." Locked into our noise, we are locked out of relation, left to the silence of isolation. "In our age," writes Wiesel, "man is obsessed by a feeling of failure and isolation. . . . one feels empty, trapped, hopeless, a stranger to the world and to oneself: between the ego and consciousness there is a rupture and lack of communication" (*Paroles* 138). From this collapse and collision, this perversion and silence, the author must summon the word.

A moment of reflection, however, will show that this isolation is more than an isolation from one another or from oneself. In Aharon Appelfeld's *The Age of Wonders*, the first-person narrator, Bruno, describes the conditions in his Austrian home during the Nazis' rise to power: "Father tried to encourage us with old, familiar words but they had no power to lift the covering of futility from the empty silence" (141-42). The exile of the word thus brings about an isolation from the father as the bearer of the word; for it is his task, as we are told in the *Shma*, to impart the word to his children.

3
The Death of the Father

The line of Jewish ancestry is matrilineal, since it is from the body of the mother that the human being is born into life. The mouth of the father, however, transmits the word that sustains life—transmits it from mouth to mouth, not from mouth to ear. When handed down through tales, the word "belongs as much to the listener as to the teller," Elie Wiesel has written. "You listen to a tale and all of a sudden it is no longer the same tale" (*Beggar* 107). The telling of the tale becomes part of the tale itself; or, as Bakhtin expresses it, "thought, drawn into an event, becomes itself part of the event" (*Problems* 10). The one who receives the word is transformed into a messenger who must in turn become the bearer of life through the utterance of the word. "I'll transmit my experience to him," Azriel says in Wiesel's *The Oath*, "and he, in turn, will be compelled to do the same. He in turn will become a messenger. And once a messenger, he has no alternative. He must stay alive until he has transmitted his message" (42). For the Holocaust novelist, the effort to fetch the word from exile is just such an endeavor to draw life out of death. The poet who engages in that struggle does so in the capacity of a son who receives and passes on the word of the father—but with this difference: the son in this case proceeds in the imposed absence of the father. He is orphaned by silence, and his path of return to life, in one way or another, leads him toward the father. For the father represents a "metatext," to borrow a term from Todorov, that "is actually an intertext" (40). What is beyond inevitably finds its way into what is within.

Operating in the absence of the father, of course, may breed not only a longing for the father but also a rebellion against the father. As the bearer of the word, the father bears a promise; when the word is emptied of its meaning, the promise goes unfulfilled. The effort to regain the word of the father, who harbors the seminal seed of life, may take the form of a struggle with the father, to wrestle from him what death has swallowed up. Yet death has claimed the father and all he signifies, so the writer-wrestler is continually thrown back to the zero point. From there he proceeds once again to affirm what he rejects, opposing the word to the silence that instills it with substance, opposing the father to the death that threatens his seed. Like Isaac, the survivor descends from the altar to become a poet, whose task is to

Death of the Father

transform suffering "into prayer and love rather than rancor and malediction" (Wiesel, *Messengers* 97). This he undertakes despite and because of the death of the father. Neher has astutely noted, "For the man of the Promise, God suddenly vanishes to the rear; but there is no purpose in seeking Him in that rear, . . . for God is already waiting out there in front, on the horizon-edge of a Promise which only restores what it has taken, without ever being fulfilled" (123). The Holocaust author is just such a man of the Promise.

The Bearer of the Legacy of Life

The father transmits the legacy of life by becoming a link not only between one generation and another, between the past and the future, but also between the Tree of Knowledge and the Tree of Life. "I do not know what life is," writes Paltiel Kossover to his son in Wiesel's *The Testament*, "and I shall die without knowing. My father, whose name you bear, knew. But he is dead. That is why I can only say to you—remember that he knew what his son does not" (20). The novelist writes not because he knows but because he has been charged with the task of remembering the one who knew. In *If This Is a Man* Primo Levi invokes the one who knows, referring to him as "Another"; this Other emerges through the lines of a text by Dante as Levi is walking one day with his friend Pibolo:

> "And three times round she went in roaring smother
> With all the waters; at the fourth the poop
> Rose, and the prow went down, as pleased Another."
>
> I keep Pibolo back, it is vitally necessary and urgent that he listen, that he understand this "as pleased Another" before it is too late; tomorrow he or I might be dead, or we might never see each other again, I must tell him, I must explain to him about the Middle Ages, about the so human and so necessary and yet unexpected anachronism, but still more, something gigantic that I myself have only just seen, in a flash of intuition, perhaps the reason for our fate, for our being here today. [134]

Such is the moment of revelation that the novelist must make into a link between creation and redemption.

Because the father is a link even—or especially—in his absence, he becomes a symbol, a silence that draws the human being elsewhere; indeed, "to let the silence in," Norman O. Brown has observed, "is symbolism" (190), and the symbol is the sustainer of life. Says Paltiel in Wiesel's *The Testament*, "The words you strangle, the words you murder, produce a kind of primary, impenetrable silence. And you will never succeed in killing a silence such as this" (30). This silence follows in the wake of the death of the father. In Rachmil Bryks's *Kiddush Hashem* Dvora Leah cries, "Fools! They think they can burn these words which are more precious than gold. Those are words of flaming fire—how can fire consume them?" (95). The words she speaks are the words of her father, passed on from mouth to mouth; though silenced, yet they return, symbols of life risen from the grave. In Saul Bellow's *Mr. Sammler's Planet*, we are told quite explicitly that "Mr. Sammler had a symbolic character. He, personally, was a symbol. His friends and family had made him a judge and a priest" (86). As a priest, the father is a bridge between what is above and what is below. He is the one who, for example, presides over the seder at the altar of the table; he is the one who engenders life by bringing order and structure to life (indeed, the word *seder* means "order").

In the days of the Tent of Meeting the priest had a rope tied around himself when he entered the Holy of Holies, so that if he should die in his service to God, his body could be retrieved without violating the Sanctuary. Yet this rope also signified his function as a link between God and man, as did his breastplate, which bore the names of the twelve tribes of Israel. The priest is not only a man but represents man as such, who stands before God and preserves what is holy, what is essential to life. In *The Dynamics of Faith* Paul Tillich observed, "The holy is the judgment over everything that is. It demands personal and social holiness in the sense of justice and love. Our ultimate concern represents what we essentially are and—therefore—ought to be. It stands as the law of our being, against us and for us" (56). So stands the father, as he hands down the holy word to the children of Israel. Thus Dvora Leah receives the word in *Kiddush Hashem*; there the words of the father are words of fire, for they are entrusted to him by the God who is a consuming fire. Similarly, in Applefeld's *Tzili: The Story of a Life* we find that the father figure, an old man, is the one who teaches Tzili to pray: "At night she would recite 'Hear O Israel' aloud, as he had instructed her, covering her face. And thus she grew" (6). Thus she "learned," *lamdah*, as the Hebrew text reads (9); thus she lived, receiving life through the prayer. For the word of the father that is the legacy of life is the word of prayer. We have seen that the language of the novel has certain features of the language of prayer; here we can see that this aspect of the novel's discourse draws the father into the novel's content.

The father who knows what life is, however, is not only a priest but also a judge. In this capacity the father represents what Bakhtin calls the authoritative word: "The authoritative word is located in a distanced zone, organically connected with a past that is felt to be hierarchically higher. It is, so to speak, the word of the fathers" (*Dialogic* 342). Because he is the one who knows, the father is the one who judges from on high, in a "distanced zone," his knowing eye forever cast upon the son. Since the son who lives in the exile of the word lives in the absence of the father, he is forever in error. In *Enemies: A Love Story* by I.B. Singer, Herman finds himself in this position: "It seemed to him that he heard his father's voice saying, 'Well, I ask you, what have you accomplished? You've made yourself and everyone else wretched. We're ashamed of you here in heaven'" (189). Thus we have an illustration of Sartre's statement that "shame is shame *of oneself before the Other*" (*Being* 303); we also realize why he insists that "the Other is not only the one whom I see but the one *who sees me*" (310). The function of the father as both priest and judge is even more evident in Wiesel's *The Testament*, particularly when Paltiel is on his way to Palestine, the Land of the Patriarchs. "From beginning to end," he relates, "my father's eyes never left me" (185). These eyes put to him the question put to the first man: Where are you? As he approaches Palestine and catches sight of Mount Carmel, Paltiel hears his father's voice calling upon him to say a prayer (187). For in saying the prayer, the son receives the word and the life that the father would bequeath to him. Saying the prayer, he affirms the responsibility, the response capacity, that Buber refers to when he declares, "Responsibility presupposes one who addresses me primarily, that is, from a realm independent of myself, and to whom I am answerable. He addresses me about something that he has entrusted to me and that I am bound to take care of loyally" (*Between* 45). In his role as judge the father does not simply judge the son's failures or transgressions, as the citation from Singer's novel might imply; rather, he judges whether or not the son lives in the fullness of the word that links heaven and earth, taking care of his trust.

This point becomes clear in Wiesel's *The Testament* when Paltiel relates a "lyrical, mystical vision" in which he sees his father leading a funeral procession. "I ask him where he is going," Paltiel explains, "and he does not answer; I ask him whence he comes, he does not answer" (321). The father is dead, yet he soon motions to Paltiel and asks him, "'What have you made of me?' And my collection of poems," says Paltiel, "is my answer" (322). Significantly, in the French text the father's question is preceded by the phrase *il me fait signe et me demande*, that is, "he makes a sign unto me and demands of me" (269). The father is the giver of signs and demands the return of a sign from the son. In this case the sign returned is the collection of signs that Paltiel's poetry comprises. His poetry, then, becomes the prayer his father would summon from him. It is a literary response in a remembrance of the words with which his father has entrusted him: "Remember this, Paltiel: with God, everything is possible; without Him nothing has value" (70). In his capacity as a link between heaven and earth, the father is the bearer of life; his is the word that invokes the Creator of life, through whom life takes on meaning. The father, therefore, is not only priest and judge; he is also savior. This function of the father comes out in Paltiel's account of his experience as a medic in the Second World War. "I felt lost," he writes. "Abandoned. Was there anyone left to turn to? I was climbing a mountain of ashes. On the other side an old man was waiting. And he was saying, 'Come, my son. Come'" (285). Thus the dead father may summon the son from death, calling him from the past and leading him into the future. Just as the father calls forth his son, so does the father figure call forth the novelist. To write a Holocaust novel is to respond to one who summons from the other side of a mountain of ashes, one who asks, "What have you made of me?" The voice that calls forth the creative process inevitably appears in the work created.

The motif of the beckoning father (or father figure) appears in Wiesel's earlier words as well. Recall, for instance, David's dream—similar to Paltiel's vision—of the old Hasid in *A Beggar in Jerusalem*. David describes him as "the beggar, the preacher of my childhood. He recognizes me and beckons me" (199). What is translated here as "beckons me" is *me fait signe* in the original French text (178). In his symbolic function, the father bears life and meaning to the extent that he gives signs. The sign given by the father "signifies an order," to use an expression from Levinas; "it orders me as one orders someone one commands, as when one says: 'Someone's asking for you'" (*Ethics* 98). Asking for me, the father asks for the fullness of my word, as in my prayer. Because it is the sign that summons one to prayer and thus to salvation, the word of the father is not simply the authoritative word but is what Bakhtin calls "the hagiographic word" (see *Problems* 248), which sanctifies life by becoming a sign of life and transforming its heir into such a sign. The destiny of the son is to become a father, just as the author must father the character. The father confers a name upon the son, and the author confers a name upon the character. Yet the creative process invariably reverses itself, so that the one whom the father names finds salvation in the name of the father. "It was my father who saved me," says a sanatorium patient in Wiesel's *Twilight*. "His face appeared before me. . . . I was sure that *he* had not forgotten *his* name. His name, his name: if only I could remember it, I would be saved" (141-42). Once again the line from Unamuno comes to mind: "Tell me thy name! is essentially the same as Save my soul!" (181). The words from Wiesel's novel might well be uttered by the author himself with respect to his character, given the double movement of creation. He is the offspring of what he creates, born of what he seeks.

In *Twilight* Wiesel introduces a character from an earlier work, *The Town beyond the Wall*, who describes what he seeks in the image of the father. His name is Pedro, and he says, "Like the question, the answer needs freedom. But while the question never changes, the answer is ever-changing: What is important for man is to know that there is an answer. What is important for man is to feel not only the existence of an answer, but the presence of one who knows the answer. When I seek that presence, I am seeking God" (197-98). In the French edition "what is important for man" is put much more strongly: *la profondeur, le sens, la vérité de l'homme,* "the depth, the meaning, the truth of man" (247)—all the things that one is to inherit from the father. As one who bears the legacy of life—as priest, judge, and savior—the father does not precisely symbolize God, but his presence signifies the presence of God, of one who knows the ever-changing answer. So we begin to have an inkling of what is lost in the death of the father. Arnost Lustig has said, "I think there were many times when I was really mad. When they killed my father [for instance], who was a beautiful man, who never did anyone any wrong" (unpublished interview with Harry James Cargas). It is from such a loss that the Holocaust novelist proceeds, working under the gaze of the dead father, a gaze like the one Wiesel describes in *Legends of Our Time:* "In dying, my father looked at me, and in his eyes where night was gathering, there was nothing but animal terror, the demented terror of one who, because he wished to understand too much, no longer understands anything. His gaze fixed on me, empty of meaning. I do not know if he saw me, if it was me he saw" (18).

The presence of the father lies in his recognition of the son; and the presence of the son rests on being thus recognized. The struggle to restore the dead father, then, is a struggle to restore the self. "Father, save me!" cries Arele in Singer's *Shosha* when his late father appears to him in a dream on the Day of Atonement (158). The Holocaust novel is just such an outcry. To understand what occurs in the death of the father is to understand, at least in part, what gives rise to the novel.

The Designification of the Other

The bearer of the legacy of life, the father is the giver of signs. With the death of the father comes not only the death of the sign but also the end of the giving of signs. Just as life emerges not only from the breath but also from breathing, so are meaning and truth born not only from the sign but also from the offering and receiving of the sign. As the giver of signs, therefore, the father signifies truth, which is not what we know but what we are, or what we are in the process of becoming. Assuming the role of priest, judge, and savior, the father takes on this signifying function with respect to the son; hence the father is the measure of the self and soul of the son. To borrow a term from Jacques Lacan, he is the Other, with a capital O. In words echoing the phenomenological stance of the Holocaust author, Lacan asks, "Who is this other to whom I am more attached than to myself, since, at the heart of my assent to my own identity, it is still he who agitates me? . . . This other is the Other that even my lie invokes as a guarantor of the truth in which it subsists. By which we can also see that is with the appearance of language that the dimension of truth emerges" (*Ecrits* 172). With the help of Lacan's insight, we realize that the exile of the word is definitively linked to the death of the father as the Other. Just as Adam, the father of all, is distinguished by his naming function, so is the father as the Other "distinguished as the locus of Speech" (Lacan, *Ecrits* 305). The signifier of truth, he is signification itself; the bearer of the word, he instills words with meaning. The problem of language so often cited in regard to Holocaust literature, then, is a problem concerning the designification of the Other that comes with the death of the father. The death of the father is the death of language. The struggle of the Holocaust novelist to summon creation from language is an effort to wrestle life from language; the writer cannot engage in that effort without engaging the father.

In *The Fifth Son*, Elie Wiesel reveals something about his own situation through the situation of his character, who describes his father's gaze as "the gaze of a living man, a serious, dignified, austere consciousness; a gaze turned inward, a consciousness thoroughly cognizant of itself. Then the gaze went dark and I told myself: this is where the mystery begins. I also told myself: this is how he is. Nothing I can do about it. Out of reach" (20-21). The passage is even more revealing when we examine the French text, where the gaze that "went dark" is the gaze that *s'èteignit* (21), "burned out, extinguished, died away." The father here is alive, a survivor of the Shoah, but there is an air of death about him. No longer a giver of signs, he is "out of reach," *hors d'atteinte,* somewhere "beyond." As Levinas has shown, proximity underlies both signification and subjectivity; "Proximity," he says, "as the 'closer and closer,' becomes the subject. It attains its *superlative* as *my* incessant restlessness, becomes unique, then one" (*Otherwise* 82). The remoteness of the father thus comes to indicate his designification, which in turn renders the self of the son problematic. In I.B. Singer's *Shosha,* Arele asserts, "From the day I left my father's house, I had existed in a state of perpetual despair" (183). From an existential standpoint, despair is a condition of disrelationship within a self who lives by its relation to the Other (cf. Kierkegaard, *Sickness* 147-48). "I come to know myself through others," Bakhtin has noted (*Estetika* 342), and the father as the Other is the primary avenue toward my determination of my self. The distance from the father thus belongs to the designification of the Other, and from the designification of the Other issues the loss of the self.

That the death of the father carries such an implication can be seen

Death of the Father

in a tale called "The Lemon" from Arnost Lustig's *Diamonds of the Night*. It is the story of a boy named Ervin who must somehow survive in a ghetto after the death of his father. If there is an afterlife, Ervin thinks, then his *"father must be able to see him. Where do you suppose he really is,* Ervin wondered, *and where am I?"* (28). The two questions are of a piece. The longing to be seen by the father is a longing for a sign from the father, a sign that will establish both the presence of the father and the identity of the son. The designification of the Other, therefore, brings about not only a loss of the significance of the father but also a loss of the sign by which the self can know itself. Understanding this, we may better understand what lies behind Manny's vision in Lustig's *Darkness Casts No Shadow:* "Before his eyes, the second boy could see a door with a brass nameplate. The plate was bare. He placed his finger on the doorbell and pushed it. This was the place he always came back to, fearful that nobody would be there" (163). The nameplate would bear the name of the father, the sign by which the son recognizes himself. With the designification of the Other the plate goes blank, and the emptiness of the dwelling is the self's own emptiness. "Glowing and awesome," Singer has written, the father sheds "his own light" (*Shosha* 158), and by the light of the father the son perceives himself. But darkness sheds no light and casts no shadow; when the sign is lost, so is the light. So is the self.

Thus the labor of the novelist to emerge from the Kingdom of Night and into the light is an endeavor to give birth to the father by whom he himself is born. For he labors to generate the word, and the word that restores him to life is the word of the father. Studying the poetry of Paltiel Kossover, we find that it expresses both the theme of Wiesel's novel and the events underlying its creation:

> In my dream
> my father
> asked me
> if he is still
> my father.
>
> I hold his hand
> and I ache.
> I talk to him
> and I ache.
>
> I tell him:
> call me,
> hold me back,
> try to understand.
>
> I tell him
> of my escapes

> into the future
> into the past.
>
> I tell him
> of the ashes
> and the scars
> on my forehead.
>
> I tell him
> to stay with me
> watch over me
> and never leave me.
>
> And so I see my father
> in my dream
> and fail to see
> myself.
> [*Testament* 294-95]

Since the father knows what life is, Paltiel summons him to determine what his own life is. But the father is dead—or exiled. His name is Gershon, from Gershom, meaning "exiled," recalling the word exiled by Paltiel's embrace of the false word of communism, of a messianism without God. Paltiel sees his father but fails to see himself because he has abandoned the word of the father; Karl Marx, he says, is his "new Rabbi" (298), one who would abolish family, father, and self (see Marx and Engles 37-38). Paltiel invokes the ashes and scars on his forehead to seek the recognition of the father, but this is not the sign by which the father knows him.

The sign by which the man is known, the sign of the Fathers, is circumcision. With the designification of the Other that occurs in the death of the father, however, the sign of the Covenant is perverted. Instead of marking the man for a life in relation to the Holy Father, it marks him for death. Hence in Yoram Kaniuk's *Adam Resurrected* Wolfovitz the Circumciser laments, "That number engraved on your arm is God!" (326). The Hebrew word for "engraved" here is *harut* (281), which also means "inscribed"; the name to be inscribed in the Book of Life is blotted out by the number registered in the ledger of death. The mute cipher eclipses the word bound as a sign upon the arm, engraved as a sign upon the phallus. In *Blood from the Sky* Piotr Rawicz explores the ramifications of the perversion of the circumcised "tool," as he pointedly calls it, since the "tool" here indicated by the phallus is the pen, which spills its words over the page like seeds over the ground, seeking an ear in which to grow. Commenting on Rawicz's main character, Edward Alexander noted that "the Sign brings Boris to the recognition that the Covenant, which has come to him, like life itself, from his ancestors, is exactly the Word become flesh" (229). Yet, as

Voloshinov/Bakhtin has argued, "there is no outer sign without an inner sign" (43). Thus in his investigation of the outer sign, Rawicz explores the inner act of writing itself, when that act is undertaken in the shadow of the death of the father, who embodies one's ancestors. "Is it not the act of writing," he asks, "of wielding the pen in pursuit of dispersing images, that most closely relates man to insect?" (311). The dispersion of images is the outcome of the designification of the Other, however, since the truth of the image rests on its relation to the Other. When the sign is lost in the death of the father, man is, indeed, little more than an insect marked for extermination.

In the novels of Aharon Appelfeld the father is often explicitly associated with writing or with books. In *The Retreat*, for example, Lotte Schloss is the first character we see, one whose father is described as "a man of books": "This simple woman spoke about her father as if he were a saint, cut off from his origins due to some terrible mistake" (46). The image of the father as saint places him in the role of the Other; cut off from his origins, however, he is designified. As Alan Mintz has observed, in Appelfeld's works "it is as if the ancestral order, as a world suffused with despair, entropy, and disintegration, was already under the star of the Holocaust" (215). Lotte's movement into the retreat, then, is a movement away from the father, guided by a different star, a different sign; it is, again, a distancing from the father and all he signifies. Hence, when she speaks at the funeral of the suicide Isadora, "all her experience on the stage seemed to drop away from her. The words scratched jarringly on the silent air. Lotte covered her face, as if she had failed shamefully" (85). The words are there, but they are without meaning, as dead as the father. Nurit Govrin asserts that for Appelfeld "the spiritual solution is in the quest for a father-image" (1593); the state of the soul is rooted in the relation to the father.

The shame over the miscarriage of the word is a shame over the death of the father, for which the son feels somehow accountable. Appelfeld demonstrates this in *The Age of Wonders*, in which Bruno views his father as a source of disgrace. After the war, he receives two letters concerning his father's writings: "The two letters suddenly coming from far away had stirred the old scar into a new pain: his father. His father. The disgrace he had not dared to touch, seething silently all these years like pus inside a wound. They said he had died half-mad in Theresienstadt, and that before he died he had tried to convert to Christianity" (209). In the Hebrew text the phrase "convert to Christianity" does not appear; rather it is *l'hemir et date*, "change his religion." What is rendered as "half-mad" is *bilbul da'at*, literally "a confusion of knowledge" (135). In this confusion the father loses the order of signs that make up his religion, which bespeaks his word. The "confusion of knowledge" emerges in the confused attempt to reorder the signs that come into collision with a reality that they cannot accommodate. The word crumbles in a failed effort to seek a new word, a new sign. The loss of the sign in the designification of the Other, moreover, does not result simply in a blank emptiness; it leaves behind a bleeding wound, in which the dead father lies buried and from which the self is poured out. It is a wound that not only "seethes" through the years but *pi'fa kol hashaniym*, "permeates all the years" (135), permeates the very lifetime of the self. The wounded I thus becomes other to itself, a point indicated in *The Age of Wonders* by the shift from the first person to the third person after the disappearance of the father. Just before the shift takes place we read, "Father was no longer with us. He was in the grip of a darkness that seemed about to overwhelm him" (154-55). Once again, darkness casts no shadow, so that the void that engulfs the father robs the son of his shadow, his *tzelem*, his image of himself.

What was referred to above as the "signifying function" Lacan calls the "Symbolic function" when he points out, "It is in the *name of the father* that we must recognize the support of the Symbolic function which, from the dawn of history, has identified his person with the figure of the law" (*Language* 41). Lacan's observation confirms what has been said about the figure of the father as judge. The Torah or the Law, indeed, begins with the father of all, followed by the Patriarchs; Moses the Lawgiver—priest, judge, savior—is the paradigm of the father, the one who wields the tables of the Law; his children are the children of Israel. Thus in the Holocaust novel the designification of the father may take the form of the crumbling of the law. Consider, for instance, these words uttered by Josek the partisan fighter in *If Not Now, When?* by Primo Levi: "If Moses was here with us, in this mill, he wouldn't think twice about changing the laws. He'd smash the tablets, the way he did that time he got mad about the golden calf, and he'd make new ones. Especially if he had seen the things we have" (185). In the Italian text the verb "smash," *spaccherebbe* (133), suggests a play on the noun *spacchino*, "stone breaker," implying an overturning of the father image itself; instead of tablet maker, he is posited as tablet breaker. Yet with the death of the father, the tablets have already been smashed, and there is no one, other than the son, to write new ones. This existential condition is reflected in the novelist's phenomenological situation, one in which he must do his work amid the rubble of a crumbled canon. "The crisis of the author," Bakhtin has said, lies in his having "to examine the position of his art within the whole of culture, in the event of being" (*Estetika* 176). In the case of the Holocaust novelist, however, culture has collapsed, and the event of being is overtaken by nothingness. With the designification of the Other there are no signs, no laws, to show the way.

The crumbling of the law is the crumbling of the Other, which is more than the breakdown of rules and regulations; it is the undoing of what is dear to human life and of what is higher than human being. Anna Langfus conveys this idea in *The Whole Land Brimstone* through the image of an angel atop a Polish church: "The angel facing south had a small bit of wing missing: nothing to speak of, yet the fact of being slightly chipped in this way was sufficient to give it a touch of humanity, to turn it into something fragile, perishable, arousing sympathy. There are times when one needs to have one's heart wrung by the sight of a piece of stone crumbling away" (32). Just as the wing makes the angel, so the law makes the man. The angel who loses its wing parallels the man who loses his father; orphaned by the death of the father, he is "fragile, perishable," left without the law from which he draws his life, like the boy Ervin in Lustig's *Diamonds of the Night*. His father dead, he collides with the realization that "there is no limit to what's 'worse.' The limit was in his father. And now Ervin had to find it, just like his father" (18). As the figure of the law, the father is the figure of the limit, the one who establishes the difference between good and evil, holy and profane, life and death. The law defines the differences that determined what matters in life; the law makes life itself something that matters. When the father dies and the law crumbles, the human being is left to the limitless hell of indifference.

We can see, then, why Mr. Sammler in Saul Bellow's novel describes hell as indifference—not simply the indifference of the father but the indifference of God the Father (215). We can sense what crumbles away in Joel's heart-wringing cry of "My God, my God, why have You forsaken me?" in Yehuda Amichai's *Not of This Time, Not of This Place* (308). And we can hear the void of what is worse when in Ka-tzetnik's *Atrocity* Moni laments, "Oh, Pa, why did you leave me?" (26). The death of the father as the designification of the Other makes for a condition not in which the father means nothing but in which the father can mean anything. The differences have not just fallen apart—they have been mutated, as shown in Ka-tzetnik's description of Piotr in *Atrocity:* "No forehead, no chin, a toothless, insucked mouth like a knife scar, and in the center a nose like a wrinkled old potato. But most important of all—his two long hands. The famous Piotr hands, with which he does his work silently, conscientiousy, solemnly, as he turns unctuous eyes on his victim. That is why he was titled Holy Dad" (35). In the original Hebrew what is translated as "unctuous" is *b'adiykut datiyt,* "devout godliness" (24), a phrase that makes more clear not only the epithet Holy Dad but the perversion of the father as well. With the death of the father, who has given the law "Thou shalt not kill," there arises a mutated father with an inverted law, a father who is himself a killer. When the father dies, death invariably rules in his place. Significantly, Piotr, Peter, bears the name of the Father of the Church, the Keeper of the Keys, who introduced a new, inverted law that locks out the Jews and who ended by being crucified upside down.

When the law crumbles, therefore, meaning collapses. With the dying of the father, the word bleeds to death. In Ka-tzetnik's *House of Dolls* Shlamek's father is branded on the forehead with the word *Jude*: "Blood gave from the seared word. And the word was as clear as the blood oozing from it. As though it were quite natural that the word *Jude* should give blood" (125). In the original text, the word rendered as "clear" is *muvenet* (131), "meaningful" or "comprehensible." Here the distinction between word and meaning is especially pronounced, and the draining of meaning from the word is especially graphic. The frontlet between the eyes, the holy word that signifies who the father is, transforms into a bleeding word that designifies the father in its identification of him. Once the sign of life's meaning, he has imposed upon him the sign of meaningless death. Perhaps Tamara speaks of such a torture when she commets on the ordeal of her father in Singer's *Enemies: A Love Story*, declaring, "Anyone who did not see my father at that moment doesn't know what it means to be a Jew" (72). Being a Jew means witnessing the life of the father poured out through the bleeding wound. As the father is emptied of life, the word is emptied of meaning. A seemingly detached, academic phrase like "the designification of the Other," therefore, has its ties with life and death. For the Other, who in Bakhtin's words is "invisibly present" (see *Estetika* 306), has its reality in the flesh that bleeds.

From the blood of the bleeding word stamped on the brow of the father, the Holocaust novelist attempts to restore life both to himself and to the father from whom the word issues. Thus struggling with the word, he writes of the father's struggle with the word. Bruno's father in Appelfeld's *The Age of Wonders* is a man of letters, one who lives by the words he writes; as soon as death begins to steal over him, he loses his command of the word. "Father stopped writing," we are told early in the novel (25), and the point is later repeated: "Ugly, tormented spirits settled on the house. Father did not write, correct proofs, or reply to the many letters piling up on his desk" (83). Yet seeing his self, his meaning, about to collapse under the weight of the ugly spirits, the father suddenly clambers to regain what would inevitably be lost. "As for father," the child narrator relates, "he was driven by a different devil, a terrible devil: his writing" (107). He was driven, *rodah*, that is, "subjugated" or "tyrannized" (72). The word that would free the man now becomes a maze of words by which he is entangled and enslaved.

Meaning breaks down into inversion, subversion, and perversion, until the word that had engendered life takes the father on a twisted spiral toward death. The deeper he plunges, the more he clings to the serpent that takes him down. His son explains, "Father's determination to remain in Austria was even stronger than before. To leave at at time like this, with evil spirits raging, meant admitting that reason had lost out, that literature was to no avail" (140). It would mean the designification of the Other; if reason and literature are to no avail, then the father himself is of no significance.

It turns out, of course, that reason and literature are indeed to no avail. With respect to the former, Jean Améry notes, "Not only was rational-analytic thinking in the camp, and particularly in Auschwitz, of no help, but it led straight into a tragic dialectic of self-destruction" (10). Améry goes on to explain, "For it was not the case that the intellectual—if he had not already been destroyed physically—had now become unintellectual or incapable of thinking. On the contrary, only rarely did thinking grant itself a respite. But it nullified itself when at almost every step it ran into its uncrossable borders. The axes of its traditional frames of reference then shattered" (19). So it happens with Bruno's father.

Regarding literature, one readily recalls the words of Piotr Rawicz: "Literature: anti-dignity exalted to a system, to a single code of behavior. The art, occasionally remunerative, of rummaging in vomit. And yet, it would appear, *navigare necesse est:* one *has* to write" (134). One writes for the sake of the father, despite the fate of the father, and in atonement for the death of the father. Because when death means designification, when it means the collapse of meaning, the task of redefining the limits outlined by the sign of the father falls to the surviving child. We have seen an example of this in the case of Ervin in Lustig's *Diamonds of the Night*. It also turns up in *The Whole Land Brimstone;* in this novel Langfus's character leaves her adamant father behind in a Polish ghetto and confesses, "I was sacrificing my father, with all the vigour of my selfishness. Shamefully. Ignominiously" (67). And who can forget the dark confession of the boy Eliezer upon the death of his father in Wiesel's *Night*? "His last word was my name," he says. "A summons, to which I did not respond. I did not weep, and it pained me that I could not weep. But I had no more tears. And, in the depths of my being, in the recesses of my weakened conscience, could I have searched it, I might perhaps have found something like—free at last!" (112-13). The son, of course, can know no freedom apart from his response to the father who summons him. The novelist writes in an endeavor to answer the father who in death calls his name.

As it often happens among the bereaved, however, death breeds rebellion, and none more so than the death of the father. "I've dethroned Frank Brody long ago," says Danny, for instance, in Lustig's *Darkness Casts No Shadow*. "Like I did with my father when the Germans came" (123). Rebellion that begins over the death of the father soon becomes a rebellion against God the Father, as Wiesel demonstrates in the argument between Gregor and the rebbe in *The Gates of the Forest*. Addressing the old man, a representative of God, Gregor cries, "He [God] turned the sentence against the judges and accusers. They, too, were taken off to the slaughter. And I tell you this: if their death has no meaning, then it's an insult, and if it does have a meaning, it's even more so" (197). With the loss of the sign comes the crumbling of the law; with the crumbling of the law comes the collapse of meaning. In the midst of this wilderness the novelist assaults the heavens in an effort to return to the earth. If his object is rebirth, he can be reborn only from the hand of the Creator. Thus, pen in hand, he does battle with God.

Wrestling in the Wilderness

And Jacob remained alone. And a strange man appeared and wrestled with him until just before dawn. And when the stranger saw that he could not defeat him, he touched the hollow of his thigh. And the hollow of Jacob's thigh was out of joint as he wrestled with him. And the stranger said, "Let me leave, for the dawn breaks." And he said, "I shall not let you leave unless you bless me." And the stranger said, "What is your name?" And he said, "Jacob." And the stranger said, "No more will you be called Jacob but Israel; for you have become like a prince before God and men, and you have prevailed." And Jacob asked and said, "Tell me your name." And he said, "Why do you ask my name?" And there he blessed Jacob. And Jacob named the place Peniel: "for I have seen God face to face and have withstood it."

—Genesis 32:24-30

Phenomenologically, the Holocaust novel is set at Peniel. The author wrestles a name from the Other, a name for his character, whereby he the author may be known as Israel. In his commentary on Jacob's encounter Wiesel writes, "No man before him had revealed to other men the battle God wages against them; no man before him had compelled God into open contest with man; and no man before him had ever established relations of provocation with God" (*Messengers* 129). The Holocaust novelist can perhaps have no other relation with God. But there is an important difference between Jacob and the Holocaust writer: in the case of the latter the man takes the battle to God. He does not receive the blessings of the father but rather survives the death of the father and the withdrawal of the word, which he struggles to extract from the Other. Once the father is dead, the writer has only God with whom to contend.

In *The Rebel* Albert Camus argues, "Human insurrection, in its exalted and tragic forms, is only, and can only be, a prolonged protest against death" (100). Yet the Holocaust novelist's protest is not only against death but also against the death of the father; because it is the death of the father—the death of the guarantor of meaning—there is nothing of the exalted or tragic about it. If we must speak of tragedy in this connection, we should recall Lev Shestov's description in *Afiny i Ierusalim:* "Tragedy is having no way out, and there is nothing great or beautiful in having no way out; there is only nothingness and formlessness" (141). To nothingness and formlessness we can add death. For death here is precisely the death of the exalted. It is the death we see, for example, in *Night*, when Wiesel describes Eliezer's father in the camp: "He was weeping. His body was shaken convulsively. Around us, everyone was weeping. Someone began to recite the Kaddish, the prayer for the dead. I do not know if it has ever happened before, in the long history of the Jews, that people have ever recited the prayer for the dead for themselves" (42). The Holocaust novel is a Kaddish said for the death of the self that transpires upon the death of the father, but it is said in a spirit of rebellion. Wiesel relates a remark made by one of his friends: "Here and now th only way to accuse Him is by praising Him" (*Legends* 61). The Holocaust novel is just such a dialectical combination of praise and accusation of God the Father. The prayer receives its dialectical utterance—*yitgadal veyitkadach shme raba*, may His name be magnified and blessed—despite and because of the death of the father, the death of the self.

Thus in remembrance and observance the novelist takes up rebellion with a cry not only of "never again" but also of "never shall I forget." Wiesel expresses it most elegantly, most hauntingly in *Night:*

Never shall I forget that night, the first night in the camp, which has turned my life into one long night, seven times cursed and seven times sealed. Never shall I forget that smoke. Never shall I forget the little faces of the children, whose bodies I saw turned into wreaths of smoke beneath a silent blue sky. Never shall I forget those flames which consumed my faith forever. Never shall I forget that noctural silence which deprived me, for all eternity, of the desire to live. Never shall I forget those moments which murdered my God and my soul and turned my dreams to dust. Never shall I forget these things, even if I am condemned to live a long as God Himself. Never. [43-44]

For "silent blue sky" the French text reads *azur muet* (60), "mute azure," suggesting a sky that does not speak, a realm robbed of the word. The French term makes more visible the link between the exile of the word and the death of the father in the conjunction of the nocturnal silence with the murdered God, with the murdered soul. In this *never*, the open wound of the self, the seeds of rebellion are planted. From that wound the Holocaust novel is born.

As the rebellion against God takes shape, however, the self becomes increasingly estranged from itself. Orphaned by the death of the father—whether physical or metaphysical—the son refuses those observances made meaningful by the father, those moments when the relation to God the Father substantiates the life of the self. In Wiesel's *Night* Eliezer's rebellion is quite pronounced on Rosh Hashanah: "This day I ceased to plead. I was no longer capable of lamentation. On the contrary, I felt very strong. I was the accuser, God the accused. My eyes were open and I was alone—terribly alone in a world without God and without man. Without love or mercy. I had ceased to be anything but ashes, yet I felt myself to be stronger than the Almighty, to whom my life had been tied for so long. I stood amid that praying congregation observing it like a stranger" (73-74). On Yom Kippur, a day of fasting, he is even more explicit: "I no longer accepted God's silence. As I swallowed my bowl of soup, I saw in the gesture an act of rebellion and protest against Him. And I nibbled my crust of bread. In the depths of my heart, I felt a great void" (75). A world without the father—the world from which the Holocaust novel emerges—is a world without God and man. Like one who nibbles bread on a day of fasting, the novelist pursues the task of re-creation in a protest against creation, implicating the Creator Himself as one who must atone—or at least listen. Hence in Wiesel's *Twilight*, when an old man, clearly a father figure, is about to be murdered by the Nazis, his last cry is "God of Israel: *Listen to the people of Israel.*" We read, "He had not recited the traditional *Shma* after all, he had not said, 'Listen, Israel, God is one God.' He had said something else, not the opposite but something else" (34). Thus the novelist says something else—not the opposite perhaps but a rebellious something else.

Like the prayer, the novel too becomes something else. The two rebelliously merge at the end of *The Last of the Just* by André Schwartz-Bart: "And praised. *Auschwitz.* Be. *Maidanek.* The Lord. *Treblinka.* And praised. *Buchenwald.* Be. *Mauthausen.* The Lord. *Belzec.* And praised. *Sobibor.* Be. *Chelmno.* The Lord. *Ponary.* And Praised. *Theresienstadt.* Be. *Warsaw.* The Lord. *Vilna.* And praised. *Sharzysko.* Be. *Bergen-Belsen.* The Lord. *Janow.* And praised. *Dora.* Be. *Neuengamme.* The Lord. *Pustkow.* And praised" (422). In this prayer—if it can be called a prayer—we have an example of what Lawrence Langer calls "the cacophony of fact" that the writer must transform into an "antiphony of art" (264). We can also see that polyphony, which is a great concern to Bakhtin (see *Problems* 40), is a structural feature of the novel with profound spiritual implications. The rebellion implied in such a prayer is made clear earlier in Schwarz-Bart's novel through the words of a young man named Yankel. He is the sole surviving son of a village wiped out by the Nazis, a man known for his prayers.

Death of the Father

I buried them all, you know, the whole village without exception—didn't miss a fingernail. And for each one of them, even for the dirty little liar Moshele—he lived next door—for each one of them, I swear it, I said all the prayers from A to Z, because in those days I was a famous praying man before the Eternal, ai-i-i-i! It lasted eight days. And nobody came. The peasants were afraid. And when it was done, I felt queer all over, you know? It was in the cemetery, I woke up and I grabbed a handful of rocks and began to throw them at the sky. And at a certain moment the sky *shattered*. You understand? . . . Then I said to myself, "Yankel, if God is in little pieces, what can it mean to be a Jew?" Let's take a closer look at that, my friend. But then, as closely as I could look I couldn't see anything but blood, and more blood, and blood again. But meaning?—none. [101]

The French word translated as "meaning" is *signification* (124), whose root, like that of the English word, is *sign:* meaning is lost as the blood washes away the sign. The blood that remains is the blood of the father, the blood of the word stamped on the brow of the father, oozing from the shattered sign of the shattered sky. For the death of a community signifies the death of the father and brings on the rebellion of the son.

The combination of prayer and rebellion underlying the Holocaust novel can also be found in *Not of This Time, Not of This Place,* where Amichai writes, "For Thine is the error, and Thou shalt reign forever. God rules only by means of an error" (310-11). If the rebellion in these words is not strong enough, then the words of Morris Feitelzohn in Singer's *Shosha* are quite unambiguous. He declares: "Mark, of all the errors Jews have made, our greatest was to delude ourselves—and later other peoples—that God is merciful, loves His creatures, hates malefactors, and all the rest of it" (142-43). Although Feitelzohn's words bear nothing of a dialectical affirmation, nothing of a prayer, in their rebellion, Singer offers us another look at this character whose rebellion is in fact an expression of what is at work in the creation and content of the novel itself. It is said that he raised an outcry against God ablaze "with religious fire"; he "castigated Him for all His sins since the Creation. He still maintained that the whole universe was a game, but he elevated this game until it became divine. That was probably how the Seer of Lublin, Rabbi Bunim, and the Kotzker spoke" (271). Like the prayer that is itself a part of the divinity, so rebellion, as we see it in the Holocaust novel, takes on an aspect of the divine. The death of the father draws its significance from the longing for the father. Since the death of the father is what gives rise to the rebellion against God the Father, that rebellion against God reveals a profound need for Him.

Wrestling in the wilderness, then, the novelist is pitted against himself in an affirmation of his need for the Other. His novel, his art, voices affirmation and need. In *The Town beyond the Wall* Wiesel's character Pedro declares: "The dialogue—or duel, if you like—between man and his God doesn't end in nothingness. Man may not have the last word, but he has the last cry. That moment marks the birth of art" (103). The words of Michael from the same novel, moreover, express what happens when the outcry is transformed into art: "The shout becomes a prayer in spite of me" (123). Written in the aftermath of the death of the father, the novel is a search for a prayer, an effort to wrestle a prayer from the wilderness. Thus in *The Town beyond the Wall* Wiesel reveals his own struggle as a novelist through his character's struggle to speak his prayer. Michael speaks the prayer in an utterance of his rebellion and his longing: "Oh God, be with me when I have need of you, but above all do not leave me when I deny you" (49). When asked about the division of this novel into prayers, Wiesel once explained, "To me, prayers are very dear. I tried to invent something new, a new approach. . . . Maybe it's no longer a prayer *for* but *against*. Usually prayers are meant as an approach to God; someone is asking for something from God. Maybe our prayers will be against God." Are they still affirmative? he was asked. "Existentially and dialectically affirmative," he answered. "For the fact that I pray means someone is there to listen, that what I am saying is not uttered to a great void. But what I *do* say, I say with anger" (Patterson, *In Dialogue* 78). In *Paroles d'etranger* he adds, "Heaven sends back the prayer that does not reflect the human condition in its agony and its pain; it is a dead prayer" (171). Said with anger, the prayer, the novel, joins rebellion with need. Said with anger, the prayer *against* is rebellion *for*.

The need to write reflects the need for God the Father, a need that arises upon the death of the father. The novelist writes despite himself, for another, just as the child Eliezer prays upon entering the camp in Wiesel's *Night*. "In spite of myself," he says, "the words formed themselves and issued in a whisper from my lips: *Yitgadal veyitkadach shme raba*. . . . May His name be blessed and magnified. . . . My heart was bursting. The moment had come. I was face to face with the Angel of Death" (43). The Angel of Death comes to claim the father, who had been the support of life, the priest, judge, and savior of life. The Angel of Death is the Angel with a Thousand Eyes, who comes to leave Eliezer with new eyes. After the death of the father, the novel closes with Eliezer's gazing into a mirror: "From the depths of the mirror, a corpse gazed back at me. The look in his eyes, as they stared into mine, has never left me" (116). Once again, the French text harbors revelations that elude the translation; for "gazed back at me" the original has *me contemplait* (178), "contemplated me," studied me, judged me. The image of the dead father is thus implied in the contemplative corpse of the dead self. As Bakhtin has said, the character is aghast at "his own face, because in it he senses the power of another person over him, the power of that other's evaluations and opinions. He himself looks on his face with another's eyes, with the eyes of the other" (*Problems* 235). If the Holocaust novelist holds up a mirror, it is not to nature but to himself, and he encounters the corpse that he must wrestle into a character. Yet what the mirror cuts in half the look of the father reconstitutes; he is the Other to whom Todorov refers: "Only the look of the Other can provide me with the feeling that I am a totality" (147). The look that never leaves the man thus becomes the look of the father; Paltiel asserts, "From beginning to end, my father's eyes never left me" (Wiesel, *Testament* 185). Fathering his character, the novelist reaffirms the significance of the father and of the father's death for his own life-and-death encounter at Peniel, where he struggles to come before the countenance. The significance of the father, then, lies above all in his connection with the longing for God couched in the rebellion against God.

Thus in Wiesel's *The Gates of the Forest* we read, "God's final victory, my son, lies in man's inability to reject Him. You think you're cursing Him, but your curse is praise; you think you're fighting Him, but all you do is open yourself to Him; you think you're crying out your hatred and rebellion, but all you're doing is telling Him how much you need His support and forgiveness" (33). These words shed much light on the rebellion of Eliezer in *Night* and of Michael in *The Town beyond the Wall*; they help us to see what underlies the rebellion of characters created by other novelists as well—Vevke in Ka-tzetnik's *Atrocity*, for example. Unlike Eliezer, Vevke chooses to fast on Yom Kippur, but the reasons for his response are the same. He cries out, "I will show You that even in Auschwitz Vevke the cobbler is equal to fasting on Yom Kippur! But You—You are to sit on Your throne in Truth! Do You hear me? *In Truth!*" (209). The Holocaust novelist cannot deal with the truth of the Shoah without first dealing with the truth of himself, and for this he needs the figure of the father. The *I insist* of his rebellion is an insistence on truth when truth has died. Yet something still glows in the embers of his longing. Levinas, in *Ethics and Infinity*, says, "The witness testifies to what was said by himself. For he has said 'Here I am!' before the Other; and from the fact that before the Other he recognizes the responsibility which is incumbent on himself, he has manifested what the face of the Other signified for him. The glory of the Infinite reveals itself through what it is capable of doing in the witness" (109). Freely translated, Levinas's words come to a simple statement made by Nadav in Wiesel's *Twilight*, for whom "the meaning of God was the yearning for God" (115). God is felt through the need for Him, so that, in Buber's words, "whoever knows God also knows God's remoteness and the agony of drought upon a frightened heart" (*I and Thou* 147). Unlike other yearnings, this longing reflects the human being's need for answerability to another, for another; and the presence of the Other is revealed through this need within the self.

"The yearning from below," it is written in the Zohar, "brings about the completion above" (33). Although we yearn for what we do not have, the presence of what we need is sensed in the yearning, just as the significance of the father is most deeply felt upon his death. In *Touch the Water, Touch the Wind*, Amos Oz writes, "Dying parents, Yotam thought, exercise a power over you that they never had before. And when your father dies you will pick him up and carry him inside you all your life like an unborn child or a malignant growth, he will accompany you through all your rebellions" (163). The Hebrew term rendered as "inside you" bears much stronger connotations than the English phrase. It is *b'hovkha*, meaning "in your guilt" or "in your debt" (172); it suggests a breakdown of relation, a distancing from the self within the self upon the death of the father. Thus an absence is made into a presence, like a wound. "His father, his father," reads the line in Appelfeld's *The Age of Wonders*, "the wound that never healed" (266). The wound spurs the rebellion that is a longing to be healed and the wrestling with God that is born from a need for God.

Obviously, then, the Holocaust novel connects the death of the father with the death of God. If the father is a Thou to whom the I responds in its effort to become I, then we can see that "extended, the lines of relationships intersect in the eternal You. Every single You is a glimpse of that. Through every single You the basic word addresses the eternal You" (Buber, *I and Thou* 123). Buber also points out that people address the eternal You by different names (123). Among the Jews a chief form of address is *avinu*, Our Father. As dreadful as it may sound, in the Holocaust novel, or in the course of its creation, the address becomes Our Dead Father. Yet through the address of the novel and despite the death of the father, there arises a response from the one who has died. The dead struggle to move inside the main character: In *The Whole Land Brimstone* by Anna Langfus, "A whole murmuring chorus was imploring me. Then another isolated voice spoke and I recognized it. 'We are all here and we are cold. Let us in,' said my father" (285). What is translated as "spoke" is *s'élève*, "rose up," in the French text (280), as if the voice were an animate entity. As these words come out of the author via her character, the voice that conveys them enters her via the character. Thus the voice speaks from beyond to reveal itself through what it is capable of doing from within.

The writing of the Holocaust novel represents a response, which is the hearing of such a voice. Creating the character, the novelist posits a face from which the one who had died may yet speak, sometimes through the image of the face itself. In Ka-tzetnik's *Sunrise over Hell* Harry Preleshnik encounters the dead face of his friend Marcel Shafran: "Prone before his eyes, he saw the values of all humanity's teachings, ethics and beliefs, from the dawn of mankind to this day.

Marcel's carcase-face revealed to him the true face of man in the image of God. He bent, stretched out his hand and caressed the head of the Twentieth Century" (111). Humanity's teachings and ethics are the teachings and ethics of the fathers, the *pirkei avot* by which human life is instilled with the presence of the living God. The God who before Ezekiel's eyes brought dead bones to life now lies among the bones of the dead. Ka-tzetnik suggests this image in *Star of Ashes*: "Admit now, Rabbi of Shilev, God of the Diaspora Himself flounders here in this snarl of bones—a Mussulman!" (179). In the Hebrew text the phrase for "Himself," *etsmo hoo*, is a play on the word meaning "bones," *etsmot* (179): the self and soul of God become the dead matter of man.

In Ka-tzetnik's images we see what becomes of the personal God when He is linked with the person of the father; indeed, that linkage, conveyed by the address Our Father, is what makes Him a personal God. As soon as rebellion becomes a personal matter, it becomes a matter of murder. "Men don't reject death, but they do immortality," says the rebel Varady in Wiesel's *The Town beyond the Wall*. "Even God, they only desire Him insofar as He's mortal: they kill Him often to prove that the themselves" (33). They also kill him to prove, like Absalom did in his rebellion against his father David, that if God will not bring justice to the world, then man will have either his own justice or chaos. In *The Rebel*, Camus observes, "Only a personal god can be asked by the rebel for a personal accounting. When the personal god begins his reign, rebellion assumes its most resolutely ferocious aspect and pronounces a definitive no. With Cain, the first act of rebellion coincides with the first crime" (31-32). The first crime is murder—murder of one's brother, one's God, and oneself. "Cain killed Cain in Abel," Wiesel notes in *Messengers of God* (61). As Wiesel also shows, Cain killed more: "Like God, he thought to offer himself a human sacrifice in holocaust. He wanted to be cruel like Him, a stranger like Him, an avenger like Him. And like Him, present and absent at the same time, absent by his presence, present *in* his absence. Cain killed to become God. To kill God" (*Messengers* 58). Just as the death of the father comes by murder, so arises the death of God.

The position of the novelist here assumes a terrifying aspect. In a life-and-death struggle the novelist is faced with becoming either Cain or Abel, one who would make the death of the father into either a murder of God or a surrender to God. In the process of writing the novel he makes a choice, and from the valley of this decision the characters emerge. Indeed, through the characters we discover the author's dangerous options. In *Twilight* Wiesel's main character, Raphael, encounters Cain, who takes Raphael for his brother. "When I killed my brother," Cain tells him, "it was really Him I wanted to kill. And he knows it. Any fool knows that whoever kills, kills God" (58).

What Cain here utters in a moment of confession a father elsewhere declares in a movement of faith, just before he and his son are about to be shot in Wiesel's *A Beggar in Jerusalem:* "Whoever kills, becomes God. Whoever kills, kills God. Each murder is a suicide, with the Eternal eternally the victim" (208). Wiesel adds, "And the survivor in all this? He will end up writing his request, which he will slip between the cracks of the Wall" (208). Thus the novelist writes a novel, a word slipped between the cracks in the wall of silence, an affirmation of life inserted into the wall of death, a cry of Our Father implanted in the wall of the fallen father. In the words of André Neher, "It is from within the void, from the depths of absence, from the heart of 'no' that there arises a 'yes.' Faith is a genesis; it appears *ex nihilo*" (207).

Commenting on his writing, Wiesel has said, "Each word corresponds to a face, a prayer, the one needing the other so as not to sink into oblivion" (*Legends* 25). In the process of its creation the novel happens at Peniel, where the wrestler encounters the face. Levinas says, "The face is exposed, menaced, as if inviting us to an act of violence. At the same time, the face is what forbids us to kill" (*Ethics* 86). Wrestling in the wilderness, the novelist is confronted with these options upon the death of the father, the one whose murder amounts to a murder of God, and one who is entrusted with teaching his son "Thou shalt not kill." Levinas goes on to show that "the important question of the meaning of being is not: why is there something rather than nothing—the Leibnizian question so much commented upon by Heidegger—but: do I not kill by being? (*Ethics* 120). The death of the father leads the Holocaust novelist to this question, the question explored through the character and put to the reader. "I believe that I can be a writer," Arnost Lustig once said, "only because I have never killed" (unpublished interview with Harry James Cargus). Knowing how the question is all too often answered, we can understand what lies behind Menahem's remark on behalf of God the Father in Wiesel's *The Town beyond the Wall:* "All He asks is to weep with us. Within us. For that our tears must remain pure and whole. Their source is the source of life" (177). The patient who believes he is God in Wiesel's *Twilight* asks Raphael to weep for him, reminding Raphael of his teacher's remark on Ecclesiastes: "According to him, this desperate book refers not to man but to the King of the Universe. 'For all my days are but sorrow!' That is not man howling, but God" (213). The tears that are the source of life are the source of the Holocaust novel. From between the lines of the novelist's outcry over the death of the father we hear the howl of God. Going deeper, we find that it is not for himself that the dead Father weeps. He weeps for his child.

4
The Death of the Child

"I want to see with my own eyes the lamb lie down with the lion," says Ivan to his brother Alyosha, "and the victim rise up and embrace his murderer. I want to be there when everyone suddenly understands what it has all been about. All the religions of the world are built on this longing, and I am a believer. But then there are the children, and what am I to do about them?" (Dostoyevsky 225). That is the question with which we now collide in our movement toward the visceral recesses of the event we term the Holocaust novel. In *A Jew Today* Elie Wiesel points out that "the Nazis exterminated the weak and the children but let the strong live. It is as though the Nazi killers knew precisely what children represent to us. According to our tradition, the entire world subsists thanks to them" (178-79). At the heart of the question of the children lies the darkness from which the light of the Creation was summoned. This is the darkness from which the Holocaust novel is created. Yet in the midst of the darkness shine points of light that make possible this impossible creation. That light is the fire hidden in the ashes; it consists of the souls of the children turned to ashes. The words arranged on the pages of the novel are made of these ashes, but their meaning is made of that fire.

Wiesel says, "The Jewish children: they haunt my writings. I see them again, I shall see them always. Huddled up. Humiliated. Bent over like old men who were surrounded for their protection, but in vain. They are thirsty, the children—and there is no one to give them a drink. They are hungry, the children—and there is no one to offer them a piece of bread. They are afraid—and there is no one to comfort them" (*Paroles* 10). Finally, they are dead, and there is no one to say Kaddish for them, except perhaps the one who, in a shriek of silence made of the children's silence, writes a novel in the saying of one long Kaddish. The Holocaust novel is as much a children's memorial as the Children's Memorial at Yad Vashem. The passage through the novel bears similarities to the passage through that memorial. A dark enclosure made of white Judean stone, it is reminiscent of a tomb. Crossing the threshold, one crosses over into a realm beyond this world, into *their* world. In the darkness burn candles multiplied into a million and a half points of light by mirrors covering the floor, walls, ceiling. Standing in the midst of those tiny beacons, the visitor hears the names read off, one by one, slowly and solemnly, like prayers. Forevermore they haunt you. The witness emerges transformed into a tomb.

"They did not even have a cemetery," Wiesel said. "We are their cemeteries" (*Against Silence* 1:168). Out of the sepulchre of the self the Holocaust novelist calls forth his offspring. If the child is the mainstay of creation, however, then the phenomenological origins of the Holocaust novel are rooted in the collapse of the child at the origin. An assessment of the death of the child with respect to the creation of the novel must therefore begin at the source of the child. Let us first consider the relation of the child to the one who bears the child: the mother. The separation and reunion of mother and child express the novelist's concern with the loss and recovery of life, with the fragmentation and redemption of the soul. In this relation we discover the critical importance of the feminine element in the phenomenology of the novel.

The Mother and Child Disunion

Mikhail Bakhtin notes that a child receives the initial sense of self from the lips of loves ones, chief among whom is the mother. "From their mouths," writes Bakhtin, "the child hears their love in emotional, loving tones and begins to recognize his name. . . . The first and most authoritative words. . . . through which he acknowledges and discovers himself as *a something* are essentially the words of a loving human being" (*Estetika* 46). This existential condition underlies Jean Améry's insistence that "everyone must be who he was in the first years of his life, even if later these were buried under. No one can become what he cannot find in his memories" (84). The figure of the child thus makes the project of redemption a movement of return. If only for a moment, the word returns from exile to be rejoined with its meaning upon the loving utterance of the name of the child.

Just as love joins mother to child, so it joins soul to word and word to meaning. Rebbe Levi Yitzhak of Berditchev once observed that all the sages and scholars of the world can never understand the babbling of a babe in its cradle. When the mother comes to the child, however, she immediately knows what the sounds mean (see Buber, *Tales* 215). Examining this relation of mother to child, we realize that the word takes on meaning as it is infused with the soul and substance of the one who speaks, "populated with his own intention," as Bakhtin puts it (*Dialogic* 293). In its primal origin the substance of the soul is love, and love is the substance of meaning. In her love for the child the mother becomes all that a mother *means*. As a mother, she signifies the child, so that in the relation between mother and child we have most fundamental instance of "the other in the same" (Levinas, *Otherwise* 25). Through this relation we see what Levinas means when he says, "The other is in me in the midst of my very identification" (*Otherwise* 125). Thus the child is in the mother, so that in her address to the child the mother recognizes herself.

Hence the one-for-the-other of signification becomes the other-in-the-one of subjectivity. Herman states this idea quite simply in I.B. Singer's *Enemies: A Love Story*: "The bearer of children remains a child herself" (135). Since the author's concern with life is generally expressed through a relation to the child, the novel frequently includes a relation to the origin of life, to the mother. Ilona Karmel articulates such a relation in *An Estate of Memory* through the tie that links two characters, Barbara to the mother, Aurelia: "For this Aurelia, Barbara felt ready to do everything. The idea of sacrifice took possession of her; never imagined clearly yet ever present, it lent her days the sense of ascent toward a towering peak. Upon this peak a transformation would occur. She, her whole being, would be suspended, someone else would take her place for that instant, and at once she would be brought back to kneel at Aurelia's side, to whisper, 'I for you—everything'" (206). Barbara's connection with Aurelia reveals something very important about the author's relation to her character. The character born of the author enters her (the other-in-the-one), so that she can be born, transformed, out of the character. "I for you—everything" means that everything I am lies in my being for you. The Holocaust novelist is not only a witness for life but a witness who comes to life through the witness she bears, as she would bear a child. Because the novelist struggles to be reborn to life, she stands in a relation to the mother.

The interidentification suggested in Singer's novel thus reveals a process of intercreation between author and character in the writing of the novel. These interactions may turn up in an overlaying of mother and child in the novel. In Aharon Appelfeld's *Tzili: The Story of a Life* the fifteen-year-old title character bears a child and is herself referred to as a child (165). The one thing that defines her as a child is her connection with her mother: "Every now and then her mother would call, 'Tzili,' and Tzili would reply, 'Here I am.' Of her entire childhood, only this was left" (158). *This* refers to both the summons and the response, both the name and the reply to the name. What remains of childhood is what remains of the self as a something, called forth upon the mother's loving utterance of the name of the child. Tzili, of course, has long since lost her mother, yet the call of the mother arises out of the distance that separates them. "We say, 'far away,'" Buber notes in *I and Thou*. "The Zulu has a sentenced-word instead that means: 'where one cries, "mother, I am lost"'" (69-70). This distance that isolates the child from the mother is a wound that cuts through the self. In her summons the mother recognizes the pain of the wound. "You're suffering," Ilana says to Elisha in Wiesel's *Dawn,* like a mother addressing a child. "That's what it means when a man speaks of his mother" (62). Thus the novelist speaks of the mother in various ways to voice the detachment of the self from life.

Because the mother is female, the child defined by a linkage to the mother is often female. Yet the identifying relation also works the other way, so that the death of the child signifies the death of the mother, that is, the death of the source of life. This underlies the prominence of the female child in the works of Ilse Aichinger, Yehuda Amichai, Aharon Appelfeld, Rachmil Bryks, Yoram Kaniuk, Ilona Karmel, Ka-tzetnik 135633, Arnost Lustig, Piotr Rawicz—nearly every Holocaust novelist. It is the terrible death that Wiesel describes in *A Jew Today:*

> She was six years old, a pale, shy and nervous child. Did she know what was happening around her? How much did she understand of the events? She saw the killers kill, she saw them kill—how did she translate these visions in her child's mind?
>
> One morning she asked her mother to hug her. Then she came to place a kiss on her father's forehead. And she said, "I think that I shall die today." And after a sigh, a long sigh: "I think I am glad."
>
> Thus my friend Shimshon learned that his little girl knew more about life and the meaning of life than many old people. [128]

Shimshon learned from his little girl that the death of the child is the death of every origin of life, that the lamb cannot dwell with the wolf nor the kid lie down with the leopard without being devoured, and that there is no child to lead them. "The child sang about the dark forests where the wolf dwelt," writes Appelfeld in *Badenheim 1939* (62). The poet sings about the child.

The novelist who wrestles with the collapse of meaning struggles with the miscarriage of life at its source. The creator faces the impossible task of regenerating life and meaning from their source. The child embodies the meaning, the mother contains the life, and both merge in the female child. Within the novel, therefore, a character's relation to the female child parallels the author's relation to the lost origins of life, not only in its meaning but also in its mystery. Consider, for example, the title character from Singer's *Shosha* in her relation to Arele. After knowing Shosha as a child, Arele encounters her years later, when he is a man. But "Shosha had neither grown nor aged," he relates. "I gaped at the mystery" (76). Arele later marries this eternal child, and when the matter of having children arises, he says to her, "I don't want children. You are my child" (216). Arele marries Shosha not so that she may become a mother but so that he may preserve her as a child and thus harbor the mystery. In this way she becomes the source of his life; the fountainhead of all significance in his life. For there is no meaning without mystery. Once the two marry, Shosha is not only the bearer of Arele's name but also the mystery who gives meaning to his name. Indeed, Singer recounts the tale of Arele's life in a book that bears the name of the female child. Shosha is the link to Arele's childhood that calls forth the child and therefore the life within him. "At the end of the name," Edmond Jabès has written, "there is the female name. One and the same name" (*Yukel* 133). For the man is nurtured by the child he nurtures, and that child, more often than not, is female.

In Lustig's *Dita Saxova*, the title character says, "The best thing I got out of the war was when I was in Theresienstadt taking care of the children" (128). Dita provides another example of the confluence of mother and child. Hardly more than a child herself, she manages to live in Theresienstadt by acting as a mother, preserving what is most precious and most fragile in life, just as the author struggles to preserve what is most dear through his female child. But his character fares no better than the children of Theresienstadt, who, like Shimshon's little girl, grew old before their time. Dita grows up only to die; the child within her, the motherly child that cared for the dying children, dies with those children. Although the circumstances vary, the death is the same for another of Lustig's title characters. Katerina Horovitzova was "a child and a woman both. Now the thing was, which of these aspects do you want to suppress and which bring to the fore?" (*Prayer* 12-13). The question is a matter of life and death, both for the child and for the woman. Or rather, it is a question of death. In the universe of the Holocaust novel the death of the child constitutes the death of the adult; death *is* the death of the child. Undertaking the creation of the novel, the author labors to give birth to what cannot live in a world where six-year-old children declare, "I think I shall die today. I think I am glad." The impossibility of post-Holocaust literature cited by writers like T.W. Adorno (125-27) and Elie Wiesel (*Dimensions* 7) does not lie in the undoing of forms or conventions. It lies in the death of the child, particularly as it is articulated in the death of the female child. The mother and child disunion brings about the novel's disintegration.

The female child's connection with the source and mystery of life is not only a tie to a past origin but also a link to any possible future; in the words of Buber, the child is "primal potential might" (*Between* 83). The death of the child is the death of the future; the Holocaust novel's interaction with the past is not just a commentary on what was but also a response to what is yet to be. This stance on the part of the novelist comes out in Lustig's *Night and Hope*, a book that began as a novel but disintegrated into tales. In a story titled "Rose Street," for example, the face of a little girl named Ruth becomes the face of a lost past and an annulled future for the old woman Elizabeth Feiner: "The girl's face with its inquisitive black eyes, such as she once used to have herself, seemed to her to represent a future reproach, because something that not even Elizabeth Feiner was able to give a name to was marking the child's face with the sorrowful expression that Jewish children so frequently have" (79-80). Looking at the Czech edition, we see that the child's face is not only "marked," it is *vpisuje*, "inscribed"; its expression is not only "sorrowful," but *bolestný*, "painful" or "agonizing" (54). The pain that marks the face of the child is the pain of death, and the inscription written into that face becomes the Holocaust novel. The epitaph on the past becomes the text of the future. "Face and discourse are tied," Levinas has argued. "The face speaks. It speaks, it is in this that it renders possible and begins all discourse" (*Ethics* 87-88). In the Holocaust novel discourse begins with the face of the child.

As the vessel of mystery, the female child is the vessel of the eternal, a light that burns from beyond death to both illuminate and darken the pages of the Holocaust novel. Such a child shapes the present and the future for Joel in Amichai's *Not of This Time, Not of This Place*. "When Ruth was burned," Joel explains, "revenge was burned, too, and the country remained empty of mercy and of vengeance and of man. Her face is the eternal light for my actions and, like all eternal lights, her face is exerting a calming effect on me and fills me with melody and happiness and sadness, instead of driving me to acts of vengeance" (112-13). The death of the child precludes vengeance, because even in death the child signifies life. The task of the novelist is not to seek revenge but to seek light, to ignite a flame of remembrance and observance. To be sure, the Hebrew word here rendered as "light" is not *or* but *ner* (182), which also means "candle." It calls to mind the Sabbath candles lit to welcome the Sabbath Bride, that feminine form who brings the eternal into time. It also calls to mind the lighting of a candle in a tale told by Elie Wiesel in *The Six Days of Destruction:*

Suddenly, Old Itzikl remembered something important. He opened the bag where he kept his tallit and tephilin, rummaged around in the bottom and brought out a candle. He tried to light it but did not succeed. He renewed his efforts, concentrating so hard he looked like a madman. Did he see his first child fall into the pit? His second? The last one? I do not know what he saw. I only know what he did: he finally succeeded in lighting his precious candle. And he lifted it high above his head. At that precise moment the life of his last child was extinguished. [25]

The Holocaust novelist writes to ignite such a candle, to remember and observe, remember and preserve.

Just as the candle goes out, however, so the word is extinguished, its meaning set adrift on a sea of words. The death of the child precludes all possiblity for the "success" of the Holocaust novel. The

Death of the Child   83

novelist knows that the flame burns in the process of the writing and not in its outcome. The writer writes just as the man runs in Wiesel's *Ani Maamin*, bearing a child in his arms:

> I run
> As far as my legs will carry me,
> Like the wind,
> Farther than the wind.
> I run,
> And while I run,
> I am thinking:
> This is insane,
> This Jewish child
> Will not be spared.
> I run and run
> And cry.
> And while I am crying,
> While I am running,
> I perceive a whisper:
> I believe,
> Says the little girl,
> Weakly,
> I believe in you.
>   [89, 91]

In the place of the Muse is the dying voice of the female child.

The Holocaust novelist, however, cannot be faithful to the silenced voice. The one who endeavors to generate a response to the dead child inevitably ends by betraying the child, just as words invariably betray silence. Again, in the death of the child—particularly the feminine child—life is extinguished at its source, both for the past and for the future. Yet to insert that child into the novel amounts to a rejection of the death that must never be denied or forgotten. Quite often, then, the child is present in the Holocaust novel by absence from it. In *Adam Resurrected* by Yoram Kaniuk, Adam declares, "Ruth. That was my daughter's name. She is the one I am looking for here, don't you know? She is the one I betrayed" (23). The Hebrew verb here translated as "looking for" is *l'hapes* (25), which may also mean "examine," as if the thing absent were somehow present; if the Holocaust novelist works through faith, it is not the faith that one day something will come but that one day it was there. If anything is found, it is found again, as we see it Piotr Rawicz's novel *Blood from the Sky*: "What of Naomi, the child who was entrusted to me? Shall I find her again here on earth? Where am I to look for her and where am I to take her?" (312). In this passage *confiée* is the French word for "entrusted" (276), from *confier*, the verb used for "commit" to memory and "plant" a seed. In this single word we see that the child is the most precious of all things entrusted to us, the vessel of life conferred upon us. In the novelist's act of remembering and preserving, the child is the one committed to memory. In the effort to regain life from the mother, from the earth, the child is the seed from which that life must spring.

Underlying the Holocaust novel is the severance of the child from the earth and therefore from the mother. The existential expression of this separation is a severance of life from the soul. From Dante's Beatrice to Goethe's Margaret the importance of the feminine aspect to the life of the soul in a literary motif; so we see the intersection of mother and child in the Holocaust novel. But neither Dante nor Goethe could fathom the darkness or the depths of the Kingdom of Night. Although these poets were versed in the spiritual agonies of the male's isolation from the female, they had no concept of the extreme version of this isolation, extreme to the point of perversion. At this extremity and proceeding beyond all extremity is the mother and child disunion. Far exceeding these poets' field of vision is the existential reality of the Holocaust novel. There is perhaps no expression of that reality more terrible than the last of Ka-tzetnik's visions in *Shivitti*: "My mother. I see her naked and marching in line, one among Them, her face pointed towards the gas chambers. 'Mama! . . . Mama! . . . Mama! . . . I behold my mother's skull in my mother's skull I see me. And I chase after me inside my mother's skull. And my mother is naked. Going to be gassed" (100-101). Hence the death of the child is expressed out of the mouth of the child himself, the death of the soul and self of the child in the absolute disunion of mother and child. From inside the skull of his mother, crying, "Mama, Mama," he writes his novel. This is the most fundamental phenomenon in the phenomenology of the Holocaust novel.

In Wiesel's *The Fifth Son*, a novel about the child of a survivor, the mother's isolation from the child is compared with the Shekhina's exile from the world. "Your mother is in exile," the boy is told. "Just like the *Shekhina* who is also in exile" (32). In this case the mother has been removed to an insane asylum, unable to live in a world gone insane. If the world has no place for the mother, no place for the Shekhina, then it has no place for the child. And so he cries out, "I look at a trembling child and I am that child. . . . I feel the need to hide, to huddle over there in the corner of my room, in the bend of the planet. . . . I am shrinking more and more until I am small, smaller, reviving the child in me, even dying in his stead in the void, in the black and scorching nothingness" (136-37). Yet the child who is revived is the child as victim, dying for the child. In the mother and child disunion everything from which the soul draws its life is lost. The death of the child, therefore, is the death of the soul.

The Child as Victim

Whether appearing among the survivors or among the murdered, the child as victim appears initially as a messenger, as one who summons the living from the heart of darkness, as one who summons the author to the task of writing. The main character in A. Anatoli's *Babi Yar*, for instance, is a child who identifies himself as a messenger for those who died at Babi Yar (147). It is not simply the status as messenger, however, that casts the child in the role of victim; it is the child's fate as the unheeded messenger, as the one whose outcry falls on deaf ears and who is therefore betrayed by those who have ears to hear. Anna Langfus demonstrates this point most unnervingly in *The Whole Land Brimstone*, where we see a "good" Christian woman who abandons and thus betrays a Jewish child. "I stopped my ears so as not to hear him," she says. "He was calling from where I had left him. He hadn't moved, for I had told him to stand still and wait for me. He was just calling out and crying" (37). Renouncing any complacency that might lead to the conviction that "They" are the ones who victimize the child, Langfus casts her first-person narrator (a figure of herself) in a similar role. Near the end of the novel she encounters a little girl in the streets of her Polish hometown. The child is crying, "Mama, mama, mama," and yet, "For some reason I started running so as not to hear her anymore" (305). In addition to a reiteration of the mother and child disunion, we note in this persona of the author the terrifying stance of the author with respect to the death of the child. Pursuing her project, the author takes on a responsibility to the point of confession in regard to the child as victim. The death of the child makes the phenomenology of the Holocaust novel a phenomenology of confession.

This phenomenological condition may help to explain a dialogic exchange that appears in Wiesel's *One Generation After*. "Don't worry," one voice declares. "I won't be the one to break your mirror: the child will. And you are powerless against him. Eyes have no hold over him. And he's not trembling. He is dead. You permitted him to escape your grasp." A second voice replies, "It's incredible: you refuse to understand. I wasn't the one who killed him. It was you" (124). A man may be abandoned to a position of having lost himself as a child, like Bruno in Appelfeld's *The Age of Wonders*, who laments, "Everything I had once known, my childhood too, was over" (100), but as soon as the man assumes the role of author, he assumes a role of response and therefore of responsibility. Levinas writes:

It is precisely insofar as the relationship between the Other and me is not reciprocal that I am subjection to the Other; and I am "subject" essentially in this sense. It is I who support all. You know the sentence in Dostoyevsky: *"We are all guilty of all and for all men before all, and I more than the others."* This is not owing to such or such a guilt which is really mine, or to offenses that I would have committed; but because I am responsible for a total responsibility, which answers for all the others and for all in the others, even for their responsibility. The I always has one responsibility *more* than all the others [*Ethics* 98-99]

Because the child is the victim, the author stands in a nonreciprocal relation to the child. Because the author would posit a world, the author is responsible for a total responsibility. Only through this accountability can one hope to regain some shred of the soul that is lost upon the death of the child. Michael, the main character in Wiesel's *The Town beyond the Wall*, reveals what transpires in the author as the novel comes into being. Early on, for example, Michael accuses God the Creator (and thus implicates the author as creator), saying, "He took my childhood; I have a right to ask Him what He did with it" (59). Yet Michael is himself pursued by a child named Yankel, one on whom he turns his back: "Michael had stood for too long at the window. When he finally turned, Yankel was no longer in the room" (83). In the nonreciprocity of this relation, Michael's responsibility announces itself upon the death of the child Yankel. At first he encounters this death as the death of a totality, as the death of a world. "Why does the earth gape at such moments?" he asks. "Why do we plunge toward the void?" (94). Further, he feels that "a child who dies becomes the center of the universe: stars and meadows die with him" (99). "The earth had titled on its axis, and the sun had ceased to govern it" (100). The emptiness into which Michael plunges is the void of the dead self. Faced with the loss of the self, Michael confronts his responsibility; it comes to him through the mouth of his absent auditor Pedro, who reveals to him that the death of the child is more than an injustice, more than a moral problem: "It is a question mark" (102). The question distinguishes the author's existential condition with respect to the child. Buber states it eloquently: "Out of the distance, out of its disappearance, comes a second cry, as soft and secret as though it came from myself: 'Where were you?' *That* is the cry of conscience. It is not my existence which calls to me, but the being which is not I" (*Between* 166). That being is the child as victim.

Placed in a position of responsibility, the character, like the author, is faced with a project of return, one by which he would account for the death of the child by assuming the place of the child. At this point Pedro asks Michael whether he wanted Yankel to die. When Michael refuses to answer, Pedro puts another question to him: "Is that why

Death of the Child

you wanted to go backwards in time? To become a child—and die?" (103). Again Michael does not answer. In his silence there is more confession than affirmation, and through his silence pours the silence of his author, who works with a picture of his childhood home over his typewriter. "That's where the town of my childhood seems to be now," we read in Wiesel's *Against Silence*. "Not here, but up there, in a Jerusalem of fire, hanging onto eternal memories of night" (3:1). This is the place to which he must return via his character, the place he can never reach except through his character. Near the end of *The Testament*, Wiesel's novel about the poet Paltiel Kossover, we see the culmination of this movement of return. "Returned to my cell," Paltiel writes, "I collapse. Finally alone, I become the child I never was, the orphan I shall cease to be" (335). In this way the child as victim established himself within the author to the extent that the author answers for the victimization of the child. If the death of the child brings with it the death of the man, then the man's hope for resurrection lies in his attempt to become a child—and die. For both author and character the novel is both womb and tomb, and in it lies the murdered child.

The contrasting images of tomb and womb come out in the title of Lustig's *Night and Hope*, a book that begins, significantly, with a piece titled "The Return." Dealing with Hynek Tausig's return to his Jewish self, the theme of his first story is amplified in the second tale, "Rose Street," in which Elizabeth Feiner is returned to herself as child upon being beaten by a Nazi. Somewhat similar to Paltiel, she awakens from her beating to behold, as a victimized child, the image of her father (99). Lustig further reveals the power of death's proximity to transform a person into a child in his piece "The Old Ones and Death" in *Diamonds of the Night*. Once again, it is the aged female figure, the wife of Aaron Shapiro, who becomes the female child victim. As Aaron is about to go outside, his wife says she will wait for him, and her voice sounded

> as if it were coming from another world, or as if that were where it was going. It sounded dry and crushed and betrayed. As though she saw something or as if she were afraid of something she couldn't put into words. As though it had to do with something for which there were no words, something that was still a part of life, but a step beyond it. Something she probably couldn't talk about to anybody else. It sounded as if she were still here, but it wasn't she anymore. Like the voice of an aged, frightened child. [79-80]

This passage reveals the eclipse of the Muse by another voice, the voice of the child as victim; it is the voice of death that makes the victim a child.

If that voice should deign to address the author, then it offers no revelation but, again, poses a question. For Ka-tzetnik, the question comes not from the mouth but from the eyes, as we see in *Sunrise over Hell:* "Nude Musselmen stare with eyes of children at the blocks, at the Heavens, their eyes a question; questioning yet staring, as they get their skeletons up on all fours into the vans. Spent, feeble, they creep in. And their eyes, the eyes of children still hold a question" (175). The Hebrew phrase translated as "their eyes hold a question" is *aynyhem shoelot davar,* that is, "their eyes ask a question" (152), where "question" is part of the verb, not the noun. This verb indicates the action by which these living dead are transformed into children and, as children, they are victimized. Looking up, they beseech the heavens in a reversal of the question that comes from above: Where are *You?* In this question is couched the prayer that Ka-tzetnik utters near the end of *Shivitti:* "God / Give me this day the silent word, like the one / Their eyes gave on their way to / The crematorium" (108). This prayer is the looking up that the author performs while looking down at the blank page and into himself in the effort to go where he can never follow.

Yet he attempts to proceed: Ka-tzetnik follows the fate of Moni, the child hero of his novel *Atrocity.* In a moment that announces his inevitable end, Moni sees traces of his own childlike face in the faces of the dying: "They are asleep. More than one will never wake again. Here and there, in such final moments of sleep, a smile will sometimes flutter on a face, like the smile of a baby asleep. They pass from this world illuminated with the pure, immaculate reflex of the first smile" (85). In the end, Moni himself dies, a babe returned to his mother: "The earth gathered him in like a mother cradling her little one to sleep. Hush . . ." (286). But this "hush"—the novel's last word, which in Hebrew is not a word but *shshshsh* (224)—is more terrifying than comforting. It is the sound of the shriek of silence, punctuated by ellipses, thus refusing closure, like a wound. In this image of the child as victim we find once more the juncture of womb and tomb, the union from which the novel and its author are born. Whether the victim is a child or an adult transformed into a child, the author beholds in the victim his own wounded soul. It is torn from him, as we see it torn from Harry Preleshnik in Ka-tzetnik's *House of Dolls.* Upon seeing his sister Daniella (another female child) turned into a "field whore," Harry swoons and falls to the floor inside a camp infirmary. "Beside him on the floor," the author relates, "lies his life like an infant of his. Any moment now the black boot will crush it, and it won't show any more from under the boot sole. Any second now. The infant lies beside him . . ." (215). Again we find the ellipses, again the open wound.

In the eyes that look to heaven, in the hush of the earth, in the life on the floor, we discover that when the child is the victim something more, something higher, is victimzed. Ka-tzetnik's hints are subtle, but if we allow ourselves a moment of midrash, we find those hints of something more. The hush consists of the letter *shin*, the letter on the doorposts signifying *Shadai*, which is one of the names of God. The life that lies on the floor next to Harry is *hayey* (223), a word that contains the double *yud*, another name of God. Who is the victim when the child is the victim? Elie Wiesel offers one response in *Ani Maamin:* "And with each hour, the most blessed and most stricken people of the world number twelve times twelve children less. And each one carries away still another fragment of the Temple in flames. Flames—never before have there been such flames. And in every one of them it is the vision of the Redeemer that is dying" (27, 29). He goes on to cry out, "These children / Have taken your countenance, / O God" (57). Levinas writes that "the face speaks" (*Ethics* 87), and this is the face that the author labors to bespeak in his engagement with the child as victim. It is the face that reveals to him, as it revealed to Wiesel, that "the death of a man is only the death of a man, but the death of a child is the death of innocence, the death of God in the heart of man. And who does not drink deep of this truth, who does not shout it from the rooftops, is a man devoid of heart, of God, he has not seen the misty eyes of a child expiring without a whimper, who dies before his parents and thus shows them the way" (*Beggar* 99). So the novelist does not write: he drinks and shouts and peers through misty eyes to show us the way.

The French text of this last quotation contains an additional phrase: the child dies not only to show them the way but also *ouvrir la voie qui les attend*, "to open up the path that awaits them" (91). These words, indeed, cast a shadow, yet they reveal a truth in a statement Wiesel makes in *Messengers of God:* "God does not wait for man at the end of the road, the termination of exile; He accompanies him there. More than that: He is the road, He is the exile" (132). If the way out of exile leads to Jerusalem, then in the post-Holocaust era it begins in Auschwitz and passes through the death of the child. The dead child who shows us the road is the dead God who is the road and therefore the exile. The sign of the exile is the death of the child, ever so innocent, ever so fragile. One sees why "in Lublin, Hasidim were urged to live not only in fear of God but also in fear for God" (Wiesel, *Somewhere* 134). One sees why, in the words of Nikos Kazantzakis, "God is not Almighty. He struggles, for he is in peril every moment; he trembles and stumbles in every living thing, and he cries out" (204). Though the child dies without a whimper, the author must make him cry out through his own outcry and thus make heard a cry from on high. As Wiesel expresses it in *Against Silence*, "The thirteenth-century Hebrew poet Eleazar Rokeah says: 'Some people complain that God is silent; they are wrong—God is not silent; God is Silence.' It is to this silence that I would like to direct my words" (2:60). It is the silence of the dead child that makes the silence that is God so deafening.

Bakhtin has noted that in the novel, "the motif of death undergoes a profound transformation in the temporally sealed-off sequence of an individual life. Here this motif takes on the meaning of an ultimate end. And the more sealed-off the individual life-sequence becomes, the more it is severed from the life of the social whole, the loftier and more ultimate becomes its significance" (*Dialogic* 216). Through the portrayal of the death of the child in the Holocaust novel we see the extremes of this transformation. Indeed, we collide with those extremes in a scene from Wiesel's first novel, one of the most dreadful in all literature:

> One day when we came back from work, we saw three gallows rearing up in the assembly place.... Roll call. SS all around us, machine guns trained: the traditional ceremony. Three victims in chains—and one of them, the little servant, the say-eyed angel.
> The SS seemed more preoccupied, more disturbed than usual. To hang a young boy in front of thousands of spectators was no light matter.... All eyes were on the child. He was lividly pale, almost calm, biting his lips. The gallows threw its shadow over him....
> "Where is God? Where is He?" someone behind me asked.
> At a sign from the head of the camp, the three chairs tipped over....
> The third rope was still moving; being so light, the child was still alive.
> For more than half an hour he stayed there, struggling between life and death, dying in slow agony under our eyes....
> Behind me, I heard the same man asking: "Where is God now?"
> And I heard a voice within me answer him: "Where is He? Here He is—He is hanging here on these gallows." [*Night* 70-71]

The persona who speaks here is the child Eliezer, who sees his soul die with the one on the gallows. If what Barbara says in Karmel's *An Estate of Memory* is true—"All of you have forgotten what a child is" (136)—then we have this passage from Wiesel to remind us. In the words of Issahar's wife, the woman in Wiesel's *A Jew Today* who sees dead children everywhere, "they are God's memory" (81). If the Holocaust author is summoned to remember, then this is the memory he must assume.

The Baal Shem Tov once said, "Oblivion is at the root of exile the way memory is at the root of redemption" (see Wiesel, *Souls* 227). At the root of memory is the word. Since the child dies in silence—dies *of* silence—the death of the child is the death of the word. As Lustig's character Elizabeth Feiner, the old woman who in death becomes a child, lay dying, "she no longer had the strength to keep death at bay by thoughts of the little girl; the only thing she knew was what from now on she was not going to speak any more" (*Night* 99-100). The Czech word translated as "not going to speak" is *nepromluví* (66), and it implies not only speaking but also addressing someone. The child who no longer addresses anyone is the one whose address the author must answer through the utterance of the death of the child. This address, this silence, is the hero of the novel, just as it is the hero of Michael's tale in Wiesel's *The Town beyond the Wall:* "The hero of my story is neither fear nor hatred; it is silence. The silence of a five-year-old Jew" (119). Such silence lends the Holocaust novel its biblical aspect, since, as André Neher has pointed out, in the Bible silence "is not only an object but most frequently a subject. . . . Silence is an actor and one of the principal actors in the vast biblical drama" (17). Pascal once cried out that the silence "of these infinite spaces" terrified him (95), yet the silence of a little child eclipses that infinity and makes infinite that terror. For it is the silence not of space but of a child who dies wordlessly, without a whimper, and whose wordlessness must therefore be transformed into the author's word. The death of the child confronts the author with the impossible task of becoming a translator of silence.

This linguistic difficulty that emerges upon the death of the child is poignantly expressed in *Herod's Children* by Ilse Aichinger. There the loss of both the child and the word is portrayed in one instance by the loss of a German child's English language notebook. "A child must have lost it," we read. "Storm riffles its pages. When the first drop fell, it fell on the red line. And the red line down the middle of the page spilled over its banks. Appalled, the meaning flew out of the words to both sides and called for a ferryman. Translate me, translate me!" (71-72). The German text contains a play on the words "appalled," *entsetzt*, and "translate," *übersetz* (70); *entsetzt* may also mean "removed" or "displaced." The image of blood in this passage calls to mind the blood of the child by which meaning is displaced. The meaning cries out to be translated—literally "carried over"—just as the child cries out to be saved. Even when the child speaks, as in Saul Bellow's *Mr. Sammler's Planet*, the words are unheard; a little one about to be shot on the streets of post-Holocaust New York begs his assailants not to kill him, but they simply didn't understand his words. Literally not the same "language" (172). The loss of the child is the loss of the language of the child. Once more we find that the problem of language that confronts the author arises upon the death of the child. What is literally not the same language must become the same language, translated through the author's literary endeavor.

The image of *übersetzen* or carrying over of meaning juxtaposed with the carrying over of the child once more calls to mind the figure who bears the little girl in his arms in Wiesel's *Ani Maamin:* "I perceive a whisper: . . . I believe in you" (91). In this utterance of *ani maamin* the child whom the man bears becomes the bearer of the man, for the utterance of the lost word may redeem the man. Faced with the project of transforming the silence of the child into the language of life, the author attempts to transform the tomb into a womb. "The sufferings of the innocent," Neher writes, "bring innocence to the guilty" (196). In the phenomenology of the Holocaust novel the victim is the savior.

The Child as Savior

The Maggid of Dubno tells the parable of a father who takes his little boy on a long, treacherous journey to a wonderous city. Whenever they came to a narrow crossing, a dangerous river, or a high mountain, the father would lift his child onto his shoulders, carry him over, and set him safely on the other side. Finally, one day they arrived at their destination, the wonderous city, at dusk. The city, however, was surrounded by a wall, and its gates were locked; the only openings in the wall were very small windows. Realizing that he had only one possible hope of gaining entrance to the city, the father had his little boy climb through a window and open the gates for him from within. Since the day when the Sanctuary was destroyed, said the Maggid, the gates of prayer have been locked. Only through the child, who is lighter than an eagle, can we be redeemed. "For the outcry of children," he said, "is formed by the breath of mouths unblemished by sin, and is therefore capable of piercing the windows of Heaven" (Kitov 1:75-76). It has already been suggested that the Holocaust novel has the characteristics of prayer; in the Maggid's parable we see who carries that prayer to heaven. There is, of course, an important difference: in the Holocaust novel the *victimized* child is the child as savior. "They will lie down so that we need not lie down," Aichinger writes (74). Yet in their lying down is a summons for us to rise up. Moshe, in Wiesel's *The Oath*, states quite explicitly the messianic significance of the child: "The Messiah. We seek him, we pursue him. We think he is in heaven; we don't know that he likes to come down as a child. And yet, every man's childhood is messianic in essence" (132). The novelist who seeks life through the word seeks resurrection through the child, and an important point of reference in this search is the child within the novelist. Whatever life he may have within him is born through that child; whatever life he may return to is voiced through that child. In the words of Paul Tillich, "the event of salvation is the birth of a child" (*New Being* 95). Hence the return to life is expressed in Primo Levi's novel *If Not Now, When?* for instance, by the birth of a child to White Rivka and Isidor at the end of the tale (346). Similarly, the yearning for life is expressed in Yehuda Amichai's *Not of This Time, Not of This Place* by Joel's desire for the child at the beginning of the novel: "I awoke with a sharp pain of longing within me. I suddenly wanted to be a child again in Weinburg, where I was born" (8). Looking at the Hebrew text, one recalls that the noun "child" and the verb "to be born" have the same root: to be born into life is to be made into a child. The original text also states that the longing *hatakh oti mibifiym*, that is, "wounded me from within" (15). Only through such an internal wound may the child here be born. Indeed, the victimized child is the wound from which the salvific word issues; if the word is to be born from the author, the author must take on the wounds of the child. Without being thus wounded, the author could not create a novel.

In one novel after another we find that the child emerges to restore life to the surrounding characters. Such a redemptive child is born in the camp in Karmel's *An Estate of Memory* (153). In Wiesel's *The Testament* the child's function as a link to life is presented quite clearly: "Let us not speak of Raissa, Citizen Magistrate," says Paltiel. "She is not the one who binds me to life; it is my son Grisha" (147). More important, Wiesel demonstrates in this novel the role of the victimized child as savior to the fallen man. As a medic in the Russian army during the Second World War, Paltiel addresses an injured soldier as if he were a child: "He was beautiful and light as a child. I spoke to him as I always did, repeating what I always said to my dead: Don't worry, my little one, we are almost there" (307). Then, carrying the "little one" on his shoulders—just as the author tries to carry meaning through his words and his silence (recall Aichinger's *übersetzen*)—Paltiel stumbles: "My guardian angel on my shoulders, I moved forward, tripping. Then I was lifted off the ground. Violent red pain. I opened my eyes: the impact had thrown me into a trench. Torn to bits, he was nothing but a decapitated, legless corpse. He had saved my life: I was only wounded" (307-8). Here the image of the trench suggests the grave from which the man rises thanks to the child, the grave in which the limbs are torn from the child like meaning torn from the world. Such is the phenomenological space in which the author works.

To the extent that the child takes on the function of savior, the space of threat must become the space of protection, like the "circle of protection" traced around the child in the "Titanium" chapter of Levi's *The Periodic Table* (165-68). *Zachor v'shamor* again comes to mind: in the death of the child we encounter not only what must be remembered but also what must be preserved. The life that must be protected and its connection to what might be lost are succinctly stated in a remark by Arele in I.B. Singer's *Shosha*. Explaining why he refuses to leave Shosha, Arele declares, "I can't kill a child. I can't break my promise either" (254). In the event of the creation of the Holocaust novel these two refusals amount to the same thing. The child's tie to life is a tie to the word; the man protects the child by protecting the integrity of his word. Struggling to remain faithful to his word, the novelist struggles to translate the outcry "formed by mouths unblemished by sin" into his own outcry. In this endeavor the child shows him the way, like

Rosemarie in Appelfeld's *To the Land of the Cattails*; a child killed for being Jewish, she "was very sensitive to words" (70). The point is made more powerfully still in Ka-tzetnik's *Phoenix over the Galilee*. Modeled after his author, Harry Preleshnik insists that "his life has been spared to voice the strangled scream of these two children" (123)—Daniella from *House of Dolls* and Moni from *Atrocity*. The Hebrew word *hishmaat* in the original (120) suggests that Harry must "make heard" that scream, not only "voice" it. Only in this way can he be spared; only by drawing the relation with the dead child into a relation with the living can he return to life.

In *Phoenix over the Galilee* the dialectic by which the victim becomes a savior is more than an empty abstraction: "The paper consumed becomes ashes. But words, where do they go? This was how they had been burned at Auschwitz, those whose bodies had turned to ash, whose lives had been unlived. Where did their souls go?" (170). In the creation of the novel we find a clue to this question. The soul of the murdered child invades the survivor and there struggles to be transformed into word, as the child becomes savior. In this struggle the intersubjectivity between author and character becomes the intrasubjectivity of both. In *Ethics and Infinity* Levinas observed: "Constituting itself in the very movement wherein being responsible for the Other devolves on it, subjectivity goes to the point of substitution for the Other. It assumes the condition—or the uncondition—of hostage. Subjectivity as such is initially hostage; it answers to the point of expiating for others" (100). To answer to the point of expiation is to bear witness. Hence the witness born by the child makes the man into a witness. When, for example, the children go on a hunger strike in Rachmil Bryks's *Kiddush Hashem*, the women who witness it are given new strength: "Dvora Leah and the other adults were astonished at the unity and perserverance displayed by the children" (81). Later, when children condemned to die are taken away, it is the child Rivkale who cries, "Hear, O Israel, the Lord is our God, the Lord is One!" (112). The *einikeit* or oneness of the children in the Yiddish text (54) expresses the oneness of God; summoned to hear, the witness is summoned to make heard that cry of faith. The message that makes the survivor into an author is not one of death alone but also one of life. The former belongs to time, the latter to eternity.

"For what is eternity in the life of man," writes Amichai, "if not to see for a second time one's childhood?" (339). What is eternity in human life, if not the drawing of human relation into divine relation? An image from Wiesel's *The Testament* strikingly depicts the function of the child as savior. Paltiel dons his phylacteries for his little one, saying, "The next day I put on the phylacteries again. This time I waited until Grisha woke up. He pulled at the straps, and that filled me with great joy" (332). Visualizing the little hands clinging to the tefilin straps, one might suppose that the child holds on to keep from falling. Yet it is the child who extends the lifeline of joy to the father, underscoring the messianic function of the child as the man's link to heaven. Elsewhere in *The Testament* this function is subtly and briefly indicated when Paltiel alludes to the sounds reverberating through the streets of Jerusalem, saying, "A mother's strident cry: 'Ahmad, you are coming?' And a child answers, 'Coming, coming'" (190). As always, Wiesel's selection of a name, however casual it may seem, is calculated and laden with significance: the name Ahmad—Ahmed in the French text (157)—signifies the Paraclete. Thus, the one who answers, "Coming, coming," to the strident cry is the Comforter, the messianic mediator between man and God.

It is not by chance that the female child in these novels is so often named Ruth, the name of the mother of the House of David, of the messianic line; recall works by Lustig, Amichai, and Kaniuk. In *Adam Resurrected* Kaniuk brings out very clearly the reflection of the author-to-character relation in the character-to-character relation; in the events that transpire between Adam and the child/dog we perceive what occurs in the event of the novel's creation. Emphasizing the phenomenology of the name, for instance, Adam says to the child/dog, "The problem before us is the selection of a name. Without a name there is no existence. . . . Therefore, child, it is a time-worn custom—every creature has a name, and you are nameless" (214). Soon he commands the child, "Write, the name will create you, the name will establish everything. . . . Write a name!" (219). Kaniuk's Adam assumes the naming function of the first Adam in an expression of the task that confronts the author himself. In the Hebrew edition the word translated as "existence" is *kiyum* (187), which also means "affirmation": in its messianic function the name of the child not only establishes being but also affirms it, bears witness to it. When the child finally writes a name, it is the name Jesus, but Adam rejects this Messiah: "No. Adam told him that story! Adam spoke—or maybe it was Herbert?—and the child cocked his ear and listened. Adam spoke about that Messiah because it was important for him to talk about him. *He was a child of this land, flesh of its flesh*" (220). Ultimately the child takes the name David (221). From his line the Messiah is born—or rather, is yet to be born.

In his effort to save the child, of course, Adam struggles to save himself; the death that threatens the child is the death that threatens the self. Once again revealing his authorial position through the existential condition of his character, Kaniuk writes, "A hunted animal is staring at Adam. A dog. A child that is an animal. Something frightfully ugly, yet beautifully ugly. And he, he knows neither what to give, nor what to say, nor how to rescue. For he himself is seeking a savior" (150). Yet the character discovers that salvation can be obtained only as it is offered; hence he sets out to save the child. We discover, then, how the victimized child becomes a savior: it is by offering the man something to save. The author bears witness to the death of the child not only for the sake of the child but also for the sake of his own soul; saving the child, the self saves itself. So we hear Michael's prayer, for example, in Wiesel's *The Town beyond the Wall*: "God of my childhood, show me the way that leads to myself" (136). For only the child can lead the self to the God of the child and thus redeem the man. Only the child can make salvation an issue for the man, because only the child can confront the man with the movement of return. As Ralph Waldo Emerson once put it, "infancy is the perpetual Messiah, which comes into the arms of fallen men, and pleads with them to return" (220). Thus bearing the child, the man bears his own soul.

This is the miracle wrought by the child as savior; given one so precious to protect, the adult has a motive to become better. So it happens for Tola in Karmel's *An Estate of Memory* when Aurelia's child is born: "Goodness seemed to her like a foreign language, which once practiced is not half so difficult as it was rumored to be" (155). The Pardo in *The Parnas* by Silvano Arieti makes a similar point after relating a tale about the death of a Jewish child. The Jews and Christians of the Italian community argued over the burial of the child; "But," says the Pardo, "think again of the little child. Everybody loved him, everybody wanted all of him, body and soul; everybody was willing to accept him, everybody was eager to save him" (54). All knew that saving the child was the one means to self-salvation. To the extent that the man responds to the child's summons, moreover, he is able to hear that summons; that which is most dear is multiplied through its preservation. In Haim Gouri's *The Chocolate Deal* Rubi saves a little girl from a burning building and in the end realizes, "Since I didn't let her die, the cry of the other girls is heard" (129). In the words of Bakhtin, "I must become for the other what God is for me" (*Estetika* 52). God is the one who declares, "Before they call I will answer" (Isaiah 65:24). Only by answering the call of the child is a person able to hear the call and thus become a living soul.

The event of finding salvation for the self in the salvation of the child occurs at the end of Ka-tzetnik's *Phoenix over the Galilee*, when Harry retrieves the body of a little girl from the wreckage of an automobile: "It was his own body now, he felt, being caried in the arms of a rescuer" (268). But let us not forget the terrible reality of what is before us; certainly Ka-tzetnik, a man who went thirty years without a night's sleep, does not forget. The novelist strives to answer the call not just of the child but of the fallen child. "The child has got to fall into the water," Aichinger writes, "if it's going to be saved" (32); and Aichinger the novelist has to pursue the child into those depths if she is to save herself. Yet this is impossible; the death of the child—even when the child is posited as savior—forever returns the author to the existential condition of a lost self. "Adam knows who the child is," we read in Kaniuk's novel, "but he doesn't know who he himself is" (330). The failure to know oneself amounts to a betrayal of the child. The horror of this realization is expressed in *Mr. Theodore Mundstock* by Ladislav Fuks, where the title character collides with his failure to respond to the child Simon: "It was the immeasurable horror of his realization that for this boy who put so much trust in him he had done nothing of use all his life" (207). Thus Mr. Mundstock sees that he has squandered his life in a vain effort to preserve it.

As always, the character's horror is the author's horror: however much he may labor, however long he may wrestle with the word, he cannot wrestle the child to life; hence he is constantly returned to the zero point. From the beginning of Fuks's novel, we see that Mr. Mundstock is shadowed by the one he cannot save, by the shadow named Mon (7). Mon is short for the child's name, Simon. This fragmentation of the name signifies both the broken identity of the child and the splitting of the self. As though looking into a mirror—which itself has a fragmenting effect—Ka-tzetnik describes the loss of identity of his character Moni, the child hero in *Atrocity*: "Nobody recognizes him. Nobody knows who he is. And Moni doesn't recognize anybody either. He dissolves among thousands of Mussulmen. He is a drop in a skeleton river flowing to a sea of ash. He shuffles across the camp, back and forth, back and forth. He does not know where he has come from or where he is going. He does not know who he is" (228-29). He also does not know what he is, the Hebrew text reads (177). Moni does not recognize himself because he does not recognize the others. The death of the child undoes the recognition of the self by destroying the recognition of the other. For the author, the child is the other whom he struggles to recognize in an act of response; but death has claimed the child, and so he does not recognize himself. For the death that rules the concentrationary universe has robbed the child of the loving word of the mother, as in the case of Theo in Appelfeld's *For Every Sin*: "It became clear to Theo beyond any doubt that he would never return to his hometown. From now on he would advance with the refugees. That language which his mother had inculcated in him with such love would be lost forever. If he spoke, he would speak only in the language of the camps. That clear knowledge made him dreadfully sad" (167). The sum of the Holocaust novelist's knowledge comes to this dark revelation uttered by a child no longer a child.

5
The Splitting of the Self

"The shattering of the 'I,'" Aharon Appelfeld has written, "is one of the deepest wounds" caused by the Shoah (*Essays* 99). The pen that descends to the page is a scalpel that cuts into the soul, incising a wound to heal this wound. In the words of Edmond Jabès, "the book is a moment of the wound, or eternity" (28). The self bled of word, father, and child splits, and the task with which the book confronts its author is to split again and thus become other to himself in an utterance of the splitting of the self. Bakhtin insists on the needfulness of this process of the author's becoming other (*Estetika* 16), for only in this act of becoming through the saying of the word can the author hope to bring the word out of exile and restore something of the relation to father and child. In short, he must die away from the death into which the death of father and child has cast him.

The Holocaust author, then, initiates the movement of return at the graveside where he is fragmented. "You are outside," writes Katzetnik in *Star of Ashes*. "On top of the earth. You weren't buried in the pit. Somebody else was" (35). We have seen this somebody else. Standing outside—even, or especially, outside the pit—the self loses itself with the loss of that somebody else. Somebody else is *sham bifniym*, the Hebrew text reads (35), "there inside" or, literally, "there within the face," leaving the man alone *al pney*, "on the face" of the earth: the Hebrew implies a removal of the face from the face and therefore a severance of the self from itself. This division underlies the brief tale of the survivor who threw himself onto a mass grave and begged the dead not to reject him in Elie Wiesel's *A Beggar in Jerusalem* (80). It suggests why the widow in Wiesel's *The Jews of Silence* goes to Babi Yar every day to call out to her dead husband and speaks to no one else (36). The other lies buried in the pit, and with him lies the word that would constitute the self, the word now in exile, splitting the self off from all others.

Because the self is exiled with the word, it becomes the place of exile. The pit, Babi Yar itself, constitutes the fissure that splits the self, as Michael discovers in Wiesel's *The Town beyond the Wall*: "The bottom of the pit: it exists. It's within us" (82-83). Hence we have a reversal of Jean-Paul Sartre's famous dictum that "hell is—other people" (*No Exit* 47). "Man carries his fiercest enemy within himself," writes Wiesel in

The Accident. "Hell isn't others. It's ourselves. Hell is the burning fever that makes you feel cold" (24). The splitting of the self breeds such a confusion of categories. Instead of harboring life, the heart becomes the house of the dead, the self transformed into a cemetery. The silence within, the silence of the pit, is indeed the silence of the grave; yet it is no more empty than the grave. It is a silence that moves, nefarious and malignant, not only splitting but also devouring the self. I.B. Singer hints at this silence in *Enemies: A Love Story* when he writes, "Herman thought of the Yiddish saying that ten enemies can't harm a man as much as he can harm himself. Yet he knew he wasn't doing it all by himself; there was his hidden opponent, his demon adversary" (162). In *Atrocity* Ka-tzetnik is more explicit: "The serpent's head. . . . He feels the beast devouring him to the last shred. Nothing is left of him. Yet, he is alive" (182). The Hebrew verb translated as "devour to the last shred" is *taraf* (132), which means "tear to pieces," a word all the more expressive of the splitting of the self. Yet the man, Hayim-Idl, is alive, his very essence consisting of this fragmentation.

In *Ecrits* Jacques Lacan writes, "Being of non-being, that is how *I* as subject comes on the scene, conjugated with the double aporia of a true survival that is abolished by knowledge of itself, and by a discourse in which it is death that sustains existence" (300). The death that invades Hayim-Idl, the beast that devours him from within, is hunger. As the metaphor suggests, however, this hunger is much more than hunger; Primo Levi has said, "Our hunger is not that feeling of missing a meal" (*If* 144). It is an absolute emptiness that cuts through the man deprived not only of bread but also of the word. It is the phenomenological nothingness that swallows the man from the inside; out of that void the man as author takes up the endeavor to return significance to the word that engenders life. Levinas, in fact, uses the simile of hunger to describe the project whereby the split self struggles to reconstitute itself. "Signification," he argues, "is signifying out of a lack, a certain negativity, an aspiration which aims emptily, like a hunger" (*Otherwise* 96). Still alive, Hayim-Idl is what he is, but "because of that," to borrow from Arnost Lustig's *Diamonds of the Night*, he has "already stopped being it without having become anything else yet" (42). The heart continues to beat when it should have come to a stop. The beating heart, the thing that fosters life, now fragments it by making the man into what he is and *no more;* robbed of his yet-to-be, he is robbed of his present, that is, of his presence. The split self is the absent self, the self made of hunger.

Bakhtin has held that "all duration confronts meaning as *yet-to-be-fulfilled,* as something incomplete, as *not-over-yet*" (*Estetika* 107). The process of the creation of the novel is a process of reintroducing this yet-to-be to the self that has been torn to pieces. Split by a past in which the self lies buried, the author assumes this orientation toward the future in an effort to heal and thus resurrect the self. The dialogic open-endedness of the novel bespeaks its orientation toward "a still *latent, unuttered future Word*," as Bakhtin puts it (*Problems* 90); its form and content, which are of a piece, reveal the split that it seeks to overcome. "The *I* of Then," Ka-tzetnik writes, "and the *I* of Now are a single identity divided by two" (*Shivitti* 100). This statement sums up the phenomenology of the novel as a phenomenology of the soul. In the novel what is divided takes on the form of a single identity, a single human voice, whose division might be overcome in an utterance of its division.

The Splitting of the Novel

In *The Symbolism of Evil* Paul Ricoeur suggests that narrative form is couched in a structure of loss (169-70). As a narrative, the Holocaust novel takes on a form expressive of what is lost, and the thing lost consists of word and meaning, father and child, self and the truth of the self. From the existential standpoint here adopted, "truth," as Kierkegaard writes, "consists not in knowing the truth but in being the truth" (*Training* 201). Truth is subjectivity, and subjectivity, like the novel, is constituted by the word. "It is from Speech [*parole* or the word]," Lacan asserts, "that Truth receives the mark that establishes it in a fictional structure" (*Ecrits* 306). This applies to the living subject as well. The fictional structure of the Holocaust novel is not a mirror held up to reality but is rather an expression of a living soul split from itself and thrown outside of reality. The novel is subjectivity, a subjectivity that is not itself. The event of the novel is the event of the split self whose truth has been lost; hence the novel takes on the fictional structure of that loss. At the heart of the novel, to borrow from Bakhtin, "lies the discovery of the *inner-man*—'one's own self,' accessible not to passive self-observation but only through an *active dialogic approach to one's own self*, destroying the naive wholeness of one's notions about the self that lies at the heart of the lyric, epic, and tragic image of man" (*Problems* 120). Bakhtin argues further that "the unity of aesthetic form is the unity of the position of the active body and soul, of the whole man" (*Estetika* 76). This interconnection of self and novel forms the core of the phenomenology of the Holocaust novel.

Bakhtin has pointed out that "a man never coincides with himself. One cannot apply to take the formula $A = A$. . . . The genuine life of the personality takes place at the point of non-coincidence between a man and himself. . . . The genuine life of the personality is made available only through a *dialogic* penetration of that personality" (*Problems* 59). Just as the event we call the self consists of such an interaction

Splitting of the Self

of voices, so does the event we call the novel. Through the shifting of voices in the novel we encounter the shifting voices—and the splitting silences—of the self; the tectonics of the self compose the architectonics of the novel. The permutations of time and space are tied to this structural/phenomenological feature of the novel. Yehuda Amichai expresses the splitting of the self in *Not of This Time, Not of This Place* through a corollary splitting of space, setting the novel at once in Weinberg and in Jerusalem. Amichai's main character, Joel, says, "I am sure there are people in Jerusalem who would swear I am still there" (36). The Hebrew text is more telling: the phrase rendered as "still there" is *nisharti sham* (53), or "I have been left behind there," implying a removal of the self from itself and setting up the shifting of the character's voice from "I" to "he" and back as he shifts from Weinberg to Jerusalem. Such a splitting of the character's self belies the split within which the author is operating.

Bakhtin has argued that *"form is a limit* aesthetically treated. The point here concerns a limit of the body, a limit of the soul, a limit of the spirit" (*Estetika* 81). The aesthetic limit, then, sets up the existential split. In *The Age of Wonders* by Aharon Appelfeld, Bruno speaks as "I" in Part 1 and is narrated as "he" in Part 2. The I who relates Part 1 is the hale and whole I of the child recounting the tale of his loss of himself; in Part 2 the novel takes on the form of third-person narration because the character is now proceeding from a position of loss. Levinas has shown that "the differing of the identical" is a manifestation of time (*Otherwise* 9). The splitting of the character into I and he parallels the splitting of time into before and after, with the event that lies between left to silence. Levinas continues, "Time and the *essence* it unfolds by manifesting *entities*, identified in the themes of statements or narratives, resound as a silence without becoming themes themselves" (*Otherwise* 38). Out of this silent between-space, in which the novel's time and essence are hidden, the author silently struggles to establish his presence in the novel; in the event left out lies the seed from which the novel emerges, for this is the event that leaves out the self.

Another example of the alternate splitting of voices into I and he can be found in Haim Gouri's *The Chocolate Deal*. Commenting on this work, Gouri has said,

The Chocolate Deal is very different. Most probably I would not have written such a book were it not for the fact that as a young man . . . I arrived in war-torn Europe soon after the Holocaust. There I saw and met the remnants of the Jewish people. This encounter changed my life. Once on a cold, wet winter night I chanced to be in a displaced persons camp in Vienna. There I met a young, lovely woman from Budapest. The camp was crowded, the air was dense with cigarette smoke, the smell of recently unpacked clothing from the

JOINT, together with the sharp aroma of ammonia and carbolic acid. People were living together and finding each other on three levels of wooden platforms. Among them were those whose sleep was haunted by nightmares and screams. These were people who were robbed of all except their will to live and wounded pride. I was then a young man unable to speak the many languages spoken there—Yiddish, Polish, Hungarian, Roumanian . . . and only later did I fully grasp what had happened to these people. I turned to the young woman and said to her that the place reminds me of Hell. She looked at me with a pensive smile and responded: "Gouri, I think you are a poet. A poet has to be careful in his choice of words. Hell is something else." On her arm was a tattooed number from Auschwitz.

The Chocolate Deal deals with Mordi and Robi. It is about their meetings among the debris of an un-named city. Perhaps there is something of Vienna and Budapest in the description. It is about a return to life. It is about the condition that allows these people to pass up the soup offered at a public kitchen because it was not hot enough. . . . You picked up the elements of time, the subtle lines that separate thought and action, dream and reality. All these come together in the choices the two heroes make among the range of possible dilemmas. There is an accounting to be made with remembrance and death, and the awful compromise of passions and life. [Personal communication with the author, 11 December 1988]

Gouri's own displacement in the displaced persons camp consists of a displacement of language; Yiddish, Polish, Hungarian, Roumanian—all indicate the displacement of the self by the exiled word. Even more revealing for the disjunction of the self is the dissociation of the word from its meaning: Hell is something else. The division of the word underlies the division of thought and action, of passion and life, that Gouri describes with respect to the novel. The divisions in the novel point up those collisions that result in the splitting of the self, both for character and for author.

Edmond Jabès articulates the question at hand by saying, "Do I know if I am in the book and when I am not? The book breaks off from the book only to rejoin it farther on. So the empty space between two pages or two works is the place and non-place where our limits of ink and screams are set up and broken down" (215). Ka-tzetnik once said that he was halfway through *Shivitti* before he realized he was writing in the first person (conversation with the author, 13 July 1989). In that work he explains, "All I've ever written is in essence a personal journal; a testimonial on paper of I/I/I: I who witnessed . . . I who experienced . . . I who lived through . . . . I, I, I, till—mid-writing—I used to be hit by the need to transform 'I' into 'he.' I feel the split, the ordeal, the alienation of it, and worst of all—may God forgive me—I feel like The Writer of Literature" (77). Reading these lines, one cannot help but notice the I-slash-I-slash-I, the slashing of the I into I and he that occurs not only in the creation but also in the structure of the novel; Ka-tzetnik's confession helps us to see what that structure reveals about its genesis. To write is to split word from silence, ink from paper, presence from absence, and self from itself, the self already split by the loss from which it writes. It is the wounding of the wound in an effort to heal. What Ka-tzetnik says about his novels Piotr Rawicz conveys within his novel *Blood from the Sky* through his character Boris: "When speaking of himself, Boris used sometimes the first and sometimes the third person. Did this wavering betoken a hidden need to objectivize his own existence, a need generally experienced by those whose existence is giving them the slip?" (139). Significantly, the French word translated as "betoken" is *traduisait* (125), which means "translates": the splitting of the author translates into the splitting of the character. One meaning, one truth, translates into another through the language that constitutes both, the language of the novel.

The discourse of the novel expresses the discursive structure of the self. The author, a translator of silence, is also the translator of the split self into the novelistic word. Yoram Kaniuk hints at this in *Adam Resurrected*: "Adam is a word: illuminate that word with the proper light and it takes on a completely different meaning, containing all human possibilities" (199). Here the Hebrew word for "human" is actually *gnozot* (175), which means "hidden"; the term for "word" in this passage is *milah*, which also means "speech." The word-to-word interaction in the novel reflects the dialogic interaction of the self with itself in an attempt to reveal what is hidden, what is lost, what is other. Hence we find that the novelist employs various means of inserting the voice of the other into the text. This insertion may take the typographic form of using italics to set off one voice from another, as in Ka-tzetnik's *Phoenix over the Galilee*, Lustig's *Darkness Casts No Shadow*, or Elie Wiesel's *The Town beyond the Wall* and *Twilight*. This use of italics not only sets up the splitting of the character-to-character relation within the novel; it also establishes a relation of what is within to what is beyond, drawing into the novel the split self that is outside the novel. The infusion of the beyond into the within takes other forms as well. Paltiel's text is injected into the text of Wiesel's *The Testament*, for example, and the inclusion of letters breaks up the text of *The Fifth Son*. In *Babi Yar* Anatoli introduces the report of the other witness (74ff.), and in *Blood from the Sky* Rawicz includes a variety of voices in the form of author, narrator, and even footnotes.

By all of these means the author endeavors to secure his presence within the novel in the aftermath of the loss of presence. When the appearance of the author takes an overt form—as in chapter 17 of Rawicz's *Blood from the Sky*, titled "In which the author speaks again" (138)—the author assumes the position of character in his own work.

The direct voicing of the author is imposed upon a context of indirect voicing and thus fragments that context in the very effort to merge with it. The same becomes the other in an alienation of the same, indicating the initial alienation from which the author proceeds. In Primo Levi's *The Periodic Table*, when the author as character hears his own words in the mouth of another character, he says, "The phrase was mine, but repeated by him it struck me as hypocritical and jarring" (219). *Stonata* is the Italian word translated as "jarring" (223); it also means "false" or "out of place." The author turned character is the author out of place, split from himself in an articulation of the phenomenological splitting of the self that underlies his creation. "To find myself," writes Levi, "man to man, having a reckoning with one of the 'others' had been my keenest and most constant desire since I left the concentration camp" (*Periodic* 215). *Ritrovarmi* means not only "to find myself" but also "to recover myself," "to become present" (219). Yet when the author becomes character, the reckoning with the other in the endeavor to recover the self only accentuates the loss of the self and the breakup of the novel.

Mindful of such dangers, some authors attempt to foster a presence both outside and inside the novel through the use of a preface. This direct address is calculated to enable the reader to hear the author's voice through the indirect address of the character-to-character interactions. Yet, struggling to establish a position in both places at once, the author, as well as the novel, is inevitably split between the two. Ka-tzetnik in *Phoenix over the Galilee* attempts to provide his audience with a key to reading the novel (vii). Wiesel begins *The Testament* with a prefatory encounter between himself and one of his characters, Grisha Kossover. In *The Parnas* Silvano Arieti, who also inserts himself as a character, includes a preface to declare the factual nature of his tale. "Only one character," he explains, "has been added: a young man I have named Angelo Luzzatto. He is a composite of several people, all real, all known to the community I describe" (3). Later in the novel Arieti is asked if he is Luzzatto (114), suggesting that not only Luzzatto but also perhaps all the characters in the novel are a composite of voices orchestrated by the voice of the author. I am Legion, the novelist all but cries out, for we are many; in the words of Jabès, "I am multiplied in my sentence as a tree unfolds its branches" (56). Hence the character threatens the author in the midst of his identity; yet this threat is just what instills the author with a sense of identity. "If I could," writes Wiesel in *Twilight*, "I would ask Lear to write a play on Shakespeare. To me, Raskolnikov's opinion of Dostoevsky is no less valid than Fyodor the Epileptic's opinion of Raskolnikov" (178). Taking on a life of his own, the character turns the author—and the novel—back on himself.

In the first volume of *Against Silence* Wiesel declares, "Novelists ought not to speak. Their mission consists in listening to other voices, including those of their own creations, of their own characters" (249). When this occurs, Bakhtin notes, "the life of the hero begins to strive to break through form and rhythm, to obtain an authoritative, meaningful significance.... An artistically convincing completion becomes impossible: the soul of the hero shifts from the category of *other* to the category of *I*—it disperses and loses itself in spirit" (*Estetika* 116). This breaking through form and rhythm is at the root of the splitting of the novel. As soon as the character becomes an I, divorced from the author, the author is returned to a divorce of himself from himself; stranded once more at the zero point, he shifts from the category of I to the category of other. In the Holocaust novel the identity of the self is no sooner confirmed than it again breaks down. As Ellen Fine has argued, if Holocaust literature "is distinguished by a deep sense of loss . . . it is essentially the loss (or lack) of identity that is its principal theme. The act of writing is closely linked to an exploration of the self" (1474).

The Breakdown of Identity

As Yehiel De-Nur lay dying in an Italian hospital immediately after World War II, he asked for writing materials. He had vowed to bear witness to what he had seen. Still in the striped shirt and trousers he had worn for two years in Auschwitz, he began his desperate tale. Two weeks later *Sunrise over Hell* was completed. He handed the manuscript to a Jewish soldier, who noticed that no name appeared on the title page. "Who is the author?" the soldier asked. De-Nur replied, "The name of the author?! The authors went to the crematorium. They wrote this book. Go on, you write their name: K. Tzetnik" (*Shivitti* 16). With the splitting of the self it is not the author as I who undertakes his task but the author as other, who has lost his I—and who tells us so in various ways through his characters. Paltiel, a character who is an author, remarks in Wiesel's *The Testament*: "The house is my house, but I . . . I am not I" (288). In *Darkness Casts No Shadow* we hear Lustig's character Manny declare, "I *am* and, at the same time, I'm not. Or as if I'm somebody else" (74). José Ortega y Gasset has said that "to feel oneself lost implies first the sensation of feeling oneself—that is, meeting oneself, finding oneself" (31). But the path that the author travels through the novel in the meeting with himself is one by which he speaks—and breaks. For here he meets a self whom he does not recognize.

Lacan raises the issue of identity in *The Language of the Self*: "In order to be recognized by the other, I utter what was in view of what will be. In order to find him, I call him by a name which he must assume or refuse in order to reply to me. I identify myself in Language, but only by losing myself in it" (63). Responding to the past in view of what is not yet, the Holocaust author confers a name upon his character by which he might recognize himself, only to lose himself once more in his discourse. Within the discourse of the novel, which is the discourse of a world, the character's place, to borrow again from Lacan, "is already inscribed at birth, if only by virtue of his proper name" (*Ecrits* 148). Indeed, to be a character is to have a name. Yet, as Jabès has said in an utterance of the conflict that harrows both author and character, "two names quarrel over my heart and mind" (28). Thus, in the breakdown of identity that comes with the splitting of the self, the character's name is often transformed into another name, into the name of the other. In *The Whole Land Brimstone* by Anna Langfus, for instance, the main character is not identified by her given name but only by the assumed name Maria, a Christian name and thus the name of the alien and alienating other. The alienating implication of that name is more pronounced in Amos Oz's *Touch the Water, Touch the Wind*, where Elisha Pomeranz takes on the name of Dziobak Przywolski, son of the virgin Mary (or Maria). Since the removal of one's name implies a removal of one's place, Pomeranz becomes a wanderer when he adopts his new name: "He passed on from darkness to darkness, as if he were cloaked in darkness" (10). The Hebrew word for "darkness" here is *mahshakh* (14), a term also used for the realm of the dead or the darkness of the grave. The breakdown of identity is a breakdown of life; the split self is the dead self.

The self assumes a new name in order to escape death only to collide with the darkness of death. This is what happens to Hynek Tausig in "The Return," the first of the tales in Lustig's *Night and Hope*: "He must convince himself in the first place that he no longer had anything in common with Hynek Tausig. Did you say Tausig? Oh, dear me, no. I would not have anything to do with him. . . . Hynek Tausig really was Alfred Janota. The identity card was genuine" (14-15). The Czech text is more expressive of the split, since the phrase "the identity card was genuine" is a translation of *legitimace není falešná* (11), literally "the forgery was legitimate." The new name is a lie, and in the lie lurks death. The sign of truth in this case is the sign of the higher relation, a relation to the One who breathes life into man and truth into life; it is the sign of the Covenant, the circumcision by which identity is inscribed upon the man. About to undergo the baptismal ritual of the bath, Tausig realizes that he "would be left behind in the baths, only Janota would come out" (23). Wishing to avoid recognition, however, he avoids the bath; ordinarily men are the same when naked, but now, in the inversion of truth and lie, they are equal only when clothed, wrapped in a cloak of darkness. In his effort to be one of Them

Tausig becomes nothing, a self that has labored itself into no self. Ultimately, then, he understands that "the worst thing that could happen to a man"—even worse than death—"was to be cast out . . . to be someone else" (36). A man cannot live if he is not who he is, if he is split from himself. Tausig, then, overcomes that split by rejoining those condemned to death. Thus he discovers life.

The breakdown of the self that comes in the wake of the name change is central to the theme of *Blood from the Sky*, where Rawicz creates the character Yuri, who assumes the identity of Boris. Noting again the shift from third to first person, we read, "It was all very well Boris's presuming on his 'legitimacy' vis-à-vis Yuri: the latter was not without weighty arguments of his own. Their quarrel, if quarrel there was, went on so long ago that it no longer even succeeded in 'harrowing' my inner self. Though (and this was the main question) was there anything whatever to harrow?" (233). The French phrase rendered as "so long ago" is *à une telle distance* (209), "at such a distance," accentuating the distancing of the self from itself in the breakdown of identity. The verb "harrow," moreover, is *déchirer*, which means "tear to pieces" or "splinter," underscoring the splitting of the self into no self. Similar to the example of Hynek Tausig, the question of whether Yuri/Boris has any self left to harrow is decided by the sign of circumcision. This sign places the character in "the true Temple" of his "crucial dream," where he is able to become himself even under the threat of death (206-9). Further, identifying the sign as the "tool," Rawicz implies a symbolic connection between the penis and the pen and therefore a linkage between character and author. Through a process of creation suggestive of procreation the author pens his character in an effort to make the character into a sign of the split that he would himself overcome.

We have seen that in the case of Ka-tzetnik the author himself adopts a different name *as author*. In *Phoenix over the Galilee*, moreover, Harry Preleshnik, a persona of his author, declares, "My name was burned with all the rest in the crematorium at Auschwitz" (28). In this instance the character does not assume a different name but loses his name, which amounts to the same thing: the death of the self. When Harry becomes number 135633 in *Sunrise over Hell*, he is told, "You're dead. Name's exactly what this number says on your arm. It's what they call you by when the furnace wants you" (161). Near the end of the novel we read, " 'Could I be wrong . . ,' he ventured, 'my name used to be Preleshnik' " (201). Harry eventually becomes an author in *Phoenix over the Galilee*. The bond between character and author is emphasized by the number they share, the number that eclipses their names and splinters their souls. The situation of Primo Levi in *The Periodic Table* is comparable. "At a distance of thirty years," writes the author/character, "I find it difficult to reconstruct the sort of human being that corresponded, in November 1944, to my name or, better, to my number: 174517" (139). Once again we note the distance, *distanza* (143), that iterates the splitting of the self. Recalling a passage from Levi's *If This Is a Man*, we note the breakdown of identity perpetrated by the number, as if the number were itself a perverted name: "My number is 174517; we have been baptized, we will carry the tatoo on our left arm until we die" (22).

In *Essays in the First Person* Appelfeld writes, "We had been taught to speak about the Holocaust in the language of big numbers, and no language distances you from contact more than such a language" (21). When the name becomes a number it is couched in this language that distances the self from itself, a language that confiscates the name in a slaying of the self. As Sartre expresses it, "ideal nothingness in-itself is *quantity*" (*Being* 263); the quantifying of the self indicates the splitting of the self into no self, into a missing self. It is as one who has been inscribed with a number that Rubi, for example, in Gouri's *The Chocolate Deal* cries, "I don't want to keep searching for my name on the list of the missing. I want to jump from here into another place. Always moving. To show them. I'll go on living. You see? I'm not dead. They haven't confiscated my name. And I haven't forgotten the names of the others" (41). Regaining the confiscated name rests on the memory of the names of the others, and this poses another question: Whose name belongs to whom? At the outset of Gouri's novel, there is a confusion in the association of the name with the face: "Now he [Rubi] sees another face upon the man [Mordi] before him. But that face also fits his name. And so it *is* him. Apparently it's him" (4-5). To be sure, the name is tied to the face; the face speaks, and the name bespeaks the face. The breakdown of identity that alters the name, then, splits the face in the midst of its speech. Thus toward the end of the novel Rubi says, "I'm telling him profound things, isn't that so?—profound and very interesting, because Mordi is speaking from my throat" (129). The face speaks, but in the splitting of the self the face splits.

Hence the motif of the double is common in the Holocaust novel, but it is not to be confused with the Jekylls, Golyadkins, or Steppenwolfs of *Doppelgänger* literature. Rather, the Holocaust novel embodies a condition of self-contradiction—*Selbst-Widerspruch*, speaking against oneself. In *I and Thou* Buber responds to the question of what self-contradiction entails:

When man does not test the *a priori* of relation in the world, working out and actualizing the innate You in what he encounters, it turns inside. Then it unfolds through the unnatural, impossible object, the I—which is to say that it unfolds where there is no room for it to unfold. Thus the confrontation within the self comes into being, and this cannot be relation, presence, the current of reciprocity, but only self-contradiction. Some men may try to interpret this as a relation, perhaps one that is religious, in order to extricate themselves from the horror of their *Doppelgänger:* they are bound to keep rediscovering the deception of any such interpretation. Here is the edge of life. What is unfulfilled was here escaped into the mad delusion of some fulfillment; now it gropes around in the labyrinth and gets lost ever more profoundly. [119-20]

The doubling in the Holocaust novel, then, does not oppose good and evil, success and failure, or animal and spirit; rather, it represents a breakdown in the relation of self and other, of I and Thou, that is critical to identity. Sidra DeKoven Ezrahi offers a helpful insight when she notes, "The characters in most of the survival novels have at least one companion who for some period shares their struggle" (79-80). Contrary to what Ezrahi implies, however, the struggle is not just for survival but for a restoration of the wholeness of the self through a relation to the other; it is not that the other assists me, but rather I must be *for the other* in my saying of I.

"What is *mine*," Bakhtin has maintained, "is not in me and for me but in the other" (*Estetika* 101). Levinas adds that the "other is the heart, and the goodness, of the same, the inspiration or the very psyche in the soul" (*Otherwise* 109). The pairing of Rubi and Mordi in Gouri's novel is one example of the double motif. Others include Danny and Manny in Lustig's *Darkness Casts No Shadow* and Gregor and Gavriel in Wiesel's *The Gates of the Forest*. In fact, from the pairing of Michael and Pedro in *The Town beyond the Wall* to the coupling of Raphael and Pedro in *Twilight*, doubles abound in Wiesel's works. In *A Beggar in Jerusalem*, the novel that follows *The Gates of the Forest*, for instance, the doubling of David and Katriel is established at the very beginning: "He [Katriel] is beckoning. Do you see him now? It is he. It is I. My name is David" (4). Shortly thereafter, David says, "People will ask in astonishment: 'Still no trace of Katriel?' I shall answer: 'His trace? I am his trace'" (7). In Wiesel's next novel, *The Oath*, the old man Azriel says to his revolutionary friend Abrasha, "You want me to be your double? You must be joking. Did you take a good look at me?" (72). Yet the doubling does not lie so much in resemblance as in the act of taking a good look, peering into the face of the other until one sees one's own face staring back: it is he, it is I.

The antecedent for this "it" is the author of the novel, which, in its form and content, articulates the breakdown of identity. As Bakhtin has pointed out, the relation between author and character in the process of creation makes it possible to say, "'I am me' in someone else's language, and in my own language, 'I am other'" (*Dialogic* 315). Therefore, Bakhtin argues elsewhere, "there can be no firm image of the hero answering to the question 'Who is he?' The only questions here are

'Who am I?' and 'Who are *you*?' But even these questions reverberate in a continuous and open-ended interior dialogue. Discourse of the hero and discourse about the hero are determined by an open dialogic attitude toward oneself and toward the other" (*Problems* 251). The questions Bakhtin invokes underlie the breakdown of identity; the author's stance toward the self as other—the stance of the split self— determines the discourse of the character as a discourse about the author. An example of the confluence of the questions "Who am I?" and "Who are you?" is found in the pairing of Leonid and Mendel in Levi's *If Not Now, When?* After Leonid died Mendel had a dream in which someone "asked Mendel who he was and Mendel couldn't answer, he didn't remember his name anymore, or where he was born, nothing" (228); near the end of the novel it is said that Mendel "had been a missing person since he had met Leonid" (341). The Italian word translated as "missing" in this last passage is *disperso* (255), "dispersed" or "scattered."

The difficulty of the self, regarding both author and character, lies not in difference but in a certain resemblance. In the event of creation the author labors to become other to himself, as Bakhtin has observed (*Estetika* 16); to become the same as the character would only exasperate the breakdown of the self and feed the sickness the author tries to overcome. In Kaniuk's *Adam Resurrected*, therefore, Adam's mental illness is indicated by, among other things, his resemblance to Herbert Stein, who is referred to as his twin (59). A more revealing example can be found in the twins who turn up in Appelfeld's *Badenheim 1939*; significantly, they are professional readers of poetry. "The readers were twin brothers who during the course of the years had become indistinguishable. But the way they read was different; it was as if their sickness had two voices" (27). Their sickness makes them indistinguishable; their sickness *is* that they are indistinguishable. That sickness has two voices; the splitting of the voice, which is the splitting of the self, is the sickness itself. It is the sickness of isolation within the self, cut off from the other who would posit the difference of I and Thou upon which identity rests. In this isolation the self is confined to the sameness, to the resemblance, of I and I. If in the relation between I and Thou one plus one equals one, in the isolation of I and I one plus one equals zero.

The Holocaust novelist, then, attempts through creation to break free of the isolation that splits the self, hence the dialogic interaction with the character. "The author speaks not *about* a character but *with* him," Bakhtin writes (*Problems* 63). Bakhtin also observes that "every dialogue proceeds as though against the background of a Third who is invisibly present, standing above the participants in the dialogue" (*Estetika* 306). The function of this Third, who is similar to Lacan's

Other, is "to introduce the dimension of Truth" (Lacan, *Language* 269). The breakdown of identity is intelligible only in the light of some truth of identity posited by the presence of the Third in the dialogic relation between I and Thou. Unsurprisingly, therefore, such a presence often shows up in the novel itself, revealing what occurs in its creation. As the author Paltiel writes his text in Wiesel's *The Testament*, for instance, he says, "I should stop writing and talking to myself, especially since I am not alone. Someone is watching me with a smile. Sitting in the opposite corner, under the skylight, his hands folded under his knees, David Aboulesia—or is it my father?—is gazing at me" (335). Both David Aboulesia and Paltiel's father function as voices of truth in the novel, as the "over-*I*," to use Bakhtin's term, "the witness and judge of every *I*" (*Estetika* 342). Aboulesia is Paltiel's witness, and his father is his judge; both constitute the Third who is positioned between the author and the text. In the words of Levinas, "the apparition of a third party is the very origin of appearing, that is, the very origin of an origin" (*Otherwise* 160). Here the origin is the origin of the novel. The Third does not appear because the author writes; rather, the author writes because the Third appears and poses the question that decides the presence of the self: Where are you?

In the lines above cited from Wiesel's novel the confusion of identity is not rooted in a breakdown of identity; instead, as Levinas has said, "the Good cannot become present or enter into a representation.... It has chosen me before I have chosen it" (*Otherwise* 11). The Third, then, is present as a trace, as a pronoun without an antecedent noun, ineffable and unidentifiable; hence only in the context of the Third can identity be an issue in the splitting of the self. Because the Third eludes identification, it often reveals itself in the novel as a question or a shadow of the self. The question "Who is with me? Who?" is repeated in Amichai's *Not of This Time, Not of This Place* (96, 111). In *Touch the Water, Touch the Wind* Oz suggests this trace of the Other: "Suddenly, in the course of an autumn in the late fifties, Pomeranz realized beyond all shadow of a doubt that he was being followed, wherever he went, cunningly, silently, patiently" (51). In the Hebrew text the root of the word "followed" is in fact *akav* (57), the word for "trace"; the term rendered as "silently," *hariyshiy*, can also mean "hushed" or "whispering." Something (or someone) is present by its absence, present as a trace, and heard only as the *kol demamah dakah*, the "thin voice of silence" of 1 Kings 19:12. The "Infinite," Levinas observes, "*anarchically* affects the I, imprinting itself as a trace in the absolute passivity—prior to all freedom—showing itself as a 'Responsibility-for-the-Other'" ("Signature" 189). What whispers not only speaks—it also summons.

With the introduction of this notion of the silently whispering trace, the Muse assumes the features of a messenger who never quite catches up with the character. As the messenger of the Third, of the Other who might introduce the radical otherness of a truth that would overcome the splitting of the self, this figure often takes the form of the madman. The madness in question, however, cannot be reduced to the madness of clinical psychology. "Mystical madness," Wiesel notes, "is redeeming. The difference between a mystical madman and a clinical madman is that a clinical madman isolates himself and others, while a mystical one wants to bring the Messiah" (*Against Silence* 3:232). Mystical madness transcends the pretensions of anything outlined by the pseudoscience of psychology; it emerges on the edge of a total breakdown of the word in both its material and spiritual aspects. As Michel Foucault has expressed it, "Language is the first and last structure of madness, its constituent form; on language are based all the cycles in which madness articulates its nature. That the essence of madness can be ultimately defined in the simple structure of a discourse does not reduce it to a purely psychological nature, but gives it a hold over the totality of soul and body" (*Madness* 100). Because the splitting of the self entails a splitting of the word, the novelist who wrestles with that split also wrestles with madness, body and soul.

Man and Madman: From the Body to the Bridge

"In the beginning," declares Dr. Benedictus in Wiesel's *Twilight*, "there was madness. . . . Christianity believes that in the beginning was the Word. But before the Word, what was there? Chaos? But what is chaos if not the loss of perception, sensitivity, language? A total pathological retrenchment. Before Creation, there was a vision of the future, and I tell you, that vision could originate only in great madness" (37-38). The beginning here described is a condition of fragmentation and loss; as such it characterizes the phenomenological condition for the creation of the Holocaust novel. In this beginning, too, is madness. Unlike the Creator of all things, however, the novelist is a human being. "The boundaries of my body," writes Jean Améry, "are also the boundaries of my self" (28). According to Jewish tradition, body and soul are of a piece. The Sages have pointed out, for example, that the performance of the *mitzvot* as an act of the soul requires the involvement of the body, that is, a confluence of body and soul. Opposite this view is the Greco-Christian tradition that pits the body against the soul. Expressions of this split are as ancient as Plato's *Phaedo* (92-93) and as modern as Descartes's *Meditations on First Philosophy*, where he argues that the soul "is more easily known than the body" (95), as if consciousness can do very well without the body. Yet this is precisely the disease that breeds madness in the splitting of the self.

In keeping with a Jewish approach, Bakhtin has maintained that "there can be a conflict between the spirit and the inner body, but there can be no conflict between the soul and the body, for they form one and the same valuable categories and express a single, creatively active relation to the givenness of man" (*Estetika* 120). In the beginning, indeed, is madness; and the body is the beginning of the self, inasmuch as the self is a subjectivity that *signifies* something. "Signification," Levinas explains, "is the one-for-the-other which characterizes an identity that does not coincide with itself. This is in fact all the gravity of an animate body" (*Otherwise* 70). This one-for-the-other has meaning, he elaborates, "only as a tearing away from oneself despite oneself. . . . And to be torn from oneself has meaning only as a being torn from the complacency in oneself characteristic of enjoyment, snatching the bread from one's mouth. Only a subject that eats can be for-the-other, can signify. Signification, and the one-for-the-other, has meaning only among beings of flesh and blood" (74). Madness is a disruption, an interruption, an eruption of this signifying activity that distinguishes the self in its flesh and blood. It is a hunger that disrupts the daily incarnation of eating bread, a hunger that erupts in an outpouring of words or a shriek of silence. Madness, therefore, begins with the body. The splitting of the self articulated through madness almost invariably finds expression in the fragmentation of the body.

A graphic indication of this fragmentation turns up in *Adam Resurrected*, Kaniuk's tale of a madman. Here the title character's madness is manifested by his imagining internal ailments and then undergoing the appropriate surgeries. Adam's body, we read, "has spat out about ten organs" (64). This chopping up of the body evinces the tearing away of body and soul in the splitting of the self. The character's here is a nameless elsewhere from which the body would extract itself in a literal rending of itself to pieces. Thus we see a further ramification of the permutations of time and space. "Today," declares one of the Schwester twins in Kaniuk's novel, "our business is to rescue as many as possible from the slaughter. Though they are already slaughtered. Yes, their bodies have reached this land, but their souls are still in the furnaces" (55). In this comment on the inmates of the insane asylum, the image of slaughter suggests that the self is not only split—it is sundered, butchered, dismembered. The Hebrew word for "soul" in this passage is *nefesh* (50), a term that suggests life, mind, human being, self, and even body. The use of this word accentuates and illuminates the split under consideration: the breakup of the self is a splitting of mind and being, of body and life itself.

In the splitting of the body the self loses all recognition of itself. Hence in *Star of Ashes* Ka-tzetnik cries out, "Body! Who are you?" (116), using the word *guf* for "body" (116); like *nefesh*, *guf* is also laden with meaning, alluding to self, substance, being, essence. Because the self-recognition that establishes substance lies in a relation to the other, the loss of recognition of oneself may be couched in the failure to recognize the other. Here too the body defines the parameters of relation; the alienation from one's own body is invoked as an alienation of the body from the body of the other. "My body," Bakhtin has observed, "is a fundamentally inner body; the body of the other is a fundamentally outer body" (*Estetika* 44). A collision of the two occurs in Ka-tzetnik's *Sunrise over Hell* when Harry encounters Marcel for the first time in the concentration camp: "Harry stared at the alien's head, the alien's body, and felt great fear. An engulfing terror washed through him. Marcel Shafran was addressing him out of an unidentifiable body" (108). Harry's terror at the sight of Marcel is a terror at the image and substance of himself, ultimately lost. Toward the end of the novel we read, "No longer his own self, he had become enthralled by a force stronger than death . . . rendering the body's purged substance translucent as sunrise" (208). "His own self" is a translation of *atsmo*, meaning "his very essence" or "his own substance"; the phrase "body's substance" is a rendering of *homer* (179), which means "matter" or "material." As the material of the self, the body is definitively tied to the essence of the self. The fragmentation of the one results in the splitting of the other; the isolation of the one leads to the loss of the other.

In its isolation from its essence the body is nothing more than so many chemicals, as Lustig indicates in *Darkness Casts No Shadow* (60). The self-contemplation that issues from this gross reduction—a contemplation in which madness stirs—arises in a state of isolation. The main character in Lustig's *Dita Saxova* insists, "'What I am fighting now is my own private invisible war, and it's nobody's business.' . . . It was not only her body she was looking at and listening to. She was listening to a voice inside her. It gave her the impression of being a person walking on a very fragile surface" (46-47). This fragile surface is the surface of sanity rubbing up against the surface of madness, just as the voice rubs up against the body in a contemplation that divides the voice from the body, the self from itself. In *Being and Nothingness* Sartre observes, "To the extent that my body indicates my possibilities in the world, seeing my body or touching it is to transform these possibilities of mine into dead-possibilities" (403). The fragile surface of which Dita speaks is the outline of possibility traced by the image in the mirror. So the author who has been reduced to a body strives to touch the body that is other, the body of the character, in a mad struggle for possibility. The character, who is but a voice, endeavors to assume a body, to break through form and rhythm, to become a self. "Self-consciousness," Bakhtin points out, "as the *artistic dominant* governing the construction of a character, cannot lie alongside other features of his image; it absorbs these other features into itself as its own material and deprives them of any power to define and finalize the hero" (*Problems* 50). Thus the author fashions a mirror that must reject him as he gazes into it. For the image in the mirror defies definition, feeds on illusion, and fosters isolation.

Foucault writes, "In this delusive attachment to himself, man generates his madness like a mirage. The symbol of madness will henceforth be that mirror which, without reflecting anything real, will secretly offer the man who observes himself in it the dream of his own presumption" (*Madness* 27). In Wiesel's *The Town beyond the Wall* Michael articulates the fragmenting effect of the mirror: "I am alone. Mother is no more. The mirror harbors other visions: the mirror itself would reject me and deny me" (149). The absence of the mother signifies the absence of life. The self alone is the self split from the origin of life and therefore from its own life; the mirror has nothing to reflect because the self is nothing but a body. "I was my body," Améry stated, "and nothing else: in hunger, in the blow that I suffered, in the blow that I dealt. My body, debilitated and crusted with filth, was my calamity" (91). Hunger, the emptiness of the stomach, the void that invades every cell, is the nothingness of the self. "I was a body," declares Eliezer in Wiesel's *Night*. "Perhaps less than that even: a starved stomach" (59). Hunger here signifies much more than a physiological condition; it is, again, the phenomenological lack from which the author proceeds and through which the character is broken apart. This schism that breeds schizophrenia comes out in *Night* when Eliezer asserts, "I was dragging with me this skeletal body which weighed so much. If only I could have got rid of it! In spite of my efforts not to think about it, I could feel myself as two entities—my body and me" (89). Transformed into nothing but a body, the I is made into an It; yet the I resists this transformation. The self begins with the body, but it is not reducible to the body. So the body renders the I that contends with it other to itself: the "me" in the phrase "my body and me" is a divided entity.

In Lustig's *Darkness Casts No Shadow* Manny "dragged the taller boy as if he were a piece of his own body which had been torn loose" (150). The taller boy is Danny, Manny's double. Split from itself, the self is split from the other; the torn body announces the isolation of the self, and the isolated self is a dead self. Thus, standing before the mirror that tears the self from itself, Eliezer ends his tale in *Night* by saying, "From the depths of the mirror, a corpse gazed back at me. The look in his eyes, as they stared into mine, has never left me" (116). Similarly, one recalls a passage from Ka-tzetnik's *Star of Ashes*: "Night about you. Auschwitz about you. Death holds your life between his hands—a circular mirror held up to your eyes" (68). Once again we find that in the Holocaust novel no mirror is held up to life; rather, death holds up the mirror to the self. The novelist gazes into the eyes of the Angel of Death, the Angel with a Thousand Eyes, until his own eyes look back at him through the visage of his character. The task, however, does not end here. The man may turn away from the mirror in an effort to return to life, but the eyes of the angel follow him. In the universe of the Holocaust novel, then, the discourse of life—and with it the life of the self—collapses. In place of that discourse is the mute stare of death that rises up from the depths of the mirror. The function of the word in the Holocaust novel is to free the self from that gaze and return it to a dialogic relation with life. The author must accomplish this not by imposing upon the character a face liberated from the mirror but by creating for his character a face that speaks.

Here we have more evidence that the recognition of the character as other is critical to the author's recognition of the self as I. As always, the author expresses the problem of self-recognition through the character. In *An Estate of Memory*, for example, Karmel's character Barbara desperately feels her face, "trying to assure herself that what lay under the yellow film was still her own face" (176). Feeling her own face, the character seeks her own word. Yet in the very act of the self's feeling itself, the noncoincidence of the self with itself, the problem of identity, is reestablished: Who is feeling whom? Which I am I? The implication of such questions emerges in Raphael's statement to Pedro in Wiesel's *Twilight:*

I am convinced, Pedro, that I am going mad. I may even be mad already. Is this me I glimpse in the mirror? Is this me speaking to you, speaking to myself? Is this me writing to you? Why is my hand trembling? Why do I feel that I'm awake even when I sleep? Why do I feel as if another were sleeping inside me? In my dream, I see two boys running toward the sea, one chasing the other, and I don't know whether I am the one or the other, or the spectator watching them, or the drowning man crying for help. Is this what madness is like? [27-28]

This is the question posed by the writing of the Holocaust novel itself: Is this what madness is like? This question is not entirely rhetorical; Foucault observes, "There is no madness except as the final instant of the work of art—the work endlessly drives madness to its limits; *where there is a work of art, there is no madness;* and yet madness is contemporary with the work of art" (*Madness* 288-89). In this *and yet* lies the problem of the splitting and the regeneration of the self.

"Madness begins," Foucault says, "where the relation of man to truth is disturbed and darkened" (*Madness* 104); this relation is grounded in the dialogic relation between self and other. The self—both as author and as character—attempts to engender this relation and hence this recognition through the word; but on the fringes of madness, "the more I talk the more I empty myself of truth" (Wiesel, *Gates* 163). The ramifications of this existential condition come to light in Grisha's comment on Dr. Mozliak in Wiesel's *The Testament*: "He extracted words from me, sentences, shreds of silence; I became more and more impoverished. The more I spoke, the less I existed; he robbed me of what I cherished most. I no longer recognized myself" (304). Dr. Mozliak, the figure of the lie, threatens Grisha's relation to the truth as a relation to his father Paltiel, to the other through whom he might recognize himself; like his father and like his author, Grisha is a poet. In order to restore the integrity of his relation to the father as a relation to truth—and therefore the integrity of himself—Grisha bites off his own tongue. He is the one who may save the word of the father and thus the relation that constitutes the truth of the self. "At the same time," Wiesel has pointed out, "in order to save it, he had to bite his tongue off. He had to become mute in order to talk. But once he is mute, he cannot talk" (Patterson, *In Dialogue* 39). The body is mutilated to restore the self, yet the breaking of the body is a splitting of the self. Hence madness looms.

In I.B. Singer's *Shosha* we see the loss of self-recognition concurrent with the loss of the higher relation when Arele asserts, "I didn't recognize myself. I was no longer formed in the image of God" (13). Arele attempts to regenerate the lost recognition through his relation to Shosha, and through Shosha the madness that threatens Arele's identity is posed; she has a dream, for example, in which a demon tries to convince her that Arele is not Arele (106-7). The problem of identity for the self has its consequences for the identity of the other, who, like Arele in his relation to Shosha, often bears the features of the father. This is a point made in Levi's *If Not Now, When?* through the character Gedaleh, the partisans' leader who proposes that they have a flag with the image of a madman on it (186). The confusion of identity unfolds the wanted poster for Gedaleh has someone else's face on it (182). "Gedaleh has many faces," we read. "That's why it's hard to understand him; because there isn't just one Gedaleh" (229). The confusion of faces underscores the confusion of the word that creates the dialogic relation on which identity is founded. "Hynek Tausig had had his moustache shaved off," Lustig relates in *Night and Hope*. "At least nobody would recognize him now" (33). Yet Tausig needs the recognition lost upon the alteration of the face in order to be Tausig. The imprint that identifies him as Alfred Janota is precisely the false word (it is, after all, his mouth that he alters) that splits him from himself, the thing that does violence to his face.

What returns Tausig to himself is the realization that the violence he would do to his identity amounts to a betrayal of the other. This concern, to be sure, is central to the existential dilemma that confronts the author: How does one bear witness without betraying those for whom the witness is borne? The dilemma is existential because in the betrayal of others the I is itself lost. In Appelfeld's *For Every Sin* an informer is told, "Don't say 'I.' You lost your 'I.' You're a nothing" (49). Appelfeld makes this point more insistently in *Tzili: The Story of a Life*. In this novel Zigi Baum, a man guilty of abandoning and then surviving his wife and children, says, "The day of judgment will come in the end. If not in this world then in the next. I can't imagine life without justice. . . . You remember how we used to fight over cigarette stubs? We lost our human image—do you say human image or divine image?" (152). You say both; each is tied to the other. Since the I is lost in both its images through its betrayal of the other, Zigi Baum ultimately kills himself (like a number of Holocaust authors). In the passage cited the Hebrew word for justice, *tzedek*, connotes rightness and righteousness. Further, the phrase "we lost" is a translation of *iyvadnu* (68), from the verb *ived*, which also means "to destroy"; indeed, this verb is used in the expression "to commit suicide," *ived atsmo*. The self that destroys the relation to the other through betrayal also destroys itself.

The self's betrayal of the other is a failure to be present before the other; the sickness of the split self lies in its being neither here nor there, marooned in a nameless elsewhere. "Being left behind is a kind of madness," Gauthier Bachman puts it in Jakov Lind's *Landscape in Concrete* (60). It is not exactly "left behind" in German, however, but "remaining behind," *zurückbleiben* (90); the problem lies with the character himself, not with another who might have abandoned him. "I'm a sick animal," Bachmann laments. "I'm neither above nor below" (130). To remain behind is to remain in the confinement of the self, in the isolation of the self and from the self. In that confinement madness threatens the self, as it does Mordi in Gouri's *The Chocolate Deal*. Hidden in a cellar that becomes the tomb of his soul, he declares, "Already madness is creeping all over me. I feel it. Creeping upward. Yesterday it passed my belt, reached close to the heart" (57). Foucault argues that "the madman is not the first and most innocent victim of confinement, but the most obscure and the most visible, the most insistent of the symbols of the confining power" (*Madness* 225). From within this confinement life's "inner infinity," as Bakhtin calls it, "struggles to break through" (*Estetika* 176-77). Madness, precisely because it symbolizes the confining power, is the sign of that infinity's struggle. The author struggles to break free of the self through the creation of a character who must break free of the structure of the novel itself. Thus in the novel madness is indicated by a text that is at once liberating and confining.

Discourse in the novel is also both liberating and confining inasmuch as it is a discourse of remembrance, a discourse that both bridges and isolates. As the film director in Amichi's *Not of This Time, Not of This Place* points out, "Memorial days bring out the madmen like mushrooms" (200). As a bridge and as a messenger, the madman is essential to the function of memory and therefore plays a prominent role in the Holocaust novel. "For this theme," Wiesel has said, "I need the madman" (Patterson, *In Dialogue* 48). In his novel *Twilight*, for instance, we see a number of madmen in the confines of a sanatorium; but in the context of confinement the madman signifies the infinite aspect of the self, the very thing that makes possible the splitting of the self. "Infinity cannot be challenged with impunity, and madness is infinite down to its fragments" (11). Hence, "when one is mad, one is everywhere . . . when one is mad, one rushes toward the unknown. When one is mad, one becomes the unknown" (148). When one is mad, one is everywhere, as the silence of the unknowable is everywhere. The infinity of space lies not in its vastness but in its silence. The madman is the author's vehicle, the messenger of the silence that both threatens the self and calls it forth. In the words of Gavriel's grandfather from Wiesel's *The Gates of the Forest*, "Madmen are just wandering messengers, and without them the world couldn't endure" (14). In *The Testament* Paltiel reiterates, "Maimonides is right: a world without madmen could never exist" (161). Nor could the novel that invokes a world exist.

The madman is the voice of the radically alien discourse that makes truth an issue in the novel; the splitting of the self can be an issue only with respect to a problematic of truth. The madman, therefore, is tied to a third position that stands above and between the dialogic interactions of the novel. In this position the madman is associated but not to be identified with Hashem, the One who poses the problem of presence through the eternal question, Where are you? Given the association of the madmen with God, we cannot declare that God is the one who summons the self, unless this is said "out of that decisive hour of personal existence when we had to forget everything we imagined we knew of God, when we dared to keep nothing handed down or learned or self-contrived, no shred of knowledge, and were plunged into the night" (Buber, *Between* 14-15). In the Holocaust novel the madman plunges us into the night and makes visible the decisive hour of personal existence that marks the phenomenology of the novel. "God is not madness," Menachem insists in Wiesel's *The Town beyond the Wall* (148), but God often makes mad those chosen to be His messengers. Thus in *Twilight* Wiesel's main character, Raphael, sets out to explore the relation between madness and prophecy (45). Indeed, his brother Yoel feigns madness before his Soviet interrogators by turning himself into the prophet Jeremiah (92-93). Significantly, in Wiesel's view one important lesson that Jeremiah teaches "all tellers of tales" is that "to transmit is more vital than to invent" (*Portraits* 126). The task that confronts the split self is to become a bridge—to God, to man, and to itself. The alien discourse of the madman, then, contains aspects of prophecy that would bridge the self with the other by way of the Third.

In Singer's *Shosha* Arele cites the Gemara to point out that "when the Temple was destroyed God gave the power of prophecy to madmen" (114). Such a connection between the discourse of the madman and that of prophetic truth as it comes from God is common in the Holocaust novel. In Kaniuk's *Adam Resurrected*, for example, one of the Schwester twins declares, "And He will again reveal Himself to and speak to the insane! They comprehend, they are sensitive, they shall see Him. Who are they, though, these madmen of ours? Tell me! . . . I'll tell you. All of us who came back" (51). Mrs. Seizling, the founder of the asylum in this tale, asserts, "God has loved them. Spoken with them. Not with the politicians, not with the kings—but with the psychotics has He spoken" (50). The Hebrew word used for "psychotic" here is *m'toraf* (45), which indeed means "mad," but it can also mean "exiled." Those who reside in Kaniuk's asylum and in the Holocaust novel itself are exiled from a world reduced to ashes, like the word exiled from meaning, like the self exiled from itself. The one link that remains for them—the link to the exiled word, the dead father, the dead child—is madness. "Only in the dark days of madness," Adam comments on his relation to the child, "were we able to make a contact of hearts" (366). Hence "without my madness," Adam cries out, "I am a *tabula mortua*, blank as death, zero" (359). For without his madness he is without the bridge to that Word which posits him as a self and through which he recognizes the splitting of his self.

This linkage with the Word that signifies the presence of God is articulated in nearly all Holocaust novels dealing with madness; to be sure, Holocaust novels must deal with madness. In *The Parnas* by Silvano Arieti, Ernesto says to the Pardo, "At the price of becoming ill, you tried to save the image of man. I was right this afternoon when I said that your illness is part of the Shekhinah with which you are touched. What is ill in you is intertwined with what is strong and holy and springs from the same source. Your illness is demanded of you" (87). Illness is *intertwined* with but not the same as what is holy. Franz Rosenzweig has written, "It was a superstition of antiquity, to call insanity 'divine,' but the road *to* insanity is divine. . . . The fear of insanity need not be greater than, or different from, the fear that ought to dominate life as a whole: the 'fear of the Lord' " (Glatzer 44). Perhaps we should reverse Rosenzweig on one point and say that the road to the divine is fraught with madness. Madness is not the cure but rather the vaccine, the dose of illness, that opens the way to what is needful. "At the present level of human evolution," Saul Bellow writes in *Mr.*

Splitting of the Self

Sammler's Planet, "propositions were held . . . by which choices were narrowed down to sainthood and madness. We are mad unless we are saintly, saintly only as we soar above madness" (87). Such is the ultimate either/or that divides the self. Within the dialectic of the self's existential condition, the very thing that divides it opens the path to its reconstitution. In the splitting of the self, what lays hold of the body becomes a bridge. "The self must be broken in order to become a self," Kierkegaard has said (*Sickness* 199). So the Holocaust novelist speaks and breaks in the endeavor to restore the relation to the other that engenders the self through the relation to the character as other.

Like most authors, Lustig comments on himself as author through his comments on his character in the novel itself. In *Diamonds of the Night*, for example, he writes, "A few of the survivors will be somewhat deranged, although nobody else will be able to tell. They'll be deranged in the sense that their madness will be like an invisible bridge spanning the distance between what was and what is yet to be" (120). Thus the author becomes invisible in the text, visible through invisibility, a silence that shrouds every word, a madness that haunts the illusion of sense. In the moment of the novel's creation the one who would become a bridge stands on a bridge, like Lustig's Katerina: "She was standing on the bridge and she must cross it, not just stand there, even though she might face fire and brimstone on the other side" (*Prayer* 29). The event of the novel is the event of just such a crossing over, not from here to there but from there to here. The phenomenological task, after all, is to be here, to answer, "*Hinehni*—Here I am!" To answer, "Here I am," is to cross over. The Jewish condition is one of crossing over: to be a Hebrew, an *ivriy*, to is be one who must *avar*, that is, "cross over."

Ilse Aichinger's *übersetzen*, to "translate" or "carry over," again comes to mind. Near the end of *Herod's Children* we see her main character, the child Ellen, on the edge of that decisiveness that would make her who she is. Attempting to follow the trains into the Kingdom of Night, she says, "'I want to get to the center, to the bridges.' One more time she tried to explain everything. Yet it seemed to her while she spoke that it couldn't be explained, that her thoughts never grew voice in that silence: she was moving her lips dumbly. What she was doing could not be reasoned, for it carried its reason within. One has to go alone to the bridges" (236). The German phrase rendered as "to the center" is *in die Mitte* (235), that is, "into the middle." The bridge goes from there to here, yet it also goes from here to the middle, to the *between* that makes up the essence of relation. In the *between* body and soul are once again joined together in the embrace that constitutes relation. We can embrace only the other, as Bakhtin has rightly said, "in all the moments of his being, his body, and *in it* his soul" (*Estetika* 39).

This, indeed, is what the split self has lost and what the word might restore: the embrace of and therefore the relation to God, the other, and itself. If a resurrection of the self is possible, then it can happen only in the restoration of relation—to the word, to the father, to the child. Only from the midst of this trinity can the self be reborn.

6
The Resurrection of the Self

Elie Wiesel has written, "It is not given to man to begin; that privilege is God's alone. But it is given to man to begin again—and he does so every time he chooses to defy death and side with the living" (*Messengers* 32). Many commonly view art as a kind of hubris, whereby a mere mortal assumes or unsurps the role of the Creator to call a world into being. Such a view cannot apply to the Holocaust novel. There the mortal does not create but re-creates; there the author does not begin but begins again. "My purpose and aspirations as a writer," Wiesel explains, "are not to build but to try to rebuild a vanished universe; instead of creating characters and situations, I try to re-create them book by book, story by story, tale by tale" (*Against Silence* 1:370). The defiance at work in the Holocaust novel is not the Promethean defiance of the Creator; it is the human defiance of the Adversary, a defiance of death, despite every reason, every temptation, to surrender. The Holocaust novel occurs where by all rights every human utterance should have been swallowed up in the silence of death. Upon the utterance of the word that brings the novel into being, already a resurrection is at work. "From the moment the Word expires," André Neher has said, "everything is so regulated that it will rise again, since, assuredly, it was in view of this resurrection, after a given period of silence, that the Word was pronounced" (23). Ka-tzetnik wrote his first novel, *Sunrise over Hell*, as he lay dying. Yet upon the completion of the novel, he made a sudden and unexpected return to life, as though regenerated by the word itself (conversation with the author, 13 July 1989).

On the edge of death the man is reborn; resurrection occurs in cemeteries. "Here it is: life!" writes Ka-tzetnik in *Star of Ashes*. "Crying out at you from your own grave: live!" (31). The novel itself cries out through a voice that bounds back at the man, coming from him and from beyond him, calling him forth: "Back of him lay Auschwitz—mute, petrified. He screamed. Heard a voice. Startled, he looked around. It was his own voice bounding back at him" (190). As the sound echoes back, the scream transformed into a voice, the resurrection, the transformation of death into life, is set into motion. The death that is Auschwitz lies in the pertrified muteness that is Auschwitz. Any life that may arise from that death comes with the bounding back of a voice that breaches the muteness. Hence even over hell the sun may rise, as it does in the closing lines of *Sunrise over Hell:* "Red sunrise blazed on his raw skull. From the distance came rolling a Russian tank, closer. Rising from the mound of corpses to his knees, Harry Preleshnik appeared to be one, grown from their midst" (215). In the Hebrew text the novel's last sentence is more revealing. It reads, *V'dumah hayah k'tsumeah v'olah m'tokhah* (184), which may be translated, "And the silence was like a plant, and it rose up from their midst." Like a plant, the man is made of the silence of the dead from which he rises, and he does rise, instilled with the silence that he must make into a voice.

Like an echo, images from the passage above recur in Ka-tzetnik's *Atrocity:* "Will this cry reach an ear after we have all passed from the world? A voice cannot be burned. Roots. Mute tree roots on Auschwitz soil. When the time comes will *they* be able to recount one whit of it?" (178). Once again, the Hebrew is more suggestive, for the word "roots" is *sharashiym* (135), and in Hebrew words themselves are made from *sharashiym*, the roots. The silence that rises like a plant has hidden beneath it roots from which words might be born: a voice cannot be burned. The roots of the voice are the roots of resurrection. But the question remains: Will the words cut off at the roots be able to rise up from the mute soil of Auschwitz? It will be said that in the end something arises; after all, we hold the novel in our hands. From the phenomenological standpoint, however, the novel is not simply the object we hold. It is an event, a process of dialogic interaction undertaken by a living soul. Because the discourse of the novel is dialogic, it is open-ended. Every word seeks a response; every utterance rises up only to die away. "The word already spoken," Bakhtin has noted, "has a ring of hopelessness in its already having been pronounced: a word uttered is the dead flesh of meaning" (*Estetika* 117). Lacan observes further, "The symbol manifests itself first of all as the murderer of the thing, and this death constitutes in the subject the eternalization of his desire. The first symbol in which we recognize humanity in its vestigial traces is the sepulture" (*Language* 84). In this case the desire that is eternalized is the longing for rebirth. The novelist no sooner emerges from the tomb than the problem of resurrection reestablishes itself. Once again the author must take up a creation that is a re-creation, beginning again and ever again.

One is tempted to call to mind the image of Sisyphus descending his mountain to put his shoulder once more to the rock. To be sure, Albert Camus summons this image in his concern with "absurd creation," declaring, "When the images of earth cling too tightly to memory, when the call of happiness becomes too insistent, it happens that melancholy rises in man's heart: that is the rock's victory, that is the rock itself" (*Myth* 90). For the Holocaust novelist, however, memory does not cling; it must be pursued. What the author pursues is not the memory of earth but the memory of ashes. The rock is not the stone of his labor but the stone that seals his tomb; it is the petrified wordlessness that he opposes with his word. How does the human being transform the scream into a voice? What is the nature of the response that is couched in the voice? Where does the memory born of response take the witness? And when, if ever, does the resurrection come? These are the questions that shape the author's existential condition and that lend our concern with the novel its phenomenological aspects.

Metaphysical Laughter

In the face of the death from which the soul would be resurrected, "revolt is not a solution," as Wiesel has said, "neither is submission. Remains laughter, metaphysical laughter" (*Souls* 199). The transformation of the word that may set the self free originates in this laughter "Laughter lifts the barriers," Bakhtin writes, "and opens the way to freedom" (*Estetika* 339). In his book on Rabelais Bakhtin argues, "Laughter . . . is one of the essential forms of truth concerning the world as a whole. . . . Certain essential aspects of the world are accessible only to laughter" (66). The truth here sought, however, does not concern the world so much as the collapse of the world and with it the splitting of the self. Bakhtin makes this point with respect to the self: "Laughter is essentially not an external but an interior form of truth" (*Rabelais* 94). As an element of the inwardness of the human being, of the depth dimension of the inner being, laughter here takes on its metaphysical aspect. When the word is exiled from its meaning, when the symbols of truth become signs of nothing, when the silence of the sky transformed into a cemetery is deafening—laughter remains the one avenue to life, the sole distinction between life and death.

Thus we can take Bakhtin's assertion that "*death is inseparable from laughter*" (*Dialogic* 196) to a deeper level. Death is inseparable from laughter because laughter is inseparable from life's attachment to life, from that love, that eros, that engenders life. "You asked if I understand love," says Pedro to Michael in Wiesel's *The Town beyond the Wall*. "I understand it because I understand death, too" (126). He understands love and death because he knows how to laugh (16, 42). Henri Bergson has shown that life's attachment to life is a "love for that which is all love" (212). Pedro understands death because he understands that its opposite is love. As life's attachment to and affirmation of life, love is made manifest through laughter. Laughter sows the seed that grows life from death, word from silence. "The spermatic word," Norman O. Brown calls it. "The sower soweth the word. In the beginning was the word, in the beginning was the deed; in the resurrection, in the awakening, these two are one: poetry" (265-66). Wiesel, however, adopts a metaphysical view of laughter that leads him to an anarchic beginning, to the beginning before the beginning. Then, he writes, "there was neither the Word, nor Love, but laughter, the roaring, eternal laughter whose echoes are more deceitful than the mirage of the desert" (*Accident* 46). This is the metaphysical laughter that makes possible the word and the love that underlie human beginnings; this is the laughter that engenders the poetry that Brown associates with resurrection and awakening.

Taking poetry in its widest sense, we recall Bakhtin's claim that in the development of the novel laughter "freed consciousness from the power of the direct word, destroyed the thick walls that had imprisoned consciousness within its own discourse, within its own language" (*Dialogic* 60). While this statement may apply to the novel in the pre-Holocaust era, in the Holocaust novel the author is not trying to free himself from his own language but from the "emptiness and silence of an imposed Absence," to use Alvin Rosenfeld's phrase (15). Laughter makes that silence heard and transforms that absence into a presence. It is the articulation of the passion of which Gregor's grandfather speaks in Wiesel's *The Gates of the Forest:* "The soul needs storm and fire and dizziness. The body has time; it moves slowly and prudently, step by step, in obedience to laws of gravity, but the soul brushes time and laws aside; it wants to push forward, regardless of the cost in pain, or intoxication or even madness" (11). In the French text we see that the soul *veut courir* (19), "wants tor run" and rush ahead, a stronger statement than "wants to push forward." The novel explicitly describes this rushing forward when Gavriel rolls away the stone that seals him in the cave with Gregor and goes out to confront the soldiers who are after him: "Gavriel stood up and examined the first soldier and then the loudly panting dogs. Gavriel frowned, his shoulders twitched. Then, in the face of the soldiers and the stupefied dogs, he burst suddenly into overwhelming laughter" (50). In that laughter we hear the reverbations of the roaring, eternal laughter of the beginning.

Viewed in its metaphysical aspects, laughter is a component of the bridge between word and meaning, self and other, God and man. Metaphysical laughter takes the man beyond the confines of space and time, of fear and isolation; it has a ring of madness about it, of a mad struggle for possibility, without which there can be no resurrection. The madman in Wiesel's *Twilight* laughed in response to Raphael's question about whether he saw God at work in the horrors of the world: "And his laughter frightened Raphael more than his prophecy" (210). When neither a yes nor a no will suffice, when a no must be turned into a yes, laughter bursts forth. This confluence of neither/nor and both/and comes out elsewhere in the Holocaust novel. In *The Chocolate Deal* by Haim Gouri, for example, we read, "And what about those mouths gaping there in a terrible scream? A mistake, gentleman! They're not screaming, God forbid. They're laughing" (117). Death and life, love and death, merge in this emergence of laughter in the scream; laughter is the initial becoming-heard of the shriek of silence. "Do you know why he was crucified?" Gregor asks of a certain Jew in *The Gates of the Forest*. "I'll tell you: because he never learned to laugh" (58). In the struggle to choose life over death, to draw life out of death, the Holocaust novelist must at the outset learn to laugh.

Aharon Appelfeld opens his novel *The Age of Wonders* with the figure of a woman "who burst out laughing . . . the woman laughed and there was a kind of crazy enjoyment in her voice, as if this were what she had been waiting for all of her life" (9). In the laughter of this character rings the laughter of the author. We not only confront his words on the page, but from between the words also arise traces of the laughter that sets him into motion, raising him up from the dead. Appelfeld writes, "Angry words, such as I had never heard in our house before, rent the air between laughter and laughter like the cawing of crows" (*Age* 98). The author has not only testimony to transmit but also the power of laughter, the power of life over death. Wiesel makes this point clearly in the closing lines of *The Testament*. The stenographer Zupanev, Paltiel's reader and witness, says,

And suddenly it happens: I am laughing, I am laughing at last. . . . It's idiotic, even unjust, but it is the dead, the dead poets who will force men like me and all the others to laugh. I tell your father and I repeat it to him. Even though he is no longer living and no gravedigger will ever lower him into the ground because the ground is cursed and so is heaven. Never mind. I shall carry him, your big child of a father. I shall carry him a day, a year, ten years, for I must hear him laugh as well. [346]

In these images are gathered together the father and child that would be resurrected; in order to bring about their resurrection as well as his own, the witness must laugh until he hears the dead laugh with him.

Of course, this is madness: it is the mad, metaphysical laughter that bridges one world with another, this world with the world that was and with the world to come. One recalls a dialogic exchange from Wiesel's *One Generation After*: "But . . . why are you laughing? *So that you may remember my laughter as well as the look in my eyes.* You lie. You laugh because you are going mad. *Perfect. Remember my madness*" (48). Laughter is the means by which madness turns back on itself, back to life. Wiesel addresses this issue in *A Begger in Jerusalem*, where he relates an exchange between Moshe the Madman and the prophet

Elijah. Says Moshe, " 'My weapons? Not tears, not prayers, but laughter, only laughter. Admit then that laughter too can provoke miracles.' To which the prophet is said to have answered: 'In our day, Moshe, laughter itself is a miracle, the most astonishing miracle of all' " (33). Laughter miraculously provokes laughter and invokes a truth that laughs itself free of a lie. This is the liberation effected by the madman in his capacity as prophet and messenger. Yoram Kaniuk makes this point in *Adam Resurrected*. An important moment in Adam's resurrection comes when he, who had made his living as a clown, takes on the role of messenger for those who go out to seek God in the desert: "He, *he* is the prophet, *he* the messenger. It is hard to believe. He wants to believe just the opposite, that he must return and smack the truth in their faces like stones from a sling shot: that no, He will not show up, it's a lie, a joke, their seriousness was Adam's jest" (298). The Hebrew text does not precisely state "He will not show up" but *lo yitgalah*, that is, "He will not be revealed"; the noun translated as "joke" is *ts'hok* (258), which means "laughter." Laughter is the revelation of the one who will not be revealed.

A modern midrash: Yitzhak was resurrected not when the angel stayed the knife in his father's hand but when he was able to descend Mount Moriah in the midst of his name, laughter. Resurrection concerns not only the dead but the living as well, for "death may invade a creature though life has not yet departed" (Wiesel, *Town* 98). Thus the laughter that fuses neither/nor with both/and is the laughter that resurrects the living, as we see in a passage from Wiesel's *The Oath:* "With my laughter I drive the living to life, the dead to oblivion. With my laughter I bring together earth and sea, hell and redemption, enigma and light, my self and its shell" (86). Driving the living to life, the self returns to life, resurrected by the laughter that joins body and soul; laughter is the balm applied to the wound of the split self. The man who can laugh is, in his laughter, precisely who he is. Through his laughter he makes others become who they are by making them laugh. "When he laughs, he laughs," it is said of Signor Torquato in Silvano Arieti's *The Parnas*. "You can hear him a mile away. And he makes everybody laugh" (82). Far more than a sense of humor is at work here: there is a sense of the eternal, of what is heard from beyond the scope of hearing, "a mile away." The laughter that overcomes the splitting of the self belongs not to the physical but, like the self, to the metaphysical. For it arises in a contradiction of the law of contradiction, making *A* into *not A*. It is a bursting forth of life where there should be only death.

A passage from Ilse Aichinger's *Herod's Children* rises up through an outcry that bespeaks an age when "God had fallen into the hands of Herod" (124). Aichinger writes:

Resurrection of the Self

You keep only what you give away. Give them what they take from you, for they grow poorer thereby. Give them your toys, your coats, your lives. Give everything away. He who takes loses. Laugh when they tear the clothes from your bodies and your caps from your heads. Laugh at the surfeited, at the contented who have lost hunger and restlessness—man's most precious gifts. Give away your last piece of bread to guard yourself from hunger; give away your last bit of property and remain restless. Throw the gleam in your face to the dark, to strengthen it. [126]

The German text follows the phrase "give everything away" with *um es zu behalten*, "in order to keep it"; "when they tear . . . the caps from your heads" is followed by *denn man behält nur das, was man hergibt* (122), reiterating that "you keep only what you give away." The insistence on this truth is an insistence on laughter, for what is offered up is retained not merely in the act of offering but also in the laughter that is offered up with it. "It's very important to give," writes André Schwarz-Bart, "when you have nothing" (402), because that is how the self becomes more than nothing; that is how the lost self regains itself. What remains to be offered up when one has nothing to offer is laughter, metaphysical laughter. Laughter begins not where tears leave off; rather, like faith, it begins where thought leaves off. In laughter lie the beginnings of the novel, of the word uttered between the laughter.

In *A Beggar in Jerusalem* Wiesel writes,

Somewhere in this world, Rabbi Nachman of Bratzlav used to say, there is a certain city which encompasses all other cities in the world. And in that city there is a street which contains all other streets in the city. And on that street there stands a house which dominates all other houses on the street. And that house has a room which comprises all other rooms in the house. And in that room lives a man in whom all other men recognize themselves. And that man is laughing. That's all he ever does, ever did. He roars with laughter when seen by others, but also when alone. So I think of Katriel: could he be that man? I never heard him laugh, but that proves nothing. Laughter may be learned, may be acquired. Moshe, Moshe the Drunkard, the madman, Moshe will confirm this in his booming voice. When did he arrive? I didn't notice. But listen to him roar:

"Come on! What are you waiting for? You're not here to attend a funeral! Laugh, for heaven's sake, laugh! Let yourselves go! Don't hold back! Laugh! Louder!" [30-31]

We can see why Wiesel has asserted that for the task of response he has undertaken he needs the madman (Patterson, *In Dialogue* 48). The madman teaches him how to laugh, and laughter, metaphysical laughter, is the soil in which the seed of response is sown. "To laugh is to reap," says Neher. "Laughter is words" (236). This insight calls to mind

Bakhtin's claim that "it is in the word that laughter manifests itself most variously" (*Dialogic* 236-37). The word places laughter in a space that is between self and other, where each may offer it to the other in an act of response.

The Project of Response

Response implies relation. The project of response is an effort to resurrect the word from the ashes of words, to raise the dialogic word of relation, through which the self can work its resurrection. The responsive word, then, arises from a position of being for-the-other, from a position of difference, as Levinas describes it, that "turns into non-indifference, precisely into my responsibility". (*Otherwise* 166). Wiesel insists that "absence of fire, absence of passion, leads to indifference and resignation—in other words, to death" (*Somewhere* 128). The process of resurrection is a process of generating the nonindifference of relation, where the dialogic response summons a response, as Lazarus was summoned from the grave. In Wiesel's *The Oath* a silence is broken in order to save a life, to return a life to life: "Speak, the old man thinks. The best way. Make him speak. Speak to him. As long as we keep speaking, he is in my power. One does not commit suicide in the middle of a sentence. One does not commit suicide while speaking or listening" (22). What we see in this relation of character to character also distinguishes the relation of author to character. The author speaks and makes the character speak so that the character may come to life and thus return the author to life. Each constitutes a portion of the testimony that goes into the literary response to the event; both are required for the transformation of difference into nonindifference, thus making the survivor into a witness.

In *Blood from the Sky* Piotr Rawicz declares that "the only thing that matters, that *will* matter, is the integrity of the witness. Be witnesses" (27). The act of response is an act of bearing witness; the summons to which the author responds is a summons to become a witness. He who is resurrected is resurrected as a witness, and through the witness he bears the man is born to life. In *Phoenix over the Galilee* Ka-tzetnik asks where the words go when the paper is turned to ashes (170). Reflecting on this image, we realize not only where the words go but also whence they arise. The dead father, the dead mother, the dead child summon the witness; the words they use go into the witness's own mouth as he responds to their call. "The life of the world," Bakhtin maintains, "is contained in its transfer from one mouth to another" (*Problems* 202). Thus Ka-tzetnik cries out, "In each one's eyes was the command: Tell it!" (*Phoenix* 60). From each one's eyes, the Hebrew text reads, comes the call to take the oath, the *shvuah* (54), a word that also means "testament." Fulfilling the vow, the man becomes one with the word placed in his mouth by the other, thus drawing the word out of exile and making his return to life. In *Star of Ashes* Ka-tzetnik answers, "I vow on your ash embraced in my arms to be a voice unto you, and unto the Ka-Tzet now voiceless and consumed; I will not cease to tell of you even unto the last whisper of my breath. So help me God, amen" (191). The Hebrew word for "breath" is *n'shiymah* (191), which is a congnate of *n'shamah*, meaning "soul," or "spirit," or "life." Calling forth the last shred of the soul, the vow to become a voice, the vow to respond, calls the author back into life. Becoming a voice unto the voiceless, he is commanded and called forth by his own voice in the act of response.

Inasmuch as the act of response is an act of testimony, it is also an act of prayer; the prayer is itself the redeemer sent out of love, the *teshuvah* that is both response and redemption. "The important thing," Lustig has written, "wasn't who or what you pray to or for, but just the fact of praying" (*Darkness* 48). This feature of the literary response to the Shoah lends that response its transformational power; it makes the phenomenology of the novel a phenomenology of resurrection. "The command is stated by the mouth of him it commands," says Levinas (*Otherwise* 147). The one commanded is commanded to rise up and live. The act of writing that distinguishes the process we call the Holocaust novel, then, is itself a process of rebirth. In *The Periodic Table* Primo Levi declares, "It was exalting to search and find, or create, the right word . . . to dredge up events from my memory and describe them with the greatest rigor and the least clutter. Paradoxically, my baggage of atrocious memories became a wealth, a seed; it seemed to me that by writing, I was growing like a plant" (153). The Italian word translated as "I was growing," *crescere* (158), suggests an image of rising up, as though the blank of the page were the soil from which the soul would rise. "Perishing and death," Bakhtin writes, "are perceived as *sowing*" (*Dialogic* 207). The thing that germinates the seed is the turning back, within the novel, on the process of creation as a process of the self's re-creation.

Levi gives this event of the novel and within the novel an even greater phenomenological accent toward the end of *The Periodic Table*:

It is my brain, the brain of the *me* who is writing; and the cell in question, and within it the atom in question, is in charge of my writing, in a gigantic minuscule game which nobody has yet described. It is that which at this instant, issuing out of a labyrinthine tangle of yeses and nos, makes my hand run along a certain path on the page, mark it with these volutes that are signs: a double snap, up and down, between two levels of energy, guides this hand of mine to impress on the page this dot, here, this one. [232-33]

The scientist transforms matter into energy; the artist transforms matter into spirit, the inanimate into the animate, mute silence into eloquent word. The dead self, the split self, is one reduced to the chemicals of the periodic table; the resurrected self is the self as matter transformed into the self as spirit. Out of the ashes of the dead, life awakens upon the utterance of a responsive word. In the Holocaust novel this word is a name, one by which the author names his character in a memory of himself. This phenomenological movement occurs, for example, in Ka-tzetnik's *Phoenix over the Galilee* when his character becomes an author: "The tentacles of terror coiled around him. And to save himself his hand shot out in reflex for the pen, as, at that moment, the first words screamed themselves out of him onto the page" (66). He writes his name: Harry Preleshnik.

Transforming his outcry into response, the author seeks a resurrection of himself through the resurrection of his character. As the name Harry Preleshnik screams itself onto the page, the author rises up from the page to become who he is. "I shoot up from the launch-pile of skeletons," Ka-tzetnik relates in a vision from *Shivitti*, "into the tempest of my own cry of Passion" (104). That cry has the power to raise the man only insofar as the man would raise the pile of skeletons. "It is the call and response to one's fellow," argues Neher, "which produces the miracle. As in the Bible, the Job of the twentieth century is finally sent back to his neighbor" (222). The resurrection of the self lies in this relation to the other; the project of response is a project of offering the self to the other in a salvation of both. It happens between Ka-tzetnik and his character as the character rises up with his name, and it happens between character and character as Harry returns his wife, Galilea, to life: "Harry had rolled away the heavy stone at the mouth of her soul, and the thoughts dammed up within had burst forth, clear and flowing" (235). His response opens the mouth of her soul; her response resurrects him, so that she may declare, "Beloved, I shall put a new pen in your hands" (238). Thus we see why Galilea is called Geulah, which, as Alan Yutler has pointed out, means "redemption" (16). Harry's relation to Galilea expresses the author's relation to Harry, the character modeled after the author himself. Because the project of the novel is a project of response, the author needs this other image of himself, this image of himself as other, in order to become other. Indeed, there can be no resurrection of the self without the self's becoming other.

Only through being for-the-other can the dead self return to life. Hence the author is for-the-character, and the character is for-another, and each relationship amplifies the other. "We can lay our hands only upon the other," Bakhtin has asserted. "Only him can we embrace" (*Estetika* 39). Only through embrace can the self be resurrected. In *The*

Gates of the Forest Wiesel writes, "Two embracing bodies. Mystery dwells in their union; it is enough that a man and a woman give themselves to each other for God to confer his powers upon them and for the world to be brought once more out of chaos" (214-15). In *The Testament* Wiesel's character Paltiel writes, "Two persons embrace and the chasm in their lives is lit up" (120). Before the creation of the sun, moon, and stars, God called forth the light: the light of relation, the light of the word itself, which summons the dialogic relation before a word has been spoken. The creation of such light is the project of response, and it is most eloquent in the movement and in the moment of embrace. The mystery that dwells in this union is the mystery of the creation, by which the world is drawn out of chaos and the self is raised from the dead. It is through response—and, more important, through responsibility—that the chasm that splits the self is spanned, thus healing the self, as it becomes for-the-other in the act of embrace.

In Wiesel's *The Oath* Moshe articulates the broader implications of this responsibility: "In order to realize himself, man must fuse all levels of being into one; every man is all men. Every man can and must carry creation of his shoulders; every unit is responsible for the whole" (197). The pursuit of this responsibility is the key to the project of response, to the struggle for a return to life through the responsive word. "Before the face," Levinas has said, "I do not simply remain there contemplating it, I respond to it" (*Ethics* 88). In that response, he goes on to argue, "the glory of the Infinite reveals itself through what it is capable of doing in the witness" (*Ethics* 109). In the dialogic relation between self and other, this third presence works the resurrection. "The Word [of response] is everything," Wiesel writes in *Twilight*. "Through the Word we elevate ourselves or debase ourselves. It is refuge for the man in exile, and exile for the righteous. How would you pray without it? How would we live without it? Don't underestimate the Word, my friend. Don't fight the Word. Let it possess you and in return you will receive life's most generous offering: the impulse that brings man closer to God" (98). The translation omits an important line from the French text: "Quand tu es en danger, elle t'enveloppe; quand tu rêves, elle te protège du cauchemar" (121); "when you are in danger, it wraps itself around you; when you dream, it protects you from nightmares." The novelist is faced with an awakening from the most terrible of nightmares, and he sets out on the most dangerous of paths in his movement toward resurrection. The responsive word, the word of dialogic relation, is both the way and the light that illuminates the way.

The project of response does not consummate the resurrection of the self, but it does initiate a movement critical to that resurrection, the movement of remembrance. Thus, Wiesel has said, "'*Zachor v'shamor b'dibar echad.* . . .' We are told, 'Remember and observe' were given in one word. Just all these days were created for one day alone, the Sabbath, all other words were created for one word alone, 'Remember' " (*Dimensions* 5). This includes, above all, the responsive word. It includes every word that goes into the Holocaust novel. "Remembering," Améry says. "That is the cue" (57).

The Movement of Remembrance

"Those who lived would *have* to remember," Rawicz maintains. "They would *have* to stop others from forgetting" (149). This *have to* arises when response and responsibility make difference into nonindifference. It is the "unimpeachable assignation" of which Levinas speaks, addressing the relation between self and other: "A fraternity that cannot be abrogated, an unimpeachable assignation, proximity is an impossibility to move away without the torsion of a complex, without 'alienation' or fault" (*Otherwise* 87). Because this assignation to remember born of responsibility makes it impossible to move away, the movement of remembrance is a movement of return, a *teshuvah* that is both a response and a return. "Rebirth, resurrection, or reawakening," Derrida has claimed, "always appropriate to themselves, in their fugitive immediacy, the plentitude of presence returning to itself. The return to the presence of the origin is produced after each catastrophe" (310). Ka-tzetnik's *Phoenix over the Galilee*, as the title itself suggests, is a novel about resurrection; as such, it is a novel about return—the return of the word from exile, of the man from death. According to Sidra DeKoven Ezrahi, moreover, "Wiesel has defined his writing as an act of commemoration. It is also an act of resurrection" (120).

Because the Holocaust novel undertakes a process of re-creation rather than creation, it is an act of return. To be sure, the theme of return abounds in the Holocaust novel; the theme not only belongs to the content of the novel but also reveals something about the process of the novel's coming into being. "My ambition," says Gregor in Wiesel's *The Gates of the Forest*, "isn't to define myself by victory or defeat, but by my determination to return to the source" (213). This determination to return not only distinguishes the movement of remembrance but, as the character indicates, is also definitively tied to the life—and therefore to the resurrection—of the self. A discourse of response and remembrance, the dialogic discourse of the Holocaust novel is also a discourse of return. The movement of return in the novel is a return to prayer, for in prayer alone does the word return from exile. Aharon Appelfeld makes this point in *For Every Sin* through the character who is determined to return to his own source, to his hometown of Budapest. He explains why: "My forefathers came from there. I want to learn how to pray from them. I have a need for prayer. Do you understand me?" (125). Thus the man would seek a resurrection of the self in a resurrection of the word of the father. The return to the source is not only a physical return to the place of one's birth (although this motif is common in the Holocaust novel), but it is also a metaphysical return to the father, a resurrection of the dead father.

In Appelfeld's *To the Land of the Cattails* a woman named Toni sets out with her son Rudi to return to her mother and father. "It's good we've come back," she says to her son. "I am very content that we've returned. A person must, in the end, return" (9). The connection of this return with a resurrection of the self is established at the outset of the novel: "Wonder of wonders: she had the power to renew herself, . . . to begin anew" (5). Resurrection is a re-surrection, not a beginning but a beginning again, just as remembrance is a re-membrance. In *Tzili: The Story of a Life* Appelfeld articulates the bond between remembrance and return through a character giving a funeral oration for a suicide victim. "He spoke about memory," the author relates, "the long memory of the Jewish people, the eternal life of the tribe, and this historic necessity of the return to the motherland" (161). The Hebrew word for "motherland" here is *moledet* (72), a word that also means "fatherland" and "birthplace," the source of one's life. Rebirth occurs in this return to the birthplace, and memory here is memory of the way back, invoked at the graveside as the site from which the return is initiated. Yet the turning back in the movement of return is not a movement backward but a movement forward. Thus when Danny asks Manny in Lustig's *Darkness Casts No Shadow* why he is continually looking back, Manny declares that it is because he is moving forward, to a new life (109). The life that lies ahead is to be reached in a movement of return.

Lustig examines this truth more thoroughly in the story titled "The Return" in *Night and Hope*. Realizing that the false self, the forged self, he had tried to become meant the death of his self and soul, the main character, Hynek Tausig, longs to return to life by returning to the self he is, to himself as a Jew among Jews: "He was posssesed by the single overpowering wish: to get in among them. To be one of that yellow-branded herd" (34). The Czech word translated as "branded" is *označkovaného* (22), the root of which is *znak* or "sign." In this case the sign of the yellow star is a sign of death, but in the movement of return the sign is inverted, returned to its originl meaning, where the Magen David is the sign of life. Death, then, is turned into life. When Tausig is about to cross over the fence to join those who bear the sign, he thinks, "For you it means only a few steps and for me—just now it means everything that is called life" (36). Returning to the Jews, "he was born anew this moment" (42). Only by joining those marked for death can Tausig be born anew into life; only by dying can he be resurrected. Wiesel writes, "The problem is not: to be or not to be. But rather: to be and not to be. What it comes down to is that man lives while dying, that he represents death to the living" (*Accident* 81). Just as no man lives alone, so is no man resurrected alone. The remembrance of the other that brings about the resurrection of the self resurrects the other within the self.

Hence Ka-tzetnik's cries out in *Shivitti:* "They and the others are buried within me, and continue living each his own life within me" (18). Bakhtin remarked that "in all the cemeteries there are only others" (Todorov 151). If Levinas is correct in his claim that "subjectivity is the other in the same" (*Otherwise* 25), then the resurrection of the self entails the resurrection of the other who lies in the cemetery. In the movement of remembrance the memory of the other invades the memory of the self. Thus in *An Estate of Memory* Ilona Karmel writes, "'Dead,' said the nameless faces, 'Dead,' the voices that had no face; and more were coming, were winding around her—she was the spool, they the thread; she the pit, they the enormous fruit" (386). In the event of the Holocaust novel the living do not raise the dead, but the dead raise the living. This is why the children in Aichinger's *Herod's Children* cry out, "Our dead aren't dead!" (48). This is what underlies Yehuda Amichai's statement in *Not of This Time, Not of This Place:* "The living do not go to the dead—it is the dead who come back and dwell with the living" (262). In all the cemeteries there are only others, but the dead of the Holocaust were robbed of their cemeteries, their ashes cast upon the wind and scattered throughout the air we breathe, invading us with every breath we take, permeating the spirit that dwells in the breath and the word that vibrates on the breath. They are also scattered across the pages of the Holocaust novel. The remembrance of the dead is a remembrance not of the past but of the other before whom we stand. André Neher wrote, "The final letter of the Hebrew alphabet is *tav*, which indicates the second person of the future tense and thus a direction of the man who is summoned toward an infinitely open future" (228). The voice that summons the man from his tomb calls him into this open-ended future.

In what might at first appear to be a contradiction of Amichai's statement cited above, Wiesel writes, "Our dead take with them to the hereafter not only clothes and food, but also the future of their decendants" (*Accident* 113). The present of which Amichai speaks, however, is tied to the future that Wiesel invokes. Dwelling with the living in the present, the dead draw the living into the future. The silence of the dead is the silence of what Neher calls "the radiations of the future." Among the dimensions of time, he explains, "the future alone is completely silent, in its plentitude but also in its remarkable ambivalence" (168-69). This silence is the silence of "a still *latent, unuttered future Word,*" as Bakhtin puts it (*Problems* 90), the silence of the word that would bring about the resurrection of the self. "If I could remember, I'd be saved," Gregor reflects in Wiesel's *The Gates of the Forest*. "But memory is somehow closed" (169). The memory that would redeem and resurrect the self is a memory of the future. The connection between resurrection and remembrance lies in the connection between remembrance and the future. Gouri writes, "An abyss opens between remembering and remembered, and that's where the rivers rush, that's where the year's seasons are, and that's where dark gray snow-covered cities are—cities, marble and gold from the sun. Kindled violet. And that's where the right of the wanderers is to defy silence, to dream, and go on" (83). The rivers and the seasons rush toward the future. The abyss between remembering and remembered is the memory of the future.

Wiesel's main character in *Dawn* asks his friend Gad, "You want my future? What will you do with it?" Gad replies, "I'll make it into an outcry" (20). The movement of remembrance makes the future into an outcry, into a shriek of that silence that distinguishes the future. Without this outcry born of the memory of the future, there can be no resurrection of the self. For this is the cry of the self's coming into being, of its rebirth, the cry of the novel itself as it emerges from the silence. Thus A. Anatoli, for example, insists that he did not write his novel *Babi Yar* in order to recall the past (328); thus he includes in his novel a "Chapter from the Future" (378ff). This orientation is what makes his "document in the form of a novel" something other than a document; this is what makes his movement of remembrance a movement forward. Similarly, chapter 3 of *The Whole Land Brimstone* by Anna Langfus is titled "In Pursuit of Tomorrow," a phrase that characterizes the pursuit of the novel itself. Indeed, the closing lines of the novel open up that horizon to disclose the abyss from which the self might be resurrected: "I was still in the dark, lying on the trunk. And I told myself that, up above, one of those countless days that I still had to live through must already be dawning" (318). Alongside the image of the woman lying in the dark, as in a tomb, we have the light that is yet to be, the radiation of the future from which the novel emerges. In the French text the suggestion of resurrection is more potent, since the word "dawning" here is a rendition of *se lever* (311), "to rise up." The thing that raises up the light of tomorrow from the darkness of the self is the movement of remembrance. "What I am is only what I will be without me," Jabès has written (57). The act of memory enacts this "will be."

One of the most explicit statements concerning memory as memory of the future is found in Amichai's *Not of This Time, Not of This Place*, where Joel asserts, "Things are beginning to move. One thing impinges on another. The confusion is assuming form. And I was overcome with a strange sense of remembering things that were about to happen" (91-92). The word "thing," which appears several times in this passage, is a translation of *davar* (140), a Hebrew term that also means "word." Memory here is memory of words about to be uttered, the unuttered future word about to be drawn out of the silence of exile. From the standpoint of the memory of the future, "the present passes," as Rosenzweig has noted, "not because the past prods it on but because the future snatches it toward itself" (*Star* 328). Thus human being, Ortega y Gasset says, "consists not so much in what it is as in what it is going to be and, therefore, in that which is not yet" (43). The movement of remembrance that issues from the literary response to the Holocaust takes the human being from the silence of the ashes to the silence of the yet-to-be. This is the silence from which, in the act of remembrance, the word is about to burst forth, about to speak, about to summon the self to life. The resurrection that is yet to be, then, begins with the establishment of a new silence over against that silence with which the novelist initially collides.

Confronting the Yet-to-Be

Bakhtin writes that "the definition given to me lies not in the categories of temporal being but in the categories of the *not-yet-existing*, in the categories of purpose and meaning, in the meaningful future, which is at odds with anything I have at hand in the past or present. To be myself for myself means yet becoming myself (*to cease becoming myself . . . means spiritual death*)" (*Estetika* 109). Bakhtin goes on to explain what characterizes this life rooted in what is yet to be: "I live in the depths of myself through faith and hope in the ongoing possibility of the inner miracle of a new birth" (*Estetika* 112). This is what belongs to the yet-to-be: a new birth, a resurrection of the self. In *The Dialogic Imagination* Bakhtin describes this new birth as a metamorphosis: "The idea of metamorphosis retains enough energy . . . to comprehend the *entire life-long destiny of a man*, at all its critical *turning points*. Here lies its significance for the genre of the novel" (114). In the event of the Holocaust novel both author and character are brought to the threshold of the turning point, where past and future, death and resurrection, word and silence meet. The novelistic word is not only formed, then, "in an atmosphere of the already spoken," as Bakhtin puts it, but is also "determined by that which has not been said but which is needed" (*Dialogic* 280). On the edge of what is needed, silence invades the word and transfigures the man. What is forever needed is the resurrection of the self.

In *Touch the Water, Touch the Wind* Amos Oz takes his main character to the brink of this metamorphosis with the character's return to the land of Israel: "The time came for a new, almost idyllic reincarnation, a kind of virgin birth. Pomeranz had finally prepared himself for working on the land" (70). This is a return to the source, to the mother, to the womb of the soul from which the man might be born again. Indeed, the Hebrew word for "reincarnation," *gilgul* (76), is laden with suggestive connotations. It is the key term, for example, in the phrase *gilgul m'hilot*, the "rolling of the dead" under their graves on their way to Israel for the resurrection; it is not the resurrection, but a movement toward the resurrection *about to be* enacted. The meeting of word and silence in this movement comes out in an exchange between two of Pomeranz's students in Israel: "The air is different in his room," says one. "As if he's always expecting a visitor," replies the other. "And that silence. Even when he talks to you, it's as if he's talking in silence" (78). The expectation of the visitor orients the silence in the man's words toward the yet-to-be. The one who is yet to come is the one who may work the resurrection. In *Blood from the Sky* Rawicz asks whether "our only real betrayal is the one we commit against silence" (295). If this is the case, then the betrayal of silence is a betrayal of the one yet to come, a betrayal of what has been given but is yet to be received.

In Wiesel's *A Beggar in Jerusalem* Katriel declares, "There is the silence which preceded creation; and the one which accompanied the revelation at Mount Sinai. The first contains chaos and solitude, the second suggests presence, fervor, plentitude. I like the second. I like silence to have a history and be transmitted by it" (108). Commenting on the silence of Mount Sinai, Wiesel has said, "There are certain silences between word and word. How was this silence transmitted? This is the silence I have tried to put in my work, and I have tried to link it to that silence, the silence of Sinai" (*Against Silence* 1:273). Each year the Jews celebrate the giving of the Torah at Mount Sinai on the sixth of Sivan—the *giving*, not the receiving, for it is yet to be received. In this yet-to-be lies the silence of Sinai. It is the silence of "perfect togetherness" that Rosenzweig describes: "In eternity the spoken word fades away into the silence of perfect togetherness—for union occurs in silence only; the word unites, but those who are united fall silent. . . . The word itself must take man to the point of learning how to share silence. His preparation begins with learning to hear" (*Star* 308-9). At Sinai the word emerges through the silence that arises between word and word in a dialogic interaction. The task of the author is to generate a dialogic response to that interaction and thus become part of both the word and the silence. The act of response as a *hearing* is the key to receiving what was given, and the movement of remembrance is the key to its transmission. Response, however, engenders the need to respond, and ever again the human being is returned to the task in the movement of return. "For ultimately the choice is a limited one,"

Wiesel points out. "We can answer God's silence with human words—or respond to God's words with human silence. But there too the road is not without obstacles: What if the silence of one is the language of the other?" (*Somewhere* 200). The author, a translator of silence, must translate the silence that preceded the creation into the silence of Sinai, using words that are filled with the silence of the yet-to-be. Out of this silence emerges the resurrection of the self upon the coming of the visitor forever expected.

Yet like the next breath that is to follow upon the breath we draw, the awaited coming is not so much the coming of a personage as the coming of an event, a stretching forth of the soul toward the other in a redemption and resurrection of the self. We are speaking, of course, about the messianic event that comprises the yet-to-be of spiritual life. "Such is the disquieting beauty of the messianic adventure," says Paltiel in Wiesel's *The Testament*. "Only man, for whose sake the Messiah is expected, is capable and worthy of making his advent possible. What man? Any man. Whosoever desires may seize the keys that open the gates of the celestial palace and thus bring power to the prisoner. The Messiah, you see, is a mystery between man and himself" (72). The not-yet-existing, to recall Bakhtin's phrase, lies between man and himself—the thing sought, not the thing found. "The great thing," insists David Aboulesia in *The Testament*, "is not to be the Messiah but to seek him" (163). For to seek the Messiah is to seek the relation between self and other that brings life to both. "What is the Messiah," Moshe asks in Wiesel's *The Oath*, "if not man transcending his solitude in order to make his fellow-man less solitary? To turn a single human being back toward life is to prevent the destruction of the world, says the Talmud" (90-91). The resurrection of the self does not, cannot, occur in isolation; rather, it is an event that is yet to transpire in the *between* of relation.

Confronting this yet-to-be, one realizes that what is actualized is never what is sought. Lazarus must die and rise again; even Jesus must come again. Just as a word uttered is the dead flesh of meaning, so the relation already established must be regenerated. Here lies the tension between the hope and faith in a new birth. This is what "separates every Jewish generation," as Rosenzweig has observed, "into those whose faith is strong enough to give themselves up to an illusion, and those whose hope is so strong that they do not allow themselves to be deluded. The former are the better, the latter the stronger. The former bleed as victims on the altar of the eternity of the people, the latter are the priests who perform the service at the altar. And this goes on until the day when all will be reversed, when the belief of the believers will become truth" (Glatzer 350). On this altar of eternity the dying and rebirth in the resurrection of the self take place. The yet-to-be does not belong to the future, which will be actualized, but to the eternal, which both transcends and cuts through time. The eternity of the truth lies in the potentiality of the faith. The movement of remembrance, then, is a movement of faith that imparts an element of the eternal to what is remembered. "As long as you know *how* to remember," writes Lustig, "when people remember something that's happened, it becomes eternal" (*Diamonds* 162). Once again the character articulates the task of the author—knowing how to remember, how to re-member, re-surrect, the self.

In Lustig's *Diamond of the Night* an old man confronts the eternal aspect of the yet-to-be in a passage where the pronoun *he* can refer not only to the character but to the author as well: "He could feel that to live and to die meant an eternity made up of people who were and the people who are yet to be, that eternity which is only *now* joining life with everything beyond life. He knew now what it was. The dead are the best in what they give to the world at this moment. Because nothing is worth more than life" (174). The process of the creation of the novel is a process of joining life with everything beyond life; it is a process of receiving at this moment what the dead give to life. In the event of the novel's creation what is beyond and yet to be is couched in the present, in the novelist's becoming present upon the utterance of the word as it is forming but yet unformed—like the prayer at the end of Wiesel's *The Gates of the Forest*: "His voice trembled, timid, like that of the orphan suddenly aware of the relationship between death and eternity, between eternity and the word. He prayed for the soul of his father and also for that of God. He prayed for the soul of his childhood and, above all, for the soul of his old comrade, Leib the Lion, who, during his life, had incarnated what is immortal in man" (225-26). In these lines that come at the open-ended closure of the novel, the author gives voice to all that goes into its creation. Upon the utterance of the prayer Gregor is returned to himself, resurrected from all that had split the self. For a moment that is filled with eternity, we see the word returned from exile, the self returned to the father, the child returned to the self. We see what was merge with what is yet to be in an affirmation of all that is immortal in man.

An important phenomenological feature of what is voiced in this prayer from *The Gates of the Forest* is absent from the translation, but it appears in the French text. For the phrase "for that of God" Wiesel writes, *por celle de Dieu dont l'âme se fait prière* (236), that is, "for the soul of God who leads the soul to prayer." Here one is reminded of Buber's statement that "men believe they pray to God, but this is not so, for the prayer itself is divinity" (*Legend* 27). Paul Tillich has declared, "It is God Himself who prays through us, when we pray to Him" (*New Being* 137). The resurrection of the self bears not only the resurrection of the other but also the redemption of God. Thus God brings the redemptive prayer to the lips of the one who longs for redemption, in an effort to seek His own redemption. In Wiesel's *The Testament* a friend asks Paltiel, who is in a hospital, what he wants: "'Redemption,' I said. And I hastened to add, 'In this place I have the right to demand and receive everything; and what I demand is redemption.' 'So do I,' said my companion sadly. 'So do I. And so does He'" (316). In *Twilight* Wiesel states that "divine redemption depends on human redemption" (100), but the reverse is also true. Setting right the time out of joint requires the reestablishment of the relation between time and eternity, between the human being and the Eternal One. The author's expression of the permutation of time is an effort to regain a relation to the eternal, to open up a place where the Eternal One can enter time, as He longs to do. "The glorious resurrection of the dead is commencing," writes Gouri. "Time is amazed" (108). The event of the Holocaust novel is the commencement of the resurrection of the self—and of God—that is eternally yet to be. It is the voicing of a prayer that, though it is finished, is never fulfilled.

In *Paroles d'étranger* Wiesel posits a relation between literature and prayer: "Both prayer and literature impart to and confer upon everyday words another sense; both appeal to that which is most personal in man, to the most elevated of his needs" (166). Need is by definition what is *not yet*, and the most elevated of needs is the need for resurrection and redemption, both human and divine. It is in prayer—and the prayerlike aspects of the novel—that the silence of what is needed makes itself heard. Wiesel writes, "Through prayer man is engaged in an eternal dialogue with God. Thanks to prayer, to its intoxicating and turbulent accents, God becomes present. Better: God becomes presence. And everything becomes possible and meaningful: here the Supreme Judge, here the Father of humanity, leaves His celestial throne to live and move among His human creatures. And, in turn, here the soul transported by its prayer leaves its abode and rises to heaven. The substance of language, and the language of silence—that is what prayer is" (*Paroles* 171-72). That is what the Holocaust novel must become in its efforts to draw the resurrection of the self out of the silence of the yet-to-be. Like prayer, the novel creates an opening for the human ascent and divine descent, a portal through which time and eternity, word and silence, now and yet-to-be can merge. For "it is from the Other," to use Lacan's expression, "that the subject receives even the message he emits" (*Ecrits* 305). It is for the Other, for the Bakhtinian "over-I," that the self undertakes the labor of rebirth.

One can thus ask whether the novel, like a prayer, is itself divine. If the event of the novel is part of God's endeavor to find redemption, can the novel be viewed as an utterance of God? To reply either yes or no to this question would be misleading. The answer is both yes and no, or rather, it is a no that *is* and a yes that is *yet to be*, an affirmation silently uttered when the last word of the novel falls silent. Recall, for example, the final note from Verdi's *Requiem* as Josef Bor describes it in *The Terezin Requiem*. Verdi, says the main character, "had a master's grasp of what a prayer for the dead should be: there somewhere in eternity, where the last note of the Requiem falls silent, there even you, as dead men, set free from torment and hardship, there even you shall find liberty" (88-89). Thus the character tells us what the novel itself is trying to be. Because the resurrection of the self belongs to the eternity of the yet-to-be, the ultimate task of the novelist is not to speak but to fall silent. But you cannot be saved, as Aichinger puts it, "if you don't fall in the water" (32). You cannot be resurrected if you do not die away; you cannot fall silent—and in so falling rise up—if you do not speak. Hence the novel is a no that harbors a yes, a refusal that promises an affirmation, a going under that moves toward a rising up, in a repeated confrontation of now with what is yet to be. Lacan writes, "There where it was just now, there where it was for a while, between an extinction that is still glowing and a birth that is retarded, 'I' can come into being and disappear from what I say" (*Ecrits* 300). So it is with the discourse of the novel.

Thus we find in many novels the positing of a resurrection of the self without its fulfillment. In the opening pages of *Landscape in Concrete* by Jakov Lind, for instance, Gauthier Bachmann indicates that he had always fantasized about being buried and then rising up from the grave (13-14). Bachmann's fantasy by definition cannot be actuality. In Ka-tzetnik's *Phoenix over the Galilee* we see that even if the man should rise, it is only so that he can fall and rise again. It is said of Harry Preleshnik that "he would always be vomited forth—even as Auschwitz and the river and the bomb had vomited him forth" (167). In Karmel's *An Estate of Memory* Aurelia survives death to give birth, not only to her child but also to herself (121). And, of course, one cannot forget the title character in *Mr. Sammler's Planet* by Saul Bellow: "What besides the spirit should a man care for who has come back from the grave? However, and mysteriously enough, it happened, as Sammler observed, that one was always, and so powerfully, so persuasively, drawn back to human conditions" (109). Resurrection, as something both yet to be and forever repeated, is a matter concerning this world and this life. The project of response involves the response of a human I to a human Thou; the return that comes in the movement of remembrance is a return to human relation under human conditions. For in the realm of this relation, in the between of this relation, the spirit itself rises rom the dead—repeatedly.

I.B. Singer makes this point in *Enemies: A Love Story:* "Herman saw in Tamara's return a symbol of his mystical beliefs. Whenever he was with her, he re-experienced the miracle of resurrection" (122). In this relation between man and wife we have the highest expression of the highest relation. Here, in Buber's words, "the lines of relationships intersect in the eternal You. Every single You is a glimpse of that. Through every single You the basic word addresses the eternal You" (*I and Thou* 123). Through the human word returned from exile the human being is returned to life. With that resurrection of the human comes the resurrection of the spirit.

Spirit in its human manifestation is man's response to his You. Man speaks in many tongues—tongues of language, of art, of action—but the spirit is one; it is response to the You that appears from the mystery and addresses us from the mystery. Spirit is word. . . . Spirit is not in the I but between I and You. It is not like the blood that circulates in you but like the air in which you breathe. Man lives in the spirit when he is able to respond to his You. He is able to do that when he enters into this relation with his whole being. [Buber, *I and Thou* 89]

Entering into this relation is the whole purpose of the Holocaust novel, as the author seeks a resurrection of the self that is no sooner realized than it must be repeated. "The more I respond the more I am responsible," Levinas points out. "The more I approach the neighbor with whom I am encharged, the further away I am" (*Otherwise* 98). The task increases with its accomplishment.

7
The Implication of the Reader

In *The Dialogic Imagination* Mikhail Bakhtin argues that the novel "and the world represented in it enter the real world and enirch it, and the real world enters the work and its world as part of the process of its creation, as well as part of its subsequent life, in a continual renewing of the work through the creative perception of listeners and readers" (254). This statement describes what we have called a phenomenological approach to the novel as an event. Examining what occurs in the process of the novel's creation, we deal not only with author and character but with the reader as well. Even before the novel is read, even if it is never read, even as it is written, the reader comes into play in the midst of its creation. All of the difficulties we have addressed—exile, death, and resurrection—not only involve the author in relation to the character but also lay claim to the reader in relation to both. The reader is not a passive observer but an active participant in the process of the novel's creation; the reader encounters the text as a living human voice. In the struggle for understanding, the reader's "understanding," as Bakhtin has shown, "bears an actively responsive character" (*Estetika* 246). Hence, Bakhtin goes on to argue, "the event in the life of the text—that is, its genuine essence—develops *along the boundary between two consciousnesses, two subjects*" (*Estetika* 285). The consciousness *within* one subject is tied to that subject's consciousness *of* the other. The one, therefore, is implicated by the other. In the framework of a phenomenology of the Holocaust novel, we as readers are ultimately thrown back on ourselves in our investigation of these texts. Confronting this event that is a re-creation, we confront the re-creation of ourselves through our responsibe participation in the event.

My voice, then, must take part in that dialogic utterance that endeavors to return the word from exile. The death of father and child that splits the soul of the author also sends cracks through my own being. At the boundary between myself and this other I stand on the threshold of my own needful resurrection, where, in my act of response, I am cast into the categories of the yet-to-be. Just as the author must become for-the-other in the utterance, so must I become for-the-author in my response. Indeed, a number of these authors summon their readers in a direct address: Piotr Rawicz in *Blood from the Sky* (146), Primo Levi in *The Periodic Table* (224), and A. Anatoli in *Babi Yar* (150). In these instances the readers are positioned within the text, posited by the author in much the same way as a character might be situated in the text. Already the readers are both here and there, chosen before they choose; already the task of establishing a presence before the text requires a movement into the text and back again. This implication of the reader also arises indirectly through character-to-character relations, where one character struggles to invoke a response, a reading, from another character. In Ka-tzetnik's *Phoenix over the Galilee*, for instance, Galilea longs for Harry "to *see* her words just as she could see them, even if she could not yet get out the sounds" (217). Seeing her words, Harry is the one who would roll back "the heavy stone at the mouth of her soul" (235). Thus receiving what is offered, the reader becomes an essential participant in the author's resurrection, just as the author poses the problem of resurrection for the reader.

In *The Testament* Elie Wiesel structures his entire novel around a relation between an author and a reader, between Paltiel and Zupanev. Significantly, Zupanev is not only a reader but also a stenographer, so that his reading of Paltiel consists of a responsive rewriting of Paltiel, a process by which Zupanev is himself transformed into a witness whose testimony invokes yet another reader, Paltiel's son Grisha. "I must implant in you his memory and mine," says the stenographer to the child. "I must, my boy" (346). Here we see the merging of word, memory, and human being in the act of reading. Bakhtin insists, "The text never appears as a dead thing; beginning with any text, we always arrive . . . at the human voice, which is to say we come up against the human being" (*Dialogic* 252-53). The joining of word with word within the text implicates the joining of the reader's word with the text itself, by which the soul of the one enters into a relation with the soul of the other. "To join two words," Wiesel writes in *The Fifth Son*, "requires as much power as to join two beings" (174). To join two words is to reunite word and meaning in the space between them, and to reunite word and meaning is to resurrect the self through a relation to another. Says Menachem in Wiesel's *The Town beyond the Wall*, "What binds one word to another is no less mysterious than what binds one human being to another" (147). The mystery abides in the *between*, and it is in the realm of this between that the act of reading takes place, that the event of the novel occurs. "I require a You to become," Buber writes (*I and Thou* 62). So does the author require a reader for the novel to come into being.

The event of the novel in its phenomenological aspects, then, is an event of encounter. "The aim of every book, of every tale," Wiesel has said, "is to initiate as many encounters on as many levels as possible: between writer and reader, speaker and listener, fact and fiction, imagination and reality, past and present" (*Against Silence* 1:310). "Every encounter quickens the steps of the Redeemer; let two beings become one and . . . creation will have meaning" (Wiesel, *Souls* 33). The reader, therefore, is implicated in the exile of the word, the death of the father, and the death of the child; the reader is also a split self in need of redemption. There can be no redemption in isolation, no resurrection of the self without the resurrection of the other. To be transformed into a witness, then, is to be cast into a position of responsibility. That position is characterized by the presence of a third party whom the reader affirms in responding to the text. In this relation, too, the reader is implicated. Thus the act of reading is an "act of consciousness motivated by the presence of a third party alongside the neighbor approached. A third party is also approached; and the relationship between the neighbor and the third party cannot be indifferent to me when I approach. . . . To be on the ground of the signification of an approach is to be *with another* for or against a third party" (Levinas, *Otherwise* 16). In the case at hand the "neighbor" is the author, and the "approach" is the process of responsive reading. The reader may reject or accept but cannot refuse the third party, since from this third position the truth of the reader's relation is called into question.

Arnost Lustig has said that "between the lines of human thought there was always a space in which one could read differently" (*Night* 172). That between-space is inhabited by the third party, and it is by virtue of this Third that the reader is implicated: the reader also has a reader. The third party, the reader's reader, therefore, is the one in whose presence and through whose presence the reader is transformed into a witness. The third party implicates the reader as irreplaceable and therefore as responsible. There is no standing before the text without standing for something, answering with one's whole being for one's being.

Reader into Witness

The epigraph to the "After-Word and Fore-Word" of Ka-tzetnik's *Shivitti* is a citation of Jeremiah 32:44. "And subscribe the deeds, and seal them. And call witnesses (105). The deeds are subscribed, inscribed, and sealed upon the soul of the reader. Engaging the voice of the author, the reader receives the author's testimony in a transfer of the word not from mouth to ear but from mouth to mouth. The mouth-to-mouth transfer transforms the reader into a witness. Indeed, such an interchange distinguishes the process of becoming a self in relation to another, a reader in relation to the author. "Subjectivity is the other in the same. The other in the same determinative of subjectivity is the restlessness of the same disturbed by the other" (Levinas, *Otherwise*

25). Becoming a witness, the reader becomes one human being implicated by what befalls another; this is the restlessness of which Levinas speaks. This invasion of the self by the other finds expression in many Holocaust novels, where the character-to-character relation bespeaks the relation between author and reader. Ka-tzetnik, for example, might well be addressing the reader when he writes, "All bodies are now—your body, just as the death of any one body is now—the death of your own" (*Star* 70). In this statement the physical and metaphysical intertwine; the disturbance of the same by the other is just such a confluence of opposites, of death and life, body and soul.

The author testifying on behalf of the dead transmits to the reader the souls of the dead. Assessing such a text is not a matter of explicating form and content in a strictly aesthetic sense but of bearing witness to those voices that would not be consumed. Thus the text itself debunks those critical *isms* that constitute an attitude of flight, as when Bachmann flees from the German installation that signifies death in Jakov Lind's *Landscape in Concrete*. Suddenly, he "stopped to sniff at the air or listen to silent voices—as Schnotz had done. As if the dead man's soul had gone into him" (48). So the silent voices conveyed by the author enter the voice of the reader, who now must either bear witness to that received or betray the one summoning. There is still more at work in the restlessness of the reader, however. Paltiel, in Wiesel's *The Testament*, speaking of his dead mother and father, declares, "I was taking my family with me; my life would become their tomb" (293). Thus Paltiel becomes a witness, his life bespeaking those voices that have fallen silent; thus Paltiel implicates the reader. In the process of creating the novel the author rolls away the stone that seals the tomb signified by the character; in the process of reading the novel the witness becomes the vessel of what the author would release. Arnost Lustig expresses this in *Diamonds of the Night* through the voice of an old man who asserts, "The spirit of those who have already died has passed into the lives of those who aren't born yet" (154). Hence the event of reading is present in the event of writing.

Because the reader disturbs the author in the midst of the novel's creation, the author is able to transmit the souls of the dead to those who have not yet read the novel. This interidentification of the author as witness and the reader as witness comes out quite clearly in Anatoli's address to the reader in *Babi Yar*: "You could have been me, and I could now have been you, reading this page" (45). This expression of subjectivity in the novel as the other in the same is set up at the novel's outset, where Anatoli insists, "I am writing it as though I were giving evidence under oath in the very highest court" (2). The author's stance as witness makes the reader into a witness; taking the stand, the author places the reader on the stand. In Yehuda Amichai's *Not of This Time*,

Not of This Place the relation of Dr. Manheim to Joel parallels this relation of reader to author. "Dr. Manheim is one of the important witnesses in my life," says Joel. "He is he witness of my childhood." At this his lover Patricia asks, "Is life for you always a trial that you must have witnesses? Why, this is awful. And who is the judge?" He answers, "You" (263). Like the reader, Dr. Manheim becomes a witness as he is invoked; Joel calls him forth as he writes him in. In the process of the novel's writing, the author calls forth the reader. Just as there is a judge for Joel, so there is a judgment of the reader's relation to the novel. Neither the author nor the reader, then, acts alone. Each is for the other, and both are under the eye of a third.

"Consciousness," Levinas has said, "is born as the presence of a third party. . . . It is the entry of the third party, a permanent entry, into the intimacy of the face to face" (*Otherwise* 160). Between author and reader the character posits a third position insofar as the character bears a world or a community to which author and reader must answer. To come to consciousness is to come before a world. "No man," Amichai writes, "dies alone or loves alone; his generation is born with him and accompanies him in his loves and in his death" (320). What is translated as "accompanies him" in Hebrew is *nimtsa imo b'sha'at* (597), which means "is present with him in the hour of" his death. The third presence in the relation between two implicates the one in the face of the other. Consciousness breeds conscience. Levinas explains, "The implication of the one in the other signifies the assignation of the one by the other. This assignation is the very signifyingness of signification, or the psyche of the same. Through the psyche proximity is my approaching of the other, the fact that the proximity of the same and the other is never close enough. The summoned one is the ego—me" (*Otherwise* 137). To read a text is to approach that text—and in it a human soul—as something meaningful; to pursue the significance of the text is to bear witness to what I signify. Thus I am called into question by the act of questioning the text: this is the implication. Because I question, I must answer: this is the assignation.

In my pursuit of the text, then, the text pursues me, and yet as I approach it, it slips away. The initial silence of the eye's contact with the first syllable of the novel is followed by "another silence," to use Haim Gouri's phrase, one that announces "the inauguration of the critical period" (9). The position of the critic is critical indeed; the critic is questioned by the very act of questioning. Like Harry Preleshnik in Katzetnik's *Sunrise over Hell*, the critic turns "into a two-legged question mark" (96), a *siyman-sh'elah*, as the Hebrew texts reads (92), a "sign of question" uttered and yet to be answered, a sign of a certain absence. In the midst of the writing of the novel, the reader is present by implication, that is, by absence. Transformed into a witness, the reader must make that absence into a presence. The question that marks the reader, then, is the question that Tzili puts to an absent friend in Aharon Appelfeld's *Tzili: The Story of a Life*: " 'Where are you and why don't you speak to me?' she would ask in despair. Nothing stirred in the silence, and but for her own voice no other voice was heard" (119). Like her author, the character speaks from the silence of abandonment or exile; as she addresses her absent interlocutor, so the author addreses a reader implicated by absence. Similarly, in *To the Land of the Cattails* Appelfeld confronts his reader with another character who seeks a sign of response. Rudi, in search of his mother, asks, " 'Where are you? Give me a sign, and I'll drive that way. Without a sign, I can't reach you.' No sign was given. More than anything he set out so as not to stay in one place" (127). Under the seal of assignation the reader becomes a witness who must in turn become the sign that the author seeks through the character.

The witness must become "a sign made to another, a sign of this giving of signs, that is, of this non-indifference, a sign of this impossibility of slipping away and being replaced, of this identity, this uniqueness: here I am" (Levinas, *Otherwise* 145). Thus the two questions posed by Tzili come to the same thing. Shifting from the role of reader to the position of witness, the human being moves from a relation of difference to one of nonindifference. This is the movement of approach that cannot be abrogated. The reader does not decide to become a witness; rather, the novel chooses the reader before the reader can make a choice. For the novel itelf emerges as the already-chosen. "Before they call, I will answer"; Levinas cites Isaiah 65:24. "This obedience prior to all representation, this allegiance before any oath, this responsibility prior to commitment, is precisely the other in the same, inspiration and prophecy, the *passing itself* of the Infinite" (*Otherwise* 150). As the novel is inspired, so it inspires and thus lays claim to the reader; the witness transforms the listener into a witness.

What Levinas expresses in the rather convoluted language of the philosopher Arele suggests more poetically, more hauntingly, in I.B. Singer's *Shosha*. "We are running away," he says, "and Mount Sinai runs after us. This chase has made us sick and mad" (255). Here we have not only the inspiration but also the assignation of the reader made into a witness. One recalls Levinas's insistence that the assignation is "unimpeachable," that it is "an impossibility to move away without the torsion of a complex" (*Otherwise* 87). This assignation, of course, is a primary feature of the Jewish condition, as well as a Jewish feature of the Holocaust novel; Singer's metaphor of Sinai is not arbitrary. As Wiesel has said, "There comes a time when one cannot be a man without assuming the Jewish condition" (*Beggar* 77); to be transformed into a witness prior to any choosing of that transformation is to assume the Jewish condition. To read the Holocaust novel is to assume the assignation of the Jewish condition. "All of us are messengers," Wiesel writes in *A Beggar in Jerusalem*, "though we may not know for whom or to what purpose" (37). In the French text "though we may not know" is a bit stronger; it is *même si nous ignorons* (39-40), "even if we do not know" it. The transmission of the message or of the question makes the reader into a witness even if the reader does not realize it. "The Berditchever once said," Wiesel tells us, "that when God gave the Torah He gave not only the words but also the blanks between the words. The task of man is to be a blank between words, a messenger, a link between God and man, between man and man, between present and past" (*Against Silence* 2:82). Like the author, the reader too is a link between text and world. While the readers may decide whether or not to testify, they do not decide whether or not to become witnesses. The reader does not choose to be called.

In *The Town beyond the Wall* Wiesel's character Kalman suggests what is entrusted to the witness: "Every man has a prayer that belongs to him, as he has a soul that belongs to him. And just as it is difficult for a man to find his soul, so it is difficult for him to find his prayer" (49). In the transfer of the word from mouth to mouth the author entrusts the witness with a kind of prayer. The author charges the witness to voice what has already been given in a saying of "here I am." Offering the witness his word, the author offers the witness his soul. Transformed into a witness, the reader takes up the task of becoming a living soul by offering up in turn that which was received. Levinas declares, "The soul is the other in me" (*Otherwise* 191). To assert that the subjectivity of the witness is the other-in-the-same is to maintain that the one made into a witness must become a soul in the offering up of a testimonial word. "The soul is spirit unrealized for itself," Bakhtin has observed; it is "reflected in the loving consciousness of another (person, God)" (*Estetika* 98). Inasmuch as consciousness is tied to presence, the project of bearing witness is a project of becoming present before another through the utterance of the word with one's whole being and in an offering up of one's whole being. That which is received must be returned, and this applies not only to the message transmitted but also to the phenomenological and existential event that transpires in its utterance.

What Martin Buber says of the human being's encounter with a living situation, therefore, also applies to the reader's relation to the text: "In spite of all similarities every living situation has, like a newborn child, a new face, that has never been before and will never come again. It demands of you a reaction which cannot be prepare beforehand. It demands nothing of what is past. It demands presence, responsibility; it demands you" (*Between* 114). Viewed as an event of discourse, the novel is just such a situation; the fact that a human voice calls out from the novel makes it a *living* situation. Thus it has a human face; the face speaks. It falls to the witness to step before the countenance and answer when summoned. For the critic this means leaving behind all the *isms*, all the methods, that might eclipse the voice; fixed formulas and ready answers betray the outcry of the text and drain the soul of the witness. In Ladislav Fuks's *Mr. Theodore Mundstock* the title character struggles to hold on to life through a method that "properly prepared for everything in a logically planned manner" (120). Ultimately, however, the method for holding on to his life results in the loss of life, and he realizes "that perhaps there were things you could not prepare for" (221). Chief among those things is answering the summons to be present.

As Buber suggests, presence consists of response and responsibility. "Here," he says in *I and Thou*, "the You appeared to man out of a deeper mystery, addressed him out of the dark, and he responded with his life. Here the word has become life" (92). Like the Creator Himself, the author calls out from the midst of his creation and puts a question to his reader: Where are you? I alone can answer, "Here I am." Through my word, my response, my presence is established before the text. "I am I," Levinas puts it, "in the sole measure that I am responsible, a non-interchangeable I. I can substitute myself for everyone, but no one can substitute himself for me" (*Ethics* 101). The reader transformed into a witness becomes an I who must answer to a Thou, an I responsible for a Thou.

Response and Responsibility

In "Art and Responsibility," the first piece he ever published, Bakhtin wrote: "What can guarantee the inner bonding of the elements of personality? Only the wholeness of responsibility. With my life I must answer for what I have experienced and understood in art. . . . Art and life are not one and the same, but they must become one within me, in the wholeness of my responsibility" (*Estetika* 5-6). Coming before the text entails first a splitting of the self. The reader takes up the task of response as one who must yet undergo an "inner bonding" and therefore as one who is in error, who must become whole. The wholeness of which Bakhtin speaks is generated by drawing the voice we encounter into our own voice, our own life. Thus in the first instance the reader reads the text as if the reader's own voice were speaking; in the first instance the reader is never *here* but is cast out *there*, split from self. The project of response, however, is not to mimic but to incorporate the voice of the text into one's own voice, thus increasing one's own life. Responsibility, then, means being thrown back on oneself through this encounter with the other; the capacity to respond is a capacity to be a self. In the words of Levinas, "Subjectivity in itself is being thrown back on oneself. Concretely: accused of what the others do or suffer, or responsible for what they do or suffer. The uniqueness of the self is the very fact of bearing the fault of another" (*Otherwise* 112). In the act of response, then, the reader becomes all the more able to respond, all the more responsible. For the act of response itself bears witness to the need to respond, so that "the debt increases in the measure that it is paid" (Levinas, *Otherwise* 12). To be placed in a position of responsibility is to incur a debt that can never be discharged.

Thus in the implication of the reader, the witness is also the accused; I come before the text indebted to the voice that cries out from the text. The witness I bear in my response to the other implicates me in my being for-the-other. Levinas writes: "Constituting itself in the very movement wherein being responsible for the other devolves on it, subjectivity goes to the point of substitution for the other. It assumes the condition—or the uncondition—of hostage. Subjectivity as such is initially hostage; it answers to the point of expiating for others" (*Ethics* 100). The novelist, indeed, confirms the philosopher's insight. To the extent that Grisha, for example, is among his father's readers in Wiesel's *The Testament*, he is a poet "not like his father" but "in place of his father" (17). The condition of hostage that characterizes this substitution becomes more evident when we discover that Grisha's mother recited his father's poetry to him as he was growing up. One of those poems reads, "But the hungry child, / The thirsty stranger, / The frightened old man, / All ask for me" (38). The last line in the French text is *c'est moi qu'ils réclament* (26), or "it is I to whom they lay claim." Hence I am the one in their debt. This is what lies behind Viktor Frankl's insistence that "man should not ask what the meaning of his life is, but rather he must recognize that it is *he* who is asked" (111). We cannot encounter the death of the father in the Holocaust novel without being implicated in that death; we cannot collide with the death of the child without incurring responsibility for that death.

Recall, for instance, the old man in Ka-tzetnik's *House of Dolls*. When his forehead is branded and bleeding with the word *Jude*, that word calls me by name. When in Wiesel's *Night* that child is hanged and a prisoner asks, "Where is God?" (70), I am the one who must answer. But no matter how deeply I recognize my answerability, I can neither go to the gallows for him or take him down from there. This exasperating connection between character and reader is illustrated by a relation between two characters in Ilona Karmel's *An Estate of Memory*, Barbara and an infant child. "The child would not be gone; hunger made him present, hunger joined them together, until above the boy's wheezing she could hear its cry demanding what she did not have to give" (237). Something is demanded that the reader does not have to give. Thus the reader owes a great debt, one that surrounds an important aspect of the tension between word and silence. Buber has said, "Only silence toward the You, the silence of *all* tongues, the taciturn waiting in the unformed, undifferentiated, prelinguistic word leaves the You free and stands together with it in reserve where the spirit does not manifest itself but is. All response binds the You into the It-world" (*I and Thou* 89). The reader responds to the text, being unable to sustain such a dizzying silence. The novel opens up an abyss; the reader stares into it until it stares back, until the reader must speak or go mad. When the shriek of silence becomes too much to bear, the reader becomes a critic who responds with words and not with life. The novelist, of course, is also aware of this existential difficulty.

In *Herod's Children* one of Ilse Aichinger's characters laments, "Paper is stony ground. I've written down too much. My whole life I've written down too much. Everything I noticed I set down, and everything I set down has fallen over. Nothing did I let grow; nothing did I pass over in silence. Nothing ever occurred to me that I didn't try to stop. First I caught butterflies and nailed them to a board, and later everything else" (182-83). The German verb translate as "set down" is *feststellen* (177), which means not only "to declare" or "to establish" but also "to secure" or "to lock in." The task of the reader is to become present before the text in an act of response; yet when the responsive word is committed to the page, the imprint eclipses the presence that the reader would establish. The great danger, the great debt, however, lies not so much in response as in explanation. Freely translated, the lament of Aichinger's character amounts to the complaint with which Saul Bellow begins *Mr. Sammler's Planet*: "Intellectual man had become an explaining creature" (7). At the end of the novel Bellow's title character returns to the same issue: "Life when it had no charm was entirely question-and-answer. The thing worked both ways. Also, the questions were bad. Also, the answers were horrible. This poverty of soul, its abstract state, you could see in faces on the street. And he too had a touch of the same disease—the disease of the single self explaining what was what and who was who" (256). Response is precisely the opposite of the explanation and the explication that Aichinger and Bellow describe. As Bakhtin has noted, "To see and understand an author's work is to see and understand another, alien consciousness and its world, that is, another subject ('*Du*'). In *explication* there is only one consciousness, one subject; in *understanding* there are two consciousnesses, two subjects. There can be no dialogical relationship to an object; therefore explication is void of dialogical features. Understanding is always, to some degree, dialogical" (*Estetika* 289). Dialogic response is tied to responsibility to the extent that it sustains rather than settles the question of presence; explanation is a flight from responsibility. Its effort to nail down meaning amounts to a crucifixion of the word.

In *One Generation After* Wiesel writes, "The Jew is in perpetual motion. He is characterized as much by his quest as by his faith, his silence as much as his outcry. He defines himself more by what troubles him than by what reassures him. . . . To me, the Jew and his questioning are one" (214). Likewise, the presence the reader must establish before the text is a state of motion; the response that expresses the reader's responsibility is made of quest and question. For the readers implicated by the novel, to answer is to ask, turning back on themselves ever again the question that implicates them: Where are you? Explanation brings human beings to a halt, locking them into the emptiness of stasis; the movement of response, on the other hand, is sustained by a refusal to explain. Thus, taking *understanding* to mean explanation, Wiesel enjoins his reader, "Let us, therefore, not make an effort to understand, but rather to lower our eyes and not understand. Every rational explanation would be more esoteric than if it were mystical. Not to understand the dead is a way of paying them an ancient debt; it is the only way to ask their pardon" (*Legends* 234). We find in Anatoli a novelist who explicitly avows this refusal. In *Babi Yar* he writes, "I know, of course, that this has been carefully analyzed by experts in all the ' -isms.' . . . Everything has been examined, proved and all is clear. All the same, *I do not understand*" (365). The reader who encounters this statement *in* the novel receives an injunction about how to go about a responsive reading *of* the novel.

One can see that all of the ideologies of literary theory—Freudianism, Marxism, structuralism, deconstruction—amount to a betrayal of the survivor and a desecration of the dead. Remember what Levinas once said: "The important question of the meaning of being is not: why is there something rather than nothing . . . but: do I not kill by being?" (*Ethics* 120). For the reader the question becomes Do I not kill by explaining? In *Dimensions of the Holocaust* Wiesel says, "First the enemy killed the Jews and then he made them disappear in smoke, in ashes, so every Jew was killed twice. In every extermination center special squads of prisoners had to unearth multitudes of corpses and then burn them. Now he tries to kill them for the third time by depriving them of their past, and nothing could be more heinous, more vicious than that. I repeat, nothing is or could be as ugly, as inhuman as the wish to deprive the dead victims of their death" (16). We must not allow ourselves the smug supposition that these words apply only to the revisionists. Any reader, however well intentioned, runs the risk of incurring this debt in the effort to respond to the outcry that rises up from the pages of the novel.

Levinas points out, "The fear for the death of the other is certainly at the basis of the responsibility for him" (*Ethics* 119). In the novel itself the reader is implicated. In *Darkness Casts No Shadow*, for instance, Lustig writes, "To kill or not to kill had gotten into man like blood in his heart or the air he inhales and exhales" (142). Indeed, the process of reading is rather like inhaling and exhaling; the reader receives the word and returns it in an act of response that decides the life and death of the one to whom the response is made. Echoing Levinas, Lustig has written that "killing is the key to explaining man and life" (*Diamonds* 84). It is also the key to responding to texts. If this should appear to be an exaggeration, we can recall an insight from Primo Levi's *If Not Now, When?*: "Of course Mendel wasn't his keeper, and still less had he shed Leonid's blood. He hadn't killed him in the field. And yet the itch persisted: maybe this is really how it is, maybe each of us is Cain to some Abel, and slays him in the field without knowing it, through the things he does to him, the things he says to him, and the things he should say to him and doesn't" (83-84). One will recall that Wiesel regards this murder as a suicide. "Every murder is a suicide," he declares. "Cain killed Cain in Abel" (*Messengers* 61). Not only are the life and death of the other at stake in the effort to respond, but the life and death of oneself also hang in the balance.

If life is to overcome death in the reader's response to the text, then the reader must abandon all security, all the protective measures, that distinguish the conventional categories and pat answers of literary explication. The reader must pursue responsibility to the point of profound vulnerability, to the vulnerability of the victim. "He who is not among the victims," as Wiesel says in *The Gates of the Forest*, "is with the executioners" (166). Sitting in the armchair comfort of our studies, this strikes us at first glance as all too easily said. Those of us who were not there must be very careful about our presumption. We cannot follow the woman who rushed to comfort the condemned child at the cost of her own life. We dare not equate ourselves with the rebbe in Wiesel's *A Beggar in Jerusalem* who in the hour of death cried to his followers, "He demands our lives in sacrifice, which proves that He remembers us, He has not turned His face from us. And so it is with joy—pure, desperate, mad joy—that we shall say to Him: 'So be it. Thy will be done.' Perhaps He needs our joy more than our tears, our deaths more than our deeds" (71-72). We are called to the witness stand to answer with our comfortable lives, and that position harbors more fear and trembling than we may think. "Where then do the difficult tasks arise?" Kierkegaard asks. "In the living-room and on the Shore Road leading to the Deer Park" (*Postscript* 430). We may not be able to follow Abraham or Isaac to Moriah, but each takes us with him as he descends from the mountain to return to life. In this we can see why "the Temple was built on Moriah. Not on Sinai" (Wiesel, *Messengers* 97). The victims' loss of security and assurance strips us of our own guarantees.

Thus in the collisions with the character, the reader, as one who must respond, is forced into the subjectivity that Levinas describes: "The subjectivity of a subject is vulnerability, exposure to affection, sensibility, a passivity more passive still than any passivity, an irrecuperable time, an unassemblable diachrony of patience, an exposedness always to be exposed the more, an exposure to expressing, and thus to saying, thus to giving" (*Otherwise* 50). The saying of the author is an offering up of the soul in a mad struggle to heal the soul. Receiving that offering, the reader is implicated as the one who must now give, who must now respond. Levinas goes on to argue, "In the exposure to wounds and outrage, in the feeling proper to responsibility, the oneself is provoked as irreplaceable, as devoted to the others, without being able to resign, and thus as incarnated in order to offer itself, to suffer and to give" (*Otherwise* 105). In *The Last of the Just* André Schwarz-Bart breaks off his narrative to address and therefore implicate his reader, saying, "I am so weary that my pen can no longer write. 'Man, strip off thy garments, cover thy head with ashes, run into the streets and dance in thy madness'" (417). Indeed, assuming the vulnerability characteristic of responsibility requires this stripping of oneself, and in the eyes of a smug and complacent world it can only pass for madness.

Michel Foucault wrote: "By the madness which interrupts it, a work of art opens a void, a moment of silence, a question without answer, provokes a breach without reconciliation where the world is forced to question itself. What is necessarily a profanation in the work of art returns to that point, and, in the time of that work swamped in madness, the world is made aware of its guilt" (*Madness* 288). As Moshe the Madman once put it, "These days honest men can do only one thing: go mad! Spit on logic, intelligence, sacrosanct reason! That's what you have to do, that's the way to stay human, to keep your wholeness!" (Wiesel, *Town* 20). The wholeness of responsibility invoked by Bakhtin is the wholeness of being human; the wholeness of the human subject lies in the subjection to wounds. Articulating a position that not only distinguishes the witness but also implicates the reader, Jean Améry writes, "On my forearm I bear the Auschwitz number; it reads more briefly than the Pentateuch or the Talmud and yet provides more thorough information. It is also more binding than basic formulas of Jewish existence. If to myself and the world, including the religious and nationally minded Jews, who do not regard me as one of their own, I say: I am a Jew, then I mean by that those realities and possibilities that are summed up in the Auschwitz number" (94). Even though darkness may cast no shadow, the Auschwitz number casts its shadow over all who would claim to be human after Auschwitz.

In *To the Land of the Cattails* Aharon Appelfeld's character Tina makes a point similar to Améry's: "I never took special pride in my Jewish origins. I'm not certain that the Jews are better than other nations. On the contrary, they have certain visible flaws that I condemn in no uncertain terms, but if someone is murdered because he is a Jew, then I proclaim myself Jewish in every respect. Am I not right?" (69). The hungry child, the thirsty stranger, the frightened old man—they all cry out from the pages of the Holocaust novel and call my name. In my responsibility, in my vulnerability, I must assume that hunger, that thirst, that fear and answer for it. As a witness, I offer my response not just as a giving of signs; rather the response itself "becomes a sign, turns into an allegiance" (Levinas, *Otherwise* 49). Situated before the voice of the other that comes to me through the text, whatever I am lies in what I am for that other. As a relation of responsibility, the relation of reader to text is a relation of I to Thou, of I-for-Thou. "The contraction and fusion into a whole being," writes Buber, "can never be accomplished by me, can never be accomplished without me. I require a You to become; becoming I, I say You. All actual life is encounter" (*I and Thou* 62). From the existential, phenomenological standpoint here adopted, responsibility does not simply mean I am responsible for myself but that I am responsible for you. In the midst of the dialogic encounter between author and reader, "I understand you" means "I am here for you."

Thus, in the words of Bakhtin, "understanding fills out the text: it is active and takes on a creative character. Creative understanding continues creativity" (*Estetika* 346). The event of creating the novel entails the creation of the reader, and the event of reading the novel entails its continued creation. So it is from the beginning of creation. "When he opened his eyes," says Wiesel in *The Oath*, "Adam did not ask God: Who are *you*? He asked: Who am *I*?" (19). But in *Messengers of God* Wiesel writes, "In the beginning, man is alone. Alone as God is alone. As he opens his eyes he does not ask: Who am I? He asks: Who are you?" (3). This is not, in truth, a contradiction. Buber writes, "The primal event pointed out by the images of the Bible does not lie under the principle of contradiction: *A* and *not-A* are here strangely concerned with one another" (*Between* 78). In the relation of I and Thou, of reader and author, we are concerned with such a primal event, as Wiesel implies when he invokes Adam's creation. The questions "Who am I?" and "Who are you?" are of a piece. In the relation to the author the reader cannot decide one question without also deciding the other. Because the novel is an event of creation, a summoning of one responsive voice by another, the one who answers, "Here I am," posits responsibility for the other; responding *to* the novel the reader becomes responsible *for* the novel.

Wiesel sets up this relation in *The Oath* early on when he states, "In the final stage of every equation, the key is responsibility. Whoever says 'I' creates the 'You.' . . . The 'I' signifies both solitude and the rejection of solitude" (17). The event of the novel is the event of this interanimation of author and reader; the novel rises up in a realm between the two, in the realm of the between that distinguishes response and responsibility. The implication of the reader lies in the positing of this space, in the positioning of the reader along the edges of this space, where the wholeness of being is rooted in being for-the-other. This constitution of the self by its capacity to be for-the-other is expressed in the novel through certain character-to-character relationships. Encountering such relations within the novel, the reader is implicated in relation to the novel. In Ka-tzetnik's *Atrocity* Hayim Idl realizes that "taking care of the Rabbi had given him strength. He protected the Rabbi, and because of that he was himself protected" (256). The Hebrew word for "protected" here is *shamar* (200), which implies watching over, looking after, caring for something very precious that has been entrusted. Hayim Idl chooses to protect the rebbe, but he cannot choose his responsibility for the rebbe. "With his body," we read, "he kept the Rabbi from being trampled. And for that he was not himself asphyxiated" (256). The breath he draws arises from his enabling the rebbe to breathe. Similarly, the word that the reader receives lies in the offering of a responsive word. As in the case of the character, the life of the reader is nurtured by nurturing the life that cries out from the novel.

We see, then, how the relation between characters may articulate the relation between author and reader. In *The Whole Land Brimstone* by Anna Langfus, the main character's husband says to her, "If I exist, it is because you still believe I do" (144). In this simple statement we hear the author's plea to the reader, we see what is entrusted to the reader, and we realize what is at stake in the reader's response. Typifying this plight of the author in relation to the reader is a man from Wiesel's childhood who also turns up in his tales, Moshe the Beadle. In *One Generation After* Wiesel writes,

Few came back. One who did was Moshe the Beadle. He was unrecognizable. . . . He now wore the mysterious face of a messenger pursued by those whose message he carried. . . . He told and told again tales so heinous as to make your skin crawl. . . . Shot, all of them. In broad daylight. He too had been shot, falling only a fraction of a second before it would have been too late. Protected by those who followed, he alone had survived. Why? So that he could come back to his town and tell the tale. . . . But his audience, weary and naive, would not, could not believe. [28-29]

The reader's debt to the author is a debt of belief, and belief comes only in the act of response. In responding, the reader, too, becomes a messenger, with a face changed by the message it speaks. Failing to respond, fleeing to cookbook methods of textual analysis, the reader casts another handful of dirt onto the graves of those who cry out from beyond the grave.

"If you'd had more experience," says Leon to Ruth in Aichinger's *Herod's Children*, "you'd know that in front of every stage there's a sighing darkness that wants to be comforted" (120). The stage is the stage of dialogic encounter; the darkness is the darkness of that massive grave known as the Kingdom of Night; the sighing—or "moaning," from the German verb *seufzen* (116)—is the utterance of the messenger who summons us; and the comfort is what is called for in the reader's response. The nature of that response is not, must not be, confined to writing books or giving lectures. The reader must comfort that sigh by comforting other people. Colliding with the child who was hanged on the gallows of Buna must add depth to my embrace of my children. Encountering the persecuted must lead me to react to persecution. Anytime the truth is threatened, anytime things mean more than people, anytime technology eclipses humanity—I must speak up. It is not enough to weep over the testimony that comes to me from the distant shores of the novel. It is not enough to analyze form and content, language and silence, word and meaning. Beyond lamentation and analysis, I am implicated in my capacity for affirmation, precisely when I have lost all basis for affirmation. As Wiesel has said, "Man is not defined by what denies him, but by that which affirms him" (*Accident* 71). If in deciding something about the novel I decide something about myself, then whatever is decided is determined by the depth and the passion of my affirmation.

The Affirming Flame

The closing stanza of W.H. Auden's "September 1, 1939," reads,

> Defenceless under the night
> Our world in stupor lies;
> Yet, dotted everywhere,
> Ironic points of light
> Flash out wherever the Just
> Exchange their messages:
> May I, composed like them
> Of Eros and of dust,

> Beleaguered by the same
> Negation and despair,
> Show an affirming flame.
> [537].

In these lines is announced the task common to author and reader. To read these Holocaust authors is to burn with them. Wiesel tells a tale about a poet who was asked what he would fetch from his house if it were on fire. The poet answered, "The fire, naturally." Says Wiesel, "We steal the fire, but our fire does not destroy. Our fire burns and burns and burns—and we burn forever" (*Against Silence* 1:318). In the openness of the vulnerability that characterizes responsibility the reader must become fuel for the flame of affirmation—over against the flames of darkness and negation that rose into the Auschwitz sky. André Neher asserts, "Every dialogue, then, implies an aggression, a renunciation, a death to oneself, and an absolute silence, which are attitudes preliminary to opening up, to communication, to dialogue, to life-within-dialogue, and to love" (48).

The novel and the response to it arise in a realm between author and reader. When these events occur amid the flame of affirmation, they are steeped in love; the act of response is an act of love. In *I and Thou* Buber notes, "Feelings one 'has'; love occurs. Feelings dwell in man, but man dwells in his love. This is no metaphor but actuality: love does not cling to an I, as if the You were merely its 'content' or object; it is between I and You" (66). One is reminded of a line from Appelfeld's *For Every Sin*: "Anyone who was in the camp deserves a lot of love. Without love, there can be no existence" (139). There is no life, no human presence, outside of that presence that is love; affirmation is an embrace of what is most precious, most dear, of what there is to love. As much as the survivor deserves love, the reader as one made into a witness needs love for the survivor; the witness lives by love for the dead father, the dead child, and the exiled word. For in its struggle for redemption, the novel implicates the readers in their own need for redemption, and there can be no redemption without love. "Do you know why God demands that you love him?" writes Wiesel in *The Gates of the Forest*. "He doesn't need your love, he can do without it, but you can't.... Your love, rather than his, can save you" (224). There is no response with the wholeness of one's life apart from this passionate affirmation of life; there is no affirmation of life without this love.

Elsewhere in *The Gates of the Forest* Wiesel relates an exchange between Gregor and Gavriel. Says Gregor, "You used to live them [your tales] by giving them your breath, out of which they made love and prayer" (208). When the reader's response to the tale is one of affirmation, it is made into love and prayer. "When you love your friend as you love yourself," Wiesel has pointed out, "God is the third partner. The only way to love God is to love Him through mankind" (*Against Silence* 2:262). Love is tied to prayer, and prayer to love. When the readers responds with their whole beings—as the author has responded—that response takes on certain characteristics of prayer. Recall Katriel's insight from Wiesel's *A Beggar in Jerusalem*: "Do you know that it is given to us to enrich a legend simply by listening to it? It belongs as much to the listener as to the teller. You listen to a tale, and all of a sudden it is no longer the same tale" (107). The tale is heard and thus deepened through the listener's responsive word, the wholeness of which lies in its union with the life of the listener. To the extent that the word is whole, one with its meaning and with the one who utters it, it is akin to prayer. The readers are implicated, therefore, according to their capacity for prayer, for pursuing the truth of the word uttered and to which they respond—to the very end.

"Who doesn't go to the end," writes Wiesel in *The Gates of the Forest*, "can only know a truth that is partial and mutilated" (155). Yet, he goes on to declare, "in taking a single word by assault it is possible to discover the secret of creation, the center where all threads come together" (166). The whole point of this phenomenological approach to the event of the novel's creation has been to take the novelistic word by assault to determine what it might reveal about the life that brings it into being. We have struggled to follow the novelist into the word, into the saying of creation that pronounces it to be good. The word then, is to be returned from exile by joining it with that place where human presence is reestablished through its relation to the place. "Sometimes it happens," we read in Wiesel's *The Town beyond the Wall*, "that we travel for a long time without knowing that we have made the long journey solely to pronounce a certain word, a certain phrase, in a certain place. The meeting of the place and the word is a rare accomplishment" (118). The place—or the "space," *l'espace* (129)—of which Wiesel speaks is the between-space of dialogic encounter between I and Thou. In the case at hand it is the space between author and reader. Through the novelistic word the author opens up the space; in a dialogic response the reader turned witness introduces the flame of affirmation to that place. When, in this encounter, the word is returned from exile—rejoined, if only for a moment, with its meaning—truth happens. With the emergence of truth a Third, the One who is truth, also emerges in the between-space.

"Only as the You becomes present does presence come into being," Buber has said (*I and Thou* 63). Presence is precisely the presence of the Third. This Third is the One who is signified by the flame of affirmation that transforms the witness into a sign. "The glory of the Infinite," Levinas has said, "reveals itself through what it is capable of

Implication of the Reader   163

doing in the witness" (*Ethics* 109). Bakhtin insists, "Every dialogue proceeds as though against the background of a responsive understanding of a Third who is invisibly present, standing above all the participants in the dialogue" (*Estetika* 306). Reading is a dialogic encounter between self and other, between reader and author, and this encounter also has its responsive Reader, its Other. "The Other with a big 'O' " Lacan states, "is the scene of the Word insofar as the scene of the Word is always in third position between two subjects. This is only in order to introduce the dimension of Truth" (*Language* 269). If love for another is a presence between I and Thou, then this Third, this Other, is He whose presence is constituted and affirmed by that love that is affirmation.

Lacan acknowledges as much when he says, "I can only just prove to the Other that he exists, not, of course, with the proofs for the existence of God, with which over the centuries he has been killed off, but by loving him" (*Ecrits* 317). The one whose reading is not ruled by this love and affirmation of the truth, whose reading arises out of academic curiosity or aesthetic appreciation, whose reading is governed by the fashion and fad of literary theory, betrays truth, life, and all there is to love. In short, that one becomes an accomplice to the murder of the word, of the father, of mother and child—and of God. In the Torah we have what is known as the *aron ha-edut*, the Ark of Testimony (see, for example, Exodus 40:3); in that Ark abides the word of God, the presence of God. Where testimony is, there God is too. For the reader transformed into a witness, the affirming flame is the ark of testimony, even—or especially—when that testimony takes the form of a question. As Wiesel has observed, "In Hebrew the word for 'question' is *she'elah*, and the *alef lamed* of God's name are part of the fabric of that word. Therefore God is in the question" (*Against Silence* 3:297). The Third is invisibly present because He is present as a question, one that is couched in a certain silence; the Third is invisibly present because, in the question that distinguishes the dialogic encounter, He is silently present.

I.B. Singer closes his novel *Shosha* with just such a question, as Arele and Haiml sit in the darkness of an Israeli night and await an answer that will not come (277). In "White Rabbit," from Lustig's *Diamonds of the Night*, the man named Thomas forever addresses a woman inside a mental ward from outside her window, knowing that she cannot hear him (67); he speaks, for there is Another who may hear, silently and invisibly. In the story "The Last Days of the Fire" from the same volume Lustig creates a character, an old man named Emil Cohen, who also implicates the position of the reader in relation to the text: "He no longer asked himself which was more important, forgiving or hope, and which to choose. We're dying, just like we've always died. . . . Why are things that way? Dying, dying, dying, and yet that long echo of past life. What price must a person pay just to survive? But he knew he'd never get an answer. Nobody ever had. . . . Yet at the same time, he knew that such an answer does exist inside every person, even if it dies with him, and that, in a way, it never dies" (173). We recall Pedro's remark in Wiesel's *Twilight:* "What is important for man is to feel not only the existence of an answer, but the presence of one who knows the answer. When I seek that presence, I am seeking God" (197-98). So we see what is lost in the internal splitting of the self and what is to be gained in the external relation to the other. He who dwells above, in the third position, dwells within.

If the universality of the Shoah lies in its uniqueness, then what threatens the author also implicates the reader. The reader too is in need of resurrection and redemption; the reader too must redeem the truth, standing before the Third, who is the truth, as one who is in error. "Here I am" harbors the questions "Where am I?" and "Where are You?" Thus question and answer merge to continually resurrect the question that raises human beings toward God, from within and from beyond. "Man raises himself toward God by the question he asks Him," says Moshe in Wiesel's *Night.* "That is the true dialogue. Man questions God and God answers. But we don't understand His answers. We can't understand them. Because they come from the depths of the soul, and they stay there until death. You will find the true answers, Eliezer, only within yourself!" (16). The French word rendered as "stay" is *demeurent* (17), which connotes "live" or "dwell," implying that the questions are alive, animate, and animating. "Do you know what the eternity of God is?" asks a teacher in Wiesel's *Legends of Our Time.* "It is we. By dancing on fire, by facing suffering and death, man creates the eternity of his creator" (159). It is not just that the Third is there, within me and before me; rather, He comes to life as my testimony comes to bear, as the affirmation that returns me to life ignites. The goal of redemption, as the Gaon of Vilna once put it, is the redemption of truth (cited by Wiesel, public lecture, Vanderbilt University, Nashville, 4 March 1990). If God is truth, then God too must be redeemed; and if truth is not something I know but something I must become, then the life of God is at stake in my capacity to come to life.

"God too must be lived," says a beggar in Wiesel's *The Oath* (129). As God is lived, so does God live. He must be lived because that is the only way the soul can live in truth; it is the only way the self can live in its relation to the other and to the Third. The life of the reader, therefore, is at stake in the response to the author, in the responsibility for the lives of those encountered in the text and beyond the text. For in the dialogic interaction with the novel, the reader engages the soul, from the depths of which comes an answer in the form of a question. In

Implication of the Reader   165

Herod's Children Aichinger's character declares, "Those who are sure they are, are not. Only those who doubt themselves, only those who have suffered, may land. For the shores of God are aflame over a dark ocean, and those who land burn. And the shores of God grow, for the burning gleams from afar; and the shores of God shrink, for the corpses of the stunted sprout from the darkness" (68). In the words of Wiesel, "He who says today that he is at peace with himself and with God is estranged from both" (*Against Silence* 1:145). God is a consuming fire (see Deuteronomy 4:24), and the one who is not consumed by that fire, by the flame of affirmation, has no life.

It has often been argued that one cannot ignore God when dealing with the Holocaust. Wiesel states it perhaps most poetically in *Ani Maamin*:

> Ani maamin, ani maamin.
> God possible—
> And impossible.
> God present? How can you?
> God absent? How can you?
> How can man
> Commit such evil?
> Without you?
> Or with you?
> Ani maamin?
> How is one to believe?
> How is one not to believe? (24)

We may embrace or refuse God, but we cannot ignore Him. Just as God haunts the literary response to the event, so is He involved in the reader's own response. "The sun and the moon and the stars are not enough for enlightenment," says Silvano Arieti. "To overcome the horizon of darkness the Divine Presence is necessary" (105). What is the point of our endeavor, if not to overcome the horizon of darkness that surrounds us? In the first utterance of creation, "Let there be light" (Genesis 1:3), we have the whole purpose of creation, both universal and particular, at all its levels. Just as the Jewish man wraps himself in the light of God each time he dons his tallith, so is every human being called to become a flaming light. The novels of the Holocaust are beacons that shine forth from the Kingdom of Night, points of light that the incomprehensible darkness cannot comprehend. As such, the voices implicate those of us who move in darkness "not of woods only and the shade of trees" (Frost 95). In this implication author, character, and reader merge. In *The Parnas* Arieti writes, "This we know, that the seven lights that carassed the body of the parnas of Pisa still shine for both the reader and the writer of these pages" (144). The character here lies beaten to death, a victim of bestial darkness. The author and reader are gathered at his body's side to bear witness and become one with the light of the menorah that signifies the divine presence of the Third.

Mikhail Bakhtin has insisted that "wherever alibi becomes a prerequisite for creation and expression there can be no responsibility, no seriousness, no significance. A special responsibility is required. . . . But this responsibility can be founded only on a profound belief in a higher truth, . . . the belief that another, higher being responds to my special responsibility, that I do not act in a utter void. Apart from this belief there can be only empty pretense" (*Estetika* 179). So we are called to emerge from the darkness, as did the first light, even before we hear the summons. For the summons is not first heard and then answered. "He who ceases to make a response ceases to hear the Word," Buber has pointed out (*Between* 45). The attitude of waiting for the word to come only underscores our deafness. "God is not mute!" the Pardo tells us in *The Parnas*. "Each crime bespeaks His lament, 'How far you are from Me!' The greater the crime, the greater is God's reminder of how much is within the realm of man's choice and grasp. But we must choose to hear Him. We do not hear" (71). We do not hear because we do not answer. Rebbe Barukh of Medzebozh once said to his grandson, "God too is unhappy; He is hiding and man is not looking for Him. Do you understand, Yehiel? God is hiding and man is not even searching for Him" (Wiesel, *Somewhere* 89). Thus God hides in the silence between the words of the Holocaust novel, abiding in the place of the word's exile. We who read are not looking for Him. Hence we are implicated.

Wiesel says that God "does not want to be talked about. He wants to be listened to, to be heard. He talks and He listens but not when people speak about Him to others. When I speak about God, my only listener should be God" (*Against Silence* 3:223). Yet, dwelling in a third position between author and reader, God listens to the reader's response to the word and the silence. He listens and talks, and to the extent that we are able to instill our response with the affirming flame of prayer, we may hear. That is when the word truly returns from exile: it returns not in its pronouncement but in its being heard:

> The love whose incandescence is awaited in the fires of suffering is not that of God but of man: the man of the first word, whom God seeks out, indicates, lays hold of ("I am the Lord *Thy* God"), the man who is always a second person, who is called upon, who is never alone in his self, whose solitude can be only a mirage and illusion, and who inevitably meets with his Seeker, in embrace or in injury, on the way or by the roadside, as a shepherd or as a wolf, as God or as Satan. The sufferings of love are those of the man who says "Yes" to this word, when it is no longer spoken but is heard across the silence. [Neher 197]

Such is the yea-saying that burns in that response that does not fall prey to the execration disguised as explication, to the anamorphosis disguised as analysis.

"Each story," says Frank in Lustig's *Darkness Casts No Shadow*, "has three versions. The first one you tell me. The second one I tell you, and the third no one knows" (123). The reader's response to the Holocaust novel is a second telling of the tale; indeed, the tale is not received until it is transmitted. What has occurred in the pages of this book, what has been rendered as a phenomenology of the Holocaust novel, simply amounts to a retelling of the tale encountered; it is the tale of its offering and its reception, of its authoring and its reading. Yet, as Lustig suggests, the tale has a third version that belongs to the One who abides in a third position above the tales written and the tales read. To Him belongs the truth of the tale, to which our lives are dedicated and by which our lives are consecrated. We come to the end of this reading only to return to it in a return to life, in that embrace of our children that is the silent telling of the true tale. Thus in *The Testament* Wiesel ends his tale of Paltiel Kossover with Paltiel's silent bequest of a tale of silence to his child Grisha: "I shall tell Grisha what I have never yet revealed to anyone; I shall tell him . . ." (336).

Epilogue

A great and strong wind rent the mountains, and broke in pieces the rocks before the Lord, but the Lord was not in the wind; and after the wind an earthquake, but the Lord was not in the earthquake; and after the earthquake a fire, but the Lord was not in the fire; and after the fire a still small voice.

—1 Kings 19:11-12

As he lay dying, Franz Rosenzweig said: "And now it comes, the point of all points, which the Lord has truly revealed to me in my sleep: the point of all points for which there . . ." (Glatzer 174). Thus in the hour of his death the man was blessed with the revelation of what cannot be conveyed, a revelation of what we the living shall have to do without. As Elie Wiesel has written, "The image of God cannot be transmitted; it can be carried away only in death" (*Beggar* 200). So the point at which we arrive is not the closure of "the point of all points" but the open-endedness that casts us into the valley of decision. There our sleep does not bring the solace of what was revealed to the great thinker; rather, like Job, we are left to cry out, "Thou dost scare me with dreams and terrify me with visions" (Job 7:14). If, however, we have not reached an end, perhaps we have at least arrived at a means for making our way through the rumbling of the shriek of silence. If we have not settled anything, perhaps we have at least been properly unsettled.

In *Ethics and Infinity* Emmanuel Levinas writes, "To escape the 'there is' one must not be posed but deposed. . . . This deposition of sovereignty by the *ego* is the social relationship with the Other. . . . I distrust the compromised word 'love,' but the responsibility for the Other, being-for-the-other, seemed to me . . . to stop the anonymous and senseless rumbling of being" (52). For author, character, and reader, this responsibility opens up the human being to the "still small voice," the *kol demamah dakah*, the "thin voice of silence" through which word may rejoin meaning to overcome the shriek of silence. Arnost Lustig insists that "no one writer but a collection of writers is needed to create a whole picture of what happened during the Holocaust" (in Knopp 310). Similarly, no one voice but a chorus of voices—the voices of authors, characters, and readers—is needed to make heard the thin voice of silence. These voices fashion the Ark of Testimony in which the word resides.

Arriving at such a view of the art and our relation to it brings us to a means or a method, one opposed to the idolatries of form and structure and even content that currently rule aesthetics. What we have is an aesthetic much like that which is found in the portrayal of the first artist to appear in the Torah. Bezalel, whose name means "in the shadow of God," was chosen to do the artwork for the Tabernacle and the Ark of Testimony as the children of Israel made their way through the wilderness. Bezalel was chosen because he was filled "with the Spirit of God, with ability, with intelligence, with knowledge, and with all craftsmanship" (Exodus 35:31). Nachmanides points out that Bezalel was entrusted with the task of creating the vessel of the word because he "knew how to combine the letters with which heaven and earth were created" (543). While the artists we have considered, even in their combined art, may not bear the wisdom and the ability of Bezalel, they are nonetheless commissioned with a similar task: to fashion a place where the word can dwell in the midst of the wilderness. Participating in that creation through our response and responsibility, we must become the place of that dwelling.

What we come to, then, is not just an aesthetic of art but, more important and more profound, an aesthetic of the soul. Indeed, Bakhtin maintains that "the problem of the soul is an aesthetic problem" (*Estetika* 89). Such a position makes the Holocaust novel a phenomenological and existential problem, one that turns our investigation back on itself. As we fathom the novel, so do we penetrate ourselves in a movement toward that place where *within* and *above* are transformed into synonyms. Here we must fashion our own ark of testimony, in the silence of a prayer that is the substance of language and the language of silence, inviolate and beyond the enclaves of exile.

Works Cited

Primary Sources

Aichinger, Ilse. *Herod's Children*. Trans. Cornelia Schaeffer. New York: Atheneum, 1964. (*Die grössere Hoffnung*. Amsterdam: Bermann Fischer Verlag, 1948.)
Amichai, Yehuda. *Not of This Time, Not of This Place*. Trans. Shlomo Katz. New York: Harper, 1968. (*Lo m'akhshiv, lo m'khan*. Tel Aviv: Schocken, 1986.)
Anatoli, A. *Babi Yar*. Trans. David Floyd. New York: Pocket, 1971. (*Babi Yar*. Frankfurt am Main: Possev Verlag, 1970.)
Appelfeld, Aharon. *The Age of Wonders*. Trans. Dalya Bilu. Boston: Godine, 1981. (*Tor hapeliot*. Tel Aviv: Hakibbutz Hameuchad, 1978.)
———. *Badenheim 1939*. Trans. Dalya Bilu. New York: Washington Square, 1980. (*Badenheim, 'ir nofesh*. Tel Aviv: Hakibbutz Hameuchad, 1979).
———. *For Every Sin*. Trans. Jeffrey M. Green. New York: Weidenfeld and Nicolson, 1989.
———. *The Retreat*. Trans. Dalya Bilu. New York: Dutton, 1984.
———. *To the Land of the Cattails*. Trans. Jeffrey M. Green. New York: Weidenfeld and Nicolson, 1986.
———. *Tzili: The Story of a Life*. Trans. Dalya Bilu. New York: Penguin, 1984. (*Haktunot v' hapasim*. Tel Aviv: Hakibbutz Hameuchad, 1983.)
Arieti, Silvano. *The Parnas*. New York: Basic, 1979.
Bellow, Saul. *Mr. Sammler's Planet*. New York: Penguin, 1977.
Bor, Josef. *The Terezin Requiem*. Trans. Edith Pargeter. New York: Avon, 1963. (*Terezínské rekviem*. Prague: Československý spisovatel, 1963.)
Bryks, Rachmil. *Kiddush Hashem*. Trans. S. Morris Engel. New York: Behrman House, 1977. (*Avif kidush hashem*. New York: Rachmiel Bruks Book Committee, 1952.)
Fuks, Ladislav. *Mr. Theodore Mundstock*. Trans. Iris Urwin. New York: Ballantine, 1969. (*Pan Theodor Mundstock*. Prague: Československý spisovatel, 1963.)
Gary, Romain. *The Dance of Genghis Cohn*. New York: World, 1968.
Gouri, Haim. *The Chocolate Deal*. Trans. Seymour Simckes. New York: Holt, 1968. (*Iskat hashokolad*. Tel Aviv: Hakibbutz Hameuchad, 1965.)
Kaniuk, Yoram. *Adam Resurrected*. Trans. Seymour Simckes. New York: Atheneum, 1971. (*Adam ben kelev*. Tel Aviv: Amikam, 1969.)
Karmel, Ilona. *An Estate of Memory*. Hertfordshire, Eng.: Panther, 1973.
Ka-tzetnik 135633. *Atrocity*. Trans. Nina De-Nur. New York: Kensington, 1977. (*Pipel*. Tel Aviv: Hakibbutz Hameuchad, 1988.)

———. *House of Dolls*. Trans. Moshe M. Kohn. New York: Pyramid, 1958. (*Beit habubot*. Tel Aviv: Hakibbutz Hameuchad, 1987.)
———. *Phoenix over the Galilee*. Trans. Nina De-Nur. New York: Harper, 1969. (*Kahol m'efer*. Tel Aviv: Am Oved, 1966.)
———. *Star of Ashes*. Trans. Nina De-Nur. Tel Aviv: Hamenora, 1971. (*Kokhev ha'efer*. Tel Aviv: Hamenora, 1971.)
———. *Sunrise over Hell*. Trans. Nina De-Nur. London: Allen, 1977. (*Salamandrah*. Tel Aviv: Hakibbutz Hameuchad, 1987.)
Kosinski, Jerzy. *The Painted Bird*. 2d ed. Boston: Houghton, 1975.
Langfus, Anna. *The Whole Land Brimstone*. Trans. Peter Wiles. New York: Pantheon, 1962. (*Le sel et le soufre*. Paris: Gallimard, 1960.)
Levi, Primo. *If Not Now, When?* Trans. William Weaver. New York: Simon, 1985. (*Se non ora, quando?* Torino: Giudio Einaudi, 1982.)
———. *The Periodic Table*. Trans. Raymond Rosenthal. New York: Schocken, 1985. (*Il sistema periodico*. Torino: Guidio Einaudi, 1975.)
Lind, Jakov. *Landscape in Concrete*. Trans. Ralph Manheim. New York: Pocket, 1968. (*Landschaft in Beton*. Neuwied am Rhein: Hermann Luchterhand, 1963.)
Lustig, Arnost. *Darkness Casts No Shadow*. Trans. Jeanne Nemcova. New York: Avon, 1978. (*Tma nemá stín*. In *Démanty noci*, 83-135. Prague: Mladá Fronta, 1958.)
———. *Diamonds of the Night*. Trans. Jeanne Nemcova. Washington, D.C.: Inscape, 1978. (*Démanty noci*. Prague: Mladá Fronta, 1958.)
———. *Dita Saxova*. Trans. Jeanne Nemcova. New York: Harper, 1979. (*Dita Saxová*. Prague: Mladá Fronta, 1969.)
———. *Night and Hope*. Trans. George Theiner. New York: Avon, 1976. (*Noc a naděje*. Prague: Noše vojsko, 1959.)
———. *A Prayer for Katerina Horovitzova*. Trans. Jeanne Nemcova. New York: Harper, 1973. (*Modlitba pro Kateřinu Horovitzovou*. Prague: Československý spisovatel, 1964.)
Oz, Amos. *Touch the Water, Touch the Wind*. Trans. Nicholas de Lange. New York: Harcourt, 1974. (*L'ga'at b'mayim, l'ga'at b'ruah*. Tel Aviv: Am Oved, 1973.)
Rawicz, Piotr. *Blood from the Sky*. Trans. Peter Wiles. New York: Harcourt, 1964. (*Le sang du ciel*. Paris: Gallimard, 1961.)
Schwarz-Bart, André. *The Last of the Just*. Trans. Stephen Becker. New York: Bantam, 1961. (*Le dernier des justes*. Paris: Editions du Seuil, 1959.)
Singer, Isaac Bashevis. *Enemies: A Love Story*. Greenwich, Conn.: Fawcett, 1972.
———. *Shosha*. Trans. Joseph Singer and I.B. Singer. New York: Farrar, 1978.
Wiesel, Elie. *The Accident*. Trans. Ann Borchardt. New York: Avon, 1962. (*Le Jour*. Paris: Editions du Seuil, 1961.)
———. *A Beggar in Jerusalem*. Trans. Lily Edelman and Elie Wiesel. New York: Random, 1970. (*Le mendiant de Jerusalem*. Paris: Editions du Seuil, 1968.)
———. *Dawn*. Trans. Frances Frenaye. New York: Hill and Wang, 1961. (*L'Aube*. Paris: Editions du Seuil, 1960.)
———. *The Fifth Son*. Trans. Marion Wiesel. New York: Summit, 1985. (*Le cinquième fils*. Paris: Bernard Grasset, 1983.)

———. *The Gates of the Forest*. Trans. Frances Frenaye. New York: Holt, 1966. (*Les portes de la forêt*. Paris: Editions du Seuil, 1964.)

———. *Night*. Trans. Stella Rodway. New York: Hill and Wang, 1961. (*La Nuit*. Paris: Editions de Minuit, 1958.)

———. *The Oath*. Trans. Marion Wiesel. New York: Avon, 1973. (*Le serment de Kolvillàg*. Paris: Editions du Seuil, 1973.)

———. *The Testament*. Trans. Marion Wiesel. New York: Summit, 1981. (*Le testament d'un poète juif assassiné*. Paris: Editions du Seuil, 1980.)

———. *The Town beyond the Wall*. Trans. Stephen Becker. New York: Avon, 1964. (*La ville de la chance*. Paris: Editions du Seuil, 1962.)

———. *Twilight*. Trans. Marion Wiesel. New York: Summit, 1988. (*Le crépuscule, au loin*. Paris: Bernard Grasset, 1987.)

Secondary Sources

Adorno, T.W. "Engagement." In *Natur zur Literatur III*, 109-35. Frankfurt am Main: Suhrkamp Verlag, 1965.

Alexander, Edward. *The Resonance of Dust: Essays on Holocaust Literature and Jewish Fate*. Columbus: Ohio State Univ. Press, 1979.

Améry, Jean. *At the Mind's Limits: Comtemplations by a Survivor on Auschwitz and Its Realities*. Trans. Sidney Rosenfeld and Stella P. Rosenfeld. Bloomington: Indiana Univ. Press, 1980.

Appelfeld, Aharon. *Essays in the First Person*. Jerusalem: Zionist Library, 1979.

Auden, W.H. "September 1, 1939." In *The Major Poets: English and American*, ed. Charles M. Coffin, 534-37. New York: Harcourt, 1969.

Bakhtin, Mikhail. *The Dialogic Imagination*. Trans. Caryl Emerson and Michael Holquist. Austin: Univ. of Texas Press, 1981.

———. *Estetika slovesnogo tvorchestva*. Moscow: Art, 1979.

———. *Esthétique et theorie du roman*. Trans. Daria Olivier. Paris: Gallimard, 1978.

———. *Problems of Dostoevsky's Poetics*. Trans. Caryl Emerson. Minneapolis: Univ. of Minnesota Press, 1984.

———. *Rabelais and His World*. Trans. Helen Isiasky. Cambridge, Mass.: MIT Press, 1968.

Bergson, Henri, *The Two Sources of Morality and Religion*. Trans. Ashley Audra and Cloudsley Brereton. Garden City, N.J.: Doubleday, 1954.

Brown, Norman O. *Love's Body*. New York: Vintage, 1966.

Buber, Martin. *Between Man and Man*. Trans. Ronald Gregor Smith. New York: Macmillan, 1965.

———. *Daniel: Dialogues on Realization*. Trans. Maurice Friedman. New York: Holt, 1964.

———. *I and Thou*. Trans. Walter Kaufmann. New York: Scribner's, 1970.

———. *The Legend of the Baal-Shem*. Trans. Maurice Friedman. New York: Schocken, 1969.

———. *Tales of the Hasidim: The Early Masters*. Trans. Olga Marx. New York: Schocken, 1947.

Works Cited

Burke, Kenneth. *The Rhetoric of Religion: Studies in Logology.* Berkeley: Univ. of California Press, 1970.
Camus, Albert. *The Myth of Sisyphus and Other Essays.* Trans. Justin O'Brien. New York: Vintage, 1955.
———. *The Rebel.* Trans. Anthony Bower. New York: Vintage, 1956.
Clark, Katerina, and Michael Holquist. *Mikhail Bakhtin.* Cambridge, Mass.: Harvard Univ. Press, 1984.
Dante. *The Inferno.* Trans. John Ciardi. New York: New American Library, 1954.
Derrida, Jacques. *Of Grammatology.* Trans. Gayatri Chakravorty Spivak. Baltimore, Md.: Johns Hopkins Univ. Press, 1976.
Descartes, René. *Selections.* Ed. Ralph M. Eaton. Trans. E.S. Haldane and G.R.T. Ross. New York: Scribner's, 1955.
Dostoyevsky, Fyodor. *The Brothers Karamazov.* Trans. Constance Garnett. New York: New American Library, 1980.
Emerson, Ralph Waldo. *Selected Writings.* Ed. William H. Gilman. New York: New American Library, 1965.
Ezrahi, Sidra DeKoven. *By Words Alone: The Holocaust in Literature.* Chicago: Univ. of Chicago Press, 1980.
Fine, Ellen S. "The Search for Identity: Post Holocaust French Literature." In *Remembering for the Future: Theme II,* 1472-80. Oxford: Pergamon, 1988.
Foucault, Michel. *The Archaeology of Knowledge and the Discourse on Language.* Trans. A.M. Sheridan Smith. New York: Pantheon, 1972.
———. *Madness and Civilization.* Trans. Richard Howard. New York: Pantheon, 1965.
———. *The Order of Things.* New York: Vintage, 1973.
Frankl, Victor E. *Man's Search for Meaning.* Trans. Ilse Lasch. Rev. ed. Boston: Beacon, 1962.
Frost, Robert. *Robert Frost's Poems.* New York: Washington Square, 1965.
Glatzer, Nahum, ed. *Franz Rosenzweig: His Life and Thought.* 2d ed. New York: Schocken, 1961.
Govrin, Nurit. "To Express the Inexpressible: The Holocaust Literature of Aharon Appelfeld." In *Remembering for the Future: Theme II,* 1580-94. Oxford: Pergamon, 1988.
Halperin, Irving. *Messengers from the Dead: Literature of the Holocaust.* Philadelphia: Westminster, 1970.
Jabès, Edmond. *The Book of Yukel and Return to the Book.* Trans. Rosemarie Waldrop. Middletown, Conn.: Wesleyan Univ. Press, 1977.
Ka-tzetnik 135633. *Shivitti.* Trans. Eliyah N. De-Nur and Lisa Herman. New York: Harper, 1989.
Kazantzakis, Nikos. *The Rock Garden.* Trans. Richard Howard and Kimon Friar. New York: Simon, 1963.
Kierkegaard, Søren. *Concluding Unscientific Postscript.* Trans. David F. Swenson and Walter Lowrie. Princeton, N.J.: Princeton Univ. Press, 1941.
———. *Fear and Trembling and The Sickness unto Death.* Trans. Walter Lowrie. Princeton, N.J.: Princeton Univ. Press, 1968.
———. *Training in Christianity.* Trans. Walter Lowrie. Princeton, N.J.: Princeton Univ. Press, 1944.

Kitov, Eliyahu. *The Book of Our Heritage*. 3 vols. Trans. Nathan Bulman. New York: Feldheim, 1973.
Knopp, Josephine. "Holocaust Literature II: Novels and Short Stories." In *Encountering the Holocaust: An Interdisciplinary Survey*, ed. Byron L. Sherwin and Susan G. Ament, 267-315. Chicago: Impact, 1979.
Kosinski, Jerzy. *Notes of the Author on the Painted Bird*. New York: Scientia-Factum, 1965.
Lacan, Jacques. *Ecrits*. Trans. Alan Sheridan. New York: Norton, 1977.
———. *The Language of the Self.* Trans. Anthony Wilden. Baltimore, Md.: Johns Hopkins Univ. Press, 1968.
Langer, Lawrence. *The Holocaust and the Literary Imagination*. New Haven, Conn.: Yale Univ. Press, 1975.
Levi, Primo. *If This Is a Man*. Trans. Stuart Wolf. New York: Orion, 1959.
Levinas, Emmanuel. *Ethics and Infinity*. Trans. Richard A. Cohen. Pittsburgh, Pa.: Duquesne Univ. Press, 1985.
———. *Otherwise Than Being; or, Beyond Essence*. Trans. Alphonso Lingis. The Hague: Nijhoff, 1981.
———. "Signature." *Research in Phenomenology* 8 (1978): 175-89.
Marx, Karl, and Frederick Engels. *Communist Manifesto*. Authorized English trans. Chicago: Kerr, 1982.
Mintz, Alan. *Hurban: Responses to Catastrophe in Hebrew Literature*. New York: Columbia Univ. Press, 1984.
Nachmanides. *Commentary on the Torah*. Vol. 2. Trans. Charles B. Chavel. New York: Shilo, 1973.
Neher, André. *The Exile of the Word: From the Silence of the Bible to the Silence of Auschwitz*. Trans. David Maisel. Philadelphia: Jewish Publication Society, 1981.
Ortega y Gasset, José. *Some Lessons in Metaphysics*. Trans. Mildred Adams. New York: Norton, 1969.
Pascal, Blaise. *Pensées*. Trans. A.J. Krailsheimer. New York: Penguin, 1966.
Patterson, David. *The Affirming Flame: Religion, Language, Literature*. Norman: Univ. of Oklahoma Press, 1988.
———. *In Dialogue and Dilemma with Elie Wiesel*. Wakefield, N.H.: Longwood Academic, 1991.
———. *Literature and Spirit: Essays on Bakhtin and His Contemporaries*. Lexington: Univ. Press of Kentucky, 1988.
Perlina, Nina. "Bakhtin and Buber: Problems of Dialogic Imagination." *Studies in Twentieth Century Literature* 9 (Fall 1984): 13-28.
Plato. *Phaedo*. Trans. R. Hackforth. New York: Bobbs, 1955.
Ricoeur, Paul. *The Symbolism of Evil*. Trans. Emerson Buchanan. Boston: Beacon, 1967.
Rosenfeld, Alvin. *A Double Dying: Reflections on Holocaust Literature*. Bloomington: Indiana Univ. Press, 1980.
Rosenzweig, Franz. *The Star of Redemption*. Trans. William H. Hallo. Boston: Beacon, 1972.
Roskies, David G. *Against the Apocalypse: Responses to Catastrophe in Modern Jewish Culture*. Cambridge, Mass.: Harvard Univ. Press, 1984.

Works Cited

Sachs, Nelly. *O the Chimneys: Selected Poems.* Trans. Michael Hamburger et al. New York: Farrar, 1967.
Sartre, Jean-Paul. *Being and Nothingness.* Trans. Hazel E. Barnes. New York: Simon, 1978.
———. *No Exit and Other Plays.* Trans. Stuart Gilbert. New York: Vintage, 1956.
Shestov, Lev. *Afiny i Ierusalim.* Paris: YMCA, 1951.
Sicher, Efriam. "'Making Good Again': Literary and Moral Reparation after the Holocaust." In *Remembering for the Future: Theme II,* 1540-48. Oxford: Pergamon, 1988.
Tillich, Paul. *The Dynamics of Faith.* New York: Harper, 1957.
———. *The Eternal Now.* New York: Scribner's, 1956.
———. *The New Being.* New York: Scribner's, 1955.
Todorov, Tzvetan. *Mikhail Bakhtine: Le principe dialogique.* Paris: Editions du Seuil, 1981.
Unamuno, Miguel de. *Tragic Sense of Life.* Trans. J.E. Crawford Fitch. New York: Dover, 1954.
Voloshinov, V.N. *Marksizm i filosofiya yazyka.* 2d ed. Leningrad: Surf, 1930.
Wardi, Charlotte. *Le génocide dans la fiction romanesque.* Paris: Presses Universitaires de France, 1986.
Wiesel, Elie. *Against Silence: The Voice and Vision of Elie Wiesel.* 3 vols. ed. Irving Abrahamson. New York: Holocaust Library, 1985.
———. *Ani Maamin.* Trans. Marion Wiesel. New York: Random, 1973.
———. *Dimensions of the Holocaust.* Evanston, Ill.: Northwestern Univ. Press, 1977.
———. *Five Biblical Portraits.* Notre Dame, Ind.: Univ of Notre Dame Press, 1981.
———. *A Jew Today.* Trans. Marion Wiesel. New York: Random, 1978.
———. *The Jews of Silence.* Trans. Neal Kozodoy. New York: Holt, 1966.
———. *Legends of Our Time.* New York: Avon, 1968.
———. *Messengers of God.* Trans. Marion Wiesel. New York: Random, 1976.
———. *One Generation After.* Trans. Lily Edelman and Elie Wiesel. New York: Pocket, 1970.
———. *Paroles d'étranger.* Paris: Editions du Seuil, 1982.
——— and Albert Friedlander. *The Six Days of Destruction.* Oxford: Pergamon, 1988.
———. *Somewhere a Master.* Trans. Marion Wiesel. New York: Summit, 1982.
———. *Souls on Fire.* Trans. Marion Wiesel. New York: Vintage, 1973.
Young, James E. *Writing and Rewriting the Holocaust: Narrative and the Consequences of Interpretation.* Bloomington: Indiana Univ. Press, 1988.
Yudkin, Leon I. *Escape into Siege: A Survey of Israeli Literature Today.* London: Routledge, 1974.
Yutler, Alan J. *The Holocaust in Hebrew Literature: From Genocide to Rebirth.* Port Washington, N.Y.: Associated Faculty Press, 1983.
Zohar: The Book of Splendor. Ed. Gershom Scholem. New York: Schocken, 1963.

Index

Abel, 75, 156
Abraham, 27, 157
Absalom, 75
absence, 4, 5, 14, 21, 30-31, 41-42, 76, 126, 149-50
Adam, 60, 95, 158
Adorno, T. W., 81
affirmation, 4, 71, 76, 95, 125, 141, 143, 160-67
Aichinger, Ilse, 39, 80, 91, 92, 93, 96-97, 121, 128-29, 136, 143, 154, 160, 165
Alexander, Edward, 7, 62
Améry, Jean, 10, 47, 67, 78, 101, 112, 115, 134, 157-58
Amichai, Yehuda, 40, 65, 71, 80, 82, 92-93, 94, 95, 111, 119, 136, 137-38, 148-49
Anatoli, A., 51, 85, 103, 137, 146, 148, 155
Appelfeld, Aharon, 6, 11, 23, 43-44, 80, 98, 108; *Tzili: The Story of a Life*, 2, 44, 56, 79, 118, 135, 150; *Badenheim 1939*, 31, 38, 41, 43, 80, 110; *The Age of Wonders*, 53, 63-64, 66-67, 74, 85, 101, 127; *The Retreat*, 43, 63; *To the Land of the Cattails*, 94, 135, 150, 158; *For Every Sin*, 97, 118, 134-35, 161
Arieti, Silvano, 96, 104, 120, 128, 165-66, 167
Auden, W. H., 160
Auschwitz, 3, 4, 10, 19, 20, 37, 38, 39, 40, 49, 67, 94, 123-24, 157-58, 161

Baal Shem Tov, 90
Babi Yar, 85, 98
Bakhtin, Mikhail, 9, 12, 15, 17, 20, 21, 22-28, 33, 44, 45, 47, 51, 52, 54, 56, 58, 60, 63, 64, 66, 70, 72, 78, 90, 96, 98, 99-100, 101, 105, 109-10, 111, 112-13, 114-15, 118, 121, 124, 125, 126, 130, 131, 132, 136, 138, 140, 145, 146, 151, 152, 154-55, 157, 158, 163, 166, 169
Barukh of Medzebozh, 166
Bellow, Saul, 52, 56, 65, 91, 120-21, 143, 154
Bergson, Henri, 125
between-space, 5, 13-14, 15, 47, 50, 101, 121, 130, 140, 146, 147, 159, 162
Bezalel, 169
body, the, 112-15, 121, 126, 148
Bor, Josef, 32, 143
Brown, Norman O., 55, 125-26
Bryks, Rachmil, 56, 80, 94
Buber, Martin, 1, 14-16, 17, 18, 22, 48, 57, 73, 74, 79, 81, 86, 108-09, 119, 141, 144, 146, 151, 152, 154, 158, 161, 162, 166
Burke, Kenneth, 4

Cain, 34, 75-76, 156
Camus, Albert, 47-48, 68-69, 75, 124-25
Cargas, Harry James, 59, 76
circumcision, 62-63, 106-07
Clark, Katerina, 22, 25
Cohen, Hermann, 22

Dante, 29, 55, 84
darkness, 38-39, 77, 106, 160, 165, 165-66
David, 75, 95
death, 32-35, 46, 49, 66, 69, 72, 81, 90, 95, 115-16, 123, 125, 127, 128, 130, 135-36
De-Nur, Yehiel. *See* Ka-tzetnik 135633

Index

Derrida, Jacques, 134
Descartes, René, 112
dialogic encounter. *See* dialogic relation
dialogic relation, 5, 6, 14-15, 22-23, 26, 51, 110, 116-17, 124, 130, 133, 154-55, 158, 160, 162, 163. *See also* human relation
Dostoevsky, Fyodor, 77, 86
double, motif of, 108-10

Ecclesiastes, 76
Elijah, 128
Emerson, Ralph Waldo, 96
Ezekiel, 75
Ezrahi, Sidra DeKoven, 8, 109, 134
faith, 4, 76, 83, 94, 140-41
Fine, Ellen, 105
Foucault, Michel, 25, 30, 112, 115, 116, 118, 157
Frankl, Viktor, 153
Friedlander, Albert, 38
Frost, Robert, 165
Fuks, Ladislav, 43, 97, 152
future, the, 26, 27, 58, 81-82, 99-100, 136-43

Gaon of Vilna, 164
Gary, Romain, 24
God, 3, 4, 14, 19, 20, 21, 27, 31-32, 35, 42, 43, 48, 55, 56, 59, 65, 68-76, 89-90, 94, 96, 119-20, 133, 140, 141-42, 163-65
Gouri, Haim, 2, 41, 96, 101-02, 108, 109, 118, 127, 137, 149
Govrin, Nurit, 63

Halperin, Irving, 6
Heine, Heinrich, 46
Holquist, Michael, 22, 25
human relation, 47-53, 108-09, 111, 113-14, 130, 132, 133, 140, 143-44, 146. *See also* dialogic relation

identity, 105-12, 116-17. *See also* soul; subjectivity
Isaac, 54, 128, 157

Jabès, Edmond, 81, 98, 102, 104, 106, 137
Jacob, 22, 68
Jeremiah, 119-20
Jesus, 95, 140
Job, 132, 168

Kafka, Franz, 34
Kaniuk, Yoram, 52, 62, 65, 80, 83, 95-96, 97, 103, 110, 113, 120, 128
Karmel, Ilona, 79, 80, 90, 93, 96, 116, 136, 143, 153-54
Ka-tzetnik 135633, 6, 11, 23, 32, 38, 40, 80, 84, 88, 100, 102-03, 105, 132, 136, 147, 148; *Star of Ashes*, 2, 75, 98, 113, 115, 123, 131; *Sunrise over Hell*, 31, 39, 49, 52, 74-75, 87-88, 107, 114, 123-24, 149; *Atrocity*, 37-38, 39-40, 65, 73, 88, 94, 97, 99, 124, 159; *House of Dolls*, 49-50, 66, 88-89, 94, 153; *Phoenix over the Galilee*, 94, 96, 103, 104, 107, 130-31, 132, 134, 143, 146
Kazantzakis, Nikos, 89
Kierkegaard, Søren, 11, 12, 13, 49, 60, 100, 121, 156
Knopp, Josephine, 7
Kosinski, Jerzy, 5, 36-37

Lacan, Jacques, 59-60, 64, 99, 100, 105-06, 110-11, 124, 142, 143, 163
Langer, Lawrence, 6, 37, 70
Langfus, Anna, 41-42, 65, 67, 74, 85, 106, 137, 159
language, 6, 9, 10-11, 13, 23-24, 29, 31-32, 45, 48, 50-51, 60, 91, 102, 103, 108, 112, 126, 142
laughter, 24-25, 39, 125-30
Law, the, 64-66
Lazarus, 130, 140
Levi, Primo, 10, 23, 47, 55, 99, 108; *If Not Now, When?* 40-41, 64, 92, 110, 117, 156; *The Periodic Table*, 93, 104, 107-08, 131-32, 146
Levinas, Emmanuel, 16-19, 20, 21, 22, 25, 31, 33, 40, 42, 49, 50, 58, 60, 73, 76, 78-79, 85-86, 89, 94, 99, 101, 109, 111, 113, 130, 131, 133, 134, 136,

Index

144, 147-48, 149, 150, 151, 152, 153, 155, 156, 157, 162-63, 168
Levi Yitzhak of Berditchev, 78, 151
Lind, Jakov, 24, 34, 42, 118, 143, 148
love, 21-22, 78-79, 125-26, 127, 131, 161-63, 166
Lustig, Arnost, 6, 7-8, 11, 50, 59, 76, 80, 95, 131, 147, 156, 168; *A Prayer for Katerina Horovitzova*, 3, 36, 46, 50, 81, 121; *Darkness Casts No Shadow*, 29, 45, 61, 67-68, 103, 105, 109, 114, 115, 135, 156, 167; *Diamonds of the Night*, 46, 61, 65, 67, 87, 99, 121, 141, 148, 163-64; *Dita Saxova*, 46-47, 50-51, 81, 114; *Night and Hope*, 81-82, 87, 90, 106-07, 117, 135

madness, 25, 112-21, 126, 127-28, 157
Maggid of Dubno, 92
Maggid of Mezeritch, 3
Maimonides, 119
Marx, Karl, 62
memory, 27, 42, 84, 89, 119, 133-38, 140-41, 143, 146
Menahem-Mendl of Kotzk, 43
Menahem-Mendl of Vitebsk, 4
Messiah, 48, 49, 92, 95-96, 112, 140
Mintz, Alan, 9-10, 63
Moses, 50, 64
mother, the, 78-84, 88, 97, 115

Nachmanides, 169
Nachman of Bratzlav, 129
Neher, André, 4, 19-22, 24, 25, 27, 32-33, 40, 55, 76, 91, 92, 123, 129, 132, 136, 161, 166
nothingness, 10, 19-20, 31, 40, 41, 64-65, 69, 99, 115

Oedipus, 12
Ortega y Gasset, José, 105, 138
other, the, 10-11, 13, 14, 16-19, 21, 23, 25, 47, 48, 57, 72-73, 79, 86, 97, 103, 104, 105-06, 109-10, 113-14, 117-18, 120, 121, 130, 132-33, 136, 140, 145, 147-48, 149, 150, 151, 152-53, 158-59, 168
Other, the. *See* Lacan, Jacques
Oz, Amos, 1, 42, 74, 106, 111, 138-39

Paraclete, 95
Pascal, Blaise, 10, 34, 91
Pentateuch. *See* Torah
Peter, 66
Plato, 112
prayer, 36, 44, 56, 57, 58, 70-72, 92, 131, 134, 141-42, 161-62, 166
presence, 5, 14-15, 16, 21-22, 29, 35, 41-43, 45, 99, 103, 104, 118, 119, 126, 134, 141, 142, 149-50, 151, 152, 155, 162. *See also* responsibility

Rawicz, Piotr, 7, 11, 23, 45, 47, 62-63, 67, 80, 83-84, 103, 107, 130, 134, 139, 146
rebellion, 54, 67-73
redemption, 4, 6, 9, 12-13, 17, 21, 29, 51, 78, 90, 131, 132, 137, 142, 147, 161, 164. *See also* movement of return; salvation
responsibility, 16-18, 21, 25-26, 28, 33, 50, 57, 73, 85-87, 94, 111, 130, 133, 144, 147, 150, 151-60, 161, 164, 166, 168-69. *See also* presence
return, movement of, 4, 45, 86-87, 96, 98, 131, 134-35, 138-39, 143-44. *See also* redemption; salvation
Ricoeur, Paul, 100
Rokeah, Eleazar, 89
Rosenfeld, Alvin, 4, 8-9, 14, 126
Rosenzweig, Franz, 12-14, 16, 17, 22, 29, 32, 40, 43, 47, 120, 138, 139, 140, 168
Roskies, David, 10
Ruth, 95

Sachs, Nelly, 3
salvation, 92-97, 137. *See also* redemption; return, movement of
Sartre, Jean-Paul, 57, 98, 108, 114
Schwartz-Bart, André, 70-71, 129, 157
Shekhina, 84, 120
Shestov, Lev, 69
Sinai, 38, 139-40, 150
Singer, I.B., 61; *Enemies: A Love Story*, 32, 43, 52, 57, 66, 79, 99, 143-44; *Shosha*, 59, 60, 61, 71, 80-81, 93, 117, 120, 150, 163

Sisyphus, 124
soul, the, 7, 8, 21, 18, 50, 78-79, 84-85, 86, 96, 100, 109, 112-13, 121, 126, 135, 142, 146, 148, 151, 157, 164, 169. *See also* identity; subjectivity
space, 40-47, 101, 113, 119
spirit, 13, 15-16, 18, 52, 105, 136, 143-44, 151
subjectivity, 16, 17, 60, 79, 94, 100, 113, 136, 147, 148, 151, 153, 157. *See also* identity; soul

Talmud, 48, 140, 157
Third, the, 15, 18-19, 110-12, 120, 147, 149, 162-64, 166, 167
Tillich, Paul, 29, 56, 92, 141
time, 13, 14, 38, 39, 40-47, 49, 101, 113, 126, 141, 142
Todorov, Tzvetan, 20, 54, 73
Torah, 64, 139, 151, 157, 163, 169
truth, 11-12, 13-14, 20, 24, 25-26, 49, 59-60, 73, 100, 106, 110-11, 116-17, 119, 125, 128, 141, 147, 162, 163, 164

Unamuno, Miguel de, 30, 46, 58

Verdi, Giuseppe, 143
Voloshinov, V. N., 52, 63

Wardi, Charlotte, 10-11
Wiesel, Elie, 1, 2, 4, 5, 6, 11, 12, 18, 19, 20, 22, 23, 24-25, 28, 29, 36, 38, 40, 41, 47, 48, 49, 51-52, 52-53, 54, 59, 68, 72, 76, 77, 78, 80, 81, 82, 83, 85, 89, 98, 105, 112, 119, 123, 125, 127, 129, 130, 133-34, 139-40, 142, 146-47, 150-51, 155, 156, 158, 159-60, 161-62, 163, 164, 165, 166, 168; *The Town beyond the Wall*, 27, 30, 35, 36, 44-45, 47-48, 71-72, 73, 75, 76, 86-87, 91, 96, 103, 109, 115, 125, 146, 151, 157, 162; *A Beggar in Jerusalem*, 30, 38, 58, 76, 98, 109, 127-28, 129, 139, 151, 156, 162; *The Testament*, 33, 35, 36, 44-45, 48, 51, 55-56, 57-58, 61-62, 73, 87, 93, 94-95, 103, 104, 105, 111, 117, 119, 127, 133, 140, 142, 146, 148, 153, 167; *Dawn*, 34, 36, 79-80, 137; *The Gates of the Forest*, 35-36, 38, 48, 68, 73, 109, 119, 126, 127, 132-33, 134, 137, 141, 156, 161, 162; *Night*, 38, 67, 69-70, 72, 73, 90, 115, 153, 164; *The Oath*, 49, 54, 92, 109, 128, 130, 133, 140, 158-59, 164; *Twilight*, 58-59, 70, 73, 75-76, 103, 104, 109, 112, 116, 119, 126, 133, 142, 164; *The Fifth Son*, 60, 84, 103, 146; *The Accident*, 98-99, 126, 135-36, 160
witness, 94, 95, 130-31, 146, 147-52, 153, 156, 157, 158, 161, 163

Yad Vashem, 77-78
Young, James, 11
Yudkin, Leon, 6
Yutler, Alan, 9, 132

Other Books by David Patterson

The Affirming Flame: Religion, Language, Literature
In Dialogue and Dilemma with Elie Wiesel
Faith and Philosophy
Literature and Spirit: Essays on Bakhtin and His Contemporaries
The Way of the Child (a novel)

Translations

Confession, by Leo Tolstoy
Diary of a Superfluous Man, by Ivan Turgenev
The Forged Coupon, by Leo Tolstoy
Winter Notes on Summer Impressions, by Fyodor Dostoyevsky

www.ingramcontent.com/pod-product-compliance
Lightning Source LLC
Chambersburg PA
CBHW032046150426
43194CB00006B/436